# HERE ARE JUST TWO OF THE TWELVE CASES YOU WILL NEVER FORGET. . . .

A 39-year-old Danish stewardess vanishes without a trace from her beautiful Connecticut home. Her husband claims she walked out of their bad marriage. The police believe him. But a dedicated private eye digs on and finally finds a tooth near the husband's property. . . .

An attractive, fortyish Los Angeles personality walks into his wife's bedroom and finds her with another man. He brutally murders both of them. Then during the subsequent investigation and trial many shocking details of their unusual marriage, sex lives, and partying begin to emerge. . . .

By Marvin J. Wolf and Katherine Mader
*Published by Ballantine Books:*

FALLEN ANGELS
ROTTEN APPLES
PERFECT CRIMES

# PERFECT CRIMES

## Marvin J. Wolf
### and
## Katherine Mader

BALLANTINE BOOKS • NEW YORK

ISBN 0-345-37477-0

Printed in Canada

First Edition: July 1995

10  9  8  7  6

# Introduction

FOR YEARS, TUBBY TEDDY NELSON, A SAN FRANCISCO bank messenger, carried a pet rabbit in a shopping bag as he made his way around town. One day he put $187,000 in the bag, set out on his bank rounds, and disappeared. Nearly thirty years later, police have no idea what happened to Nelson or his loot.

In a Chicago suburb lives a cashiered bank vault clerk whom authorities believe smuggled exactly $1 million from a high-security bank vault. Some of the money turned up, years later, in a Florida drug bust. The statute of limitations expired before charges could be brought against the clerk.

A killer disposed of a corpse by sneaking it into a Paris medical school and hiding it amid eight hundred cadavers awaiting dissection. But for a nervous temporary janitor, police might never have discovered the body.

Two rich Chicago college students kidnapped, murdered, and dismembered a nine-year-old boy—and would probably have gotten away with it. But Nathan Leopold accidentally dropped his prescription eyeglasses near the body of Bobby Franks, leading police to him and co-killer Richard Loeb. It took all of Clarence Darrow's considerable talents to save their lives.

A wealthy Miami restaurateur and his mother were murdered by two employees—who then assumed their victims' identities. Only a chance meeting with a victim's out-of-town friend unmasked the stranger-than-fiction charade.

A New York lawyer bribed retired merchant William Marsh Rice's live-in butler to forge a will increasing bequests to most of his relatives but diverting most of Marsh's fortune to the lawyer. Then he murdered Rice. But an unforeseen hitch delayed Rice's cremation long enough for relatives to demand an autopsy—and the plot was exposed.

In 1976, Peter Hogg, an airline pilot, strangled his wife, then dumped her weighted body into England's deepest lake. Eight years later, a tourist vanished near the same lake and police launched a massive search. On the bottom they found Mrs. Hogg's body, preserved by the cold. Hogg was convicted.

In August 1989, a bold extortionist made fools of everyone when he used the threat of stolen National Guard missiles to take $150,000 from a Florida bank. He crossed up the FBI by *running* across a freeway jammed with bumper-to-bumper rush-hour traffic, then hopped a wall. Dubbed "Turnpike Cooper" by the Miami media, the robber was never seen again.

So how hard is it, really, to pull off a perfect crime? And what goes on in the minds of people who risk their future on something as chancy as a major felony—even murder—in the belief they'll escape punishment?

Not everyone grows to ethical adulthood. Among us walk, largely unnoticed, thousands whose moral development ended in childhood, people who care about little but their own gratification. Most of these sociopaths, however, lack sophistication. They operate on an adolescent's level, grabbing and pushing. There is little attractive about their behavior, and many wind up behind bars, more often sooner than later.

Others, far fewer, who lack all conscience, mask their selfish greed in the cultured clothing of manners and hide their criminal inclinations behind attractive personalities.

These are people to fear.

Smugly confident in their abilities to outwit authority, knowing all there is to know about crossing the lines society places to protect the weak from the strong, they choose their time and pick their crime in the expectation that they will never have to pay the price of failure.

Because it is thrilling to imagine the fruits of such effrontery, we look with fascination—or outrage—at those who dare to find the loopholes, who contrive to beat the system—and succeed. When we hear of someone pulling off something so grand, so outrageous, so deliciously perfect that all we can do is shake our heads in wonderment, we may sometimes nurture a secret envy and marvel at the perpetrator's audacity.

Thus the attraction of a modern-day Robin Hood, the man who called himself "D. B. Cooper" when he skyjacked an airliner in 1972. Waving a bag he said contained a bomb, he demanded and got two parachutes and a bag full of cash, then forced the pilot to take off. Somewhere over western Idaho or northern Oregon, Cooper parachuted into the darkness, never to be seen again. Years later, police recovered a few bills that *might* have come from the skyjacking. Officials have speculated that the skyjacker was killed by his jump over forested mountains—but the law never caught up with D. B. Cooper.

As much as people may secretly enjoy reading about the exploits of D. B. Cooper or Robin Hood, it remains hard to profit from a serious crime. Computers have eliminated much of the drudgery required to sift through vast amounts of data, and scientific advances have made possible far more detailed analysis of crime-scene evidence. It's now possible to analyze the composition and microscopic appearance of textile fibers, paint, metal, hair, skin, blood and other body fluids, and many other heretofore inaccessible crime-scene clues.

Ironically, these capabilities have appeared at the same time that serious crime proliferates. So, while it is now possible to identify and convict far more offenders than ever before, police, prosecutors, and courts everywhere are overwhelmed by an escalating volume of cases.

Worse, competing for scarce tax dollars, police and politicians often manipulate crime statistics to their own advantage. Often they mask their failure to deal effectively with common crime by playing to voters, emphasizing the prosecution of a few highly publicized cases.

*So:* it's easier to get away with many types of crimes today than it was a generation ago. *But:* it's harder to get away with any serious crime when authorities decide to take more than a routine interest. Why? Because despite all the negative publicity surrounding police, prosecutors, and the court system, most who serve the cause of justice *are* smarter than most who seek to beat the system. Out of pride and professionalism, most detectives and prosecutors do work longer and harder to solve a baffling case than most perpetrators work to commit their crimes.

While unsolved murders have risen sharply in recent years, most of these are the product of senseless, random violence. It remains very hard to get away with planned murder. Most complex crime schemes fail because:

1) The plotter is unable to foresee every possible permutation of events—and eventually, Murphy's Law throws the plan awry.
2) The plan overlooks some strong probability—a common and basic flaw that makes failure inevitable.
3) The perpetrators fail to execute as they had planned.

Complex planning often goes into so-called white-collar crimes, where perpetrators use their insider's knowledge, power, and influence to loot a company's assets. In the 1980s, this was typical of the events that led to many savings-and-loan failures, and it has long been common in the insurance, registered-securities, banking, and other industries where large amounts of cash or fungible commodities are present. As a rule, however, those perpetrating these kinds of crimes do not expose themselves to great personal hazard and their victims are usually colorless institutions rather than individuals. While these facts do not lessen the severity of the crimes, we felt that most people would find other types of crime much more interesting.

We have also omitted crimes from one of the most common categories: insurance scams revolving around fictitious or staged events. Many succeed because insurers prefer to settle small claims when it's cheaper than litigation, so America has seen a proliferation of workers'-compensation fraud and staged auto accidents. These usually require the collusion of doctors and lawyers who, in most cases, wind up with the biggest share of the illicit profits. This subject, however, is so vast and complex that it requires a book of its own. More important for us, these kinds of cases usually lack the human drama, the excitement of the chase, the high-stakes, go-for-broke thrills of the crimes that we present here.

What sort of person *plans* a murder? According to Sweden's leading authority on the psychology of murder, Dr. Andreas Bjerre, "weakness is the essence of all crime." Most murderers, says Bjerre, are weak in the skills required to meet the demands of their daily lives. Murder, for them, represents escape from their overwhelming problems: coping with the realities that everyone must face. The strong cope while the weak kill. Thus nineteen-year-old Edward Hickman, who could barely hold down a clerk's job in a bank and so had been denied promotion to teller, chose to kidnap and murder Marion Parker, his boss's twelve-year-old daughter. In ransom notes to his victim's parents, Hickman explained that he needed the money for college!

To justify murderous actions and to allow wriggle room from the awful consequences, most murderers engage in massive self-deception. So strong is this that most convicted killers studied by Bjerre deny even the most incontrovertible facts of their daily realities, including the most onerous aspects of their incarceration. In this way Harvey Glatman, a creepy-looking television repairman with a near-genius IQ, deluded himself with fantasies of sexual conquest. In real life, women found Glatman repugnant. Rather than deal with this reality by working to improve his social skills and appearance, he posed as a photographer, duped women into letting him tie them up—then raped and strangled them.

This need to deny reality becomes so important that it can override common sense—exactly what happened to Kenneth Bianchi and Angelo Buono, convicted of nine murders in Southern California in 1977 and 1978. According to courtroom testimony, they operated by flashing phony police badges, ordering young women into an auto resembling an unmarked police car and taking them to Buono's place of business. Evidence at trial showed that after torture, rape, and murder, they disposed of nearly all physical evidence and planted the nude bodies where they would be found quickly. Many in law enforcement thought that by exhibiting an obvious understanding of criminology, the killers seemed to be taunting police. These murders got enormous publicity which led to the creation of a special task force. When yet another murder delivered one of the killers to authorities in another state, the mountain of circumstantial evidence unearthed by the task force was instrumental in their convictions.

So compulsive and deeply rooted is their need to deny reality that many criminals feel their actions are justified—and more so when their deeds are reported in newspapers and on television. They relish the publicity accompanying their crimes because it adds to their self-esteem. Probably the most famous example of this phenomenon is the "Manson family." The small group of arrested adolescents who made Charles Manson their living god missed no opportunity during their trial to get television coverage, even when it meant self-mutilation.

Another well-documented aspect of murderers is their astonishing ability to focus entirely on the task before them. At the moment they decide to kill, everything else in their lives recedes into a murky background. This phenomenon is not limited to those of minor intelligence. Even the brightest, most detail-oriented minds seem to screen out everything but the object of their wrath—for a time, nothing but the crime and its victim exist in the murderer's mind. According to Bjerre's studies, just before the act, murderers are in a state of mind akin to sleepwalking, oblivious to all consequences of their actions. This may explain the uncanny single-mindedness of Harry Thaw, the turn-of-the-century millionaire playboy who killed famed New York architect Stanford White before dozens of witnesses at Madison Square Garden. The same phenomenon was illustrated by Richard Ramirez, the so-called Night Stalker who terrorized Southern California in the 1980s. Despite a public outcry, enormous publicity, and the assignment of hundreds of officers to a manhunt, Ramirez continued to invade the homes of sleeping people and murder them, one after another, in their own beds. He was finally caught by a citizens' watch group.

Even more interesting is that having decided to kill, killers deeply believe they are empowered, that the reward of the intended murder is theirs by all legitimate standards, that by *not* murdering they would be giving up that to which they are rightfully entitled. In this way, "Tiger Woman" Clara Phillips brutally beat her husband's lover to death, justifying her action on the grounds that her husband had humiliated her and his infidelities deserved to be exposed.

Killers, when caught, may argue passionately that the tangible or intangible dividend of their murder was rightfully theirs because *they* are more deserving than their victim. Thus Mark David Chapman could murder ex-Beatle John Lennon. Chapman convinced himself that he was "the Catcher in the Rye, the Holden Caulfield of the present generation." Lennon had to die so that the world would realize this. He further justified murder because the musician had accumulated an enormous fortune and lived in luxury while millions suffered. Chapman expected to be thanked for the murder.

Other killers justify their actions as being in harmony with the natural order. They indulgently see themselves as rebels against society's overly restrictive norms. By their brute actions they seek to reject the "unnatural" constraints of civilization.

As we examined hundreds of actual or attempted "perfect" crimes, we began to notice a pattern. It seems to us that most "perfect" crimes—successful or not—regardless of technique or strategy, involve a high degree of detailed planning, complex execution, and most of all, reasoned willingness on the part of the perpetrators to risk their lives and everything they possess on the possibility that they'll not get caught.

What follows is a collection of exquisitely audacious

"perfect" crimes. Some of them succeeded; but for accidents of fate or unforeseen circumstances, others very well might have. Either way, we're betting that you won't want to stop reading until you find out why.

Marvin J. Wolf & Katherine Mader
Los Angeles, California, April 1994

# The Lone Wolf
# (1981)

**M**ANY SOPHISTICATED CRIMINALS BELIEVE THAT ONE WAY to get away with a crime is to camouflage one illegal act with another that is less serious. For example, a murder that looks like a robbery attempt gone awry may draw less attention and investigative effort than a murder that looks like an assassination. That may be enough to ensure that police never make the right connections between victim and perpetrator.

Another notion, with some foundation in truth, is that selecting the right place to commit a crime may help in evading justice. For example, if a crime occurs in a jurisdiction where authorities are stretched to the limits of their resources, they may put less effort into any one case than would those not so overloaded. This case illustrates a murder brilliantly camouflaged as the by-product of a simple robbery and carefully planned to take advantage of a police force with too many cases to investigate. Were it not for a few anti-Establishment journalists who were drawn to the killer by his swollen ego and incautious behavior, this might well have been a perfect crime.

In his native Japan, as elsewhere in a world he saw as his personal oyster, Kazuyoshi Miura stood out. Partial to lizard-skin cowboy boots and Porsche sunglasses, he wrapped his lean, sinewy six-foot frame in expensive

9

London-tailored suits. Roaming Tokyo's entertainment districts with the requisite pretty young woman nestled at his side, Miura was almost an unconscious parody of what Japanese hate most about Westerners. At thirty-something, he emerged from obscurity, styling himself the "Lone Wolf," a flamboyant sensation seeker who operated by his own rules.

Where most Japanese are unfailingly polite—in disputes, the one who first displays temper is shamed and hence the loser—Miura was highly aggressive. He liked to win—and he enjoyed rubbing the loser's nose in defeat. And unlike most Japanese businessmen, the bustling little concern he founded was dependent upon American imports. Once a month or so, Miura flew to Los Angeles to buy merchandise for his Tokyo store, Fulham Road Ltd. He prowled swap meets, garage sales, and thrift shops for Fifties furniture and antique clothing. Sensing how mad young Japanese were for anything hip, American, and wearable, he bought the first Camp Beverly Hills license for Japan.

Broadening his horizons, Miura became a sort of latter-day Lafcadio Hearn, reporting on Japanese exotica—Tokyo's kinky, sex-toy-strewn love hotels and its gay bathhouses, for example—for a Los Angeles counterculture periodical called *Wet*, "the magazine of gourmet bathing."

During one of his monthly excursions to Los Angeles, on the afternoon of August 13, 1981, Miura, then thirty-three years old, checked into the New Otani Hotel in the Little Tokyo area near downtown. He was accompanied by his beautiful wife, Kazumi, twenty-eight.

After changing clothes, Kazumi and Miura made a beeline for the hotel shopping arcade, returning in early evening with a Chinese-style dress. It needed a few nips and tucks, so Miura used the phone to summon a seamstress to their room. Then he left for a business meeting in the lobby.

In the hotel room, the seamstress asked Kazumi to pose before a bathroom mirror—and suddenly pulled a claw hammer from her bag. She struck Kazumi in the head, a glancing blow that caused a cut but no serious harm. Kazumi struggled with her attacker, but the seamstress fled.

Kazumi found her husband in the lobby, meeting with

Yoshikuni Matsumoto, his twenty-eight-year-old, Los Angeles–based assistant. Kazumi wanted to phone the police immediately.

Miura calmed her down. This wasn't a good time to get involved with the police, he explained. It would take a lot of time and effort and there was so much crime in Los Angeles that the police would probably never catch a crazy seamstress. When Kazumi remained unconvinced, Miura leveled with her: the real problem was marijuana. Miura bought a few kilos every time he came to Los Angeles; in Tokyo it was worth far more wholesale than he paid retail. If police came to the room, said Miura, they might find his marijuana.

So the couple said nothing to police. Cutting short their working vacation, they returned to Tokyo, where Kazumi told her friends and family what a horrible place Los Angeles was.

Kazumi Sasaki and Miura had been married for twenty months and had known each other scarcely two years. Her family had little time to object to Miura's whirlwind courtship. After the marriage, when they came to know him, they found little to admire in their son-in-law.

The well-connected owner of a small ironworks and welding company in suburban Tokyo, Mr. Yoshitsugu Sasaki was wary of Miura's flashy ways. But Kazumi didn't care what her father thought. She was crazy about Miura. She told her twin sister that Miura was "her destiny."

When Kazumi became pregnant, however, Miura seemed to lose interest in her. By the time she bore him a baby girl, relations were quite strained. The trip to Los Angeles was a sort of second honeymoon, a way to reignite the passion between them. Still in search of that passion, perhaps, Kazumi agreed to return to Los Angeles with Miura three months later, on November 18.

After landing at Los Angeles International Airport, the couple rented a car and drove to Seventh Street, just west of the downtown area, where they checked into the City Center Motel. Miura was anxious to make use of every hour of daylight, he explained, so without bathing or changing clothes, the couple went for a drive. Miura brought along his camera. He was looking for a pair of palm trees, like those in the Camp Beverly Hills logo, so he could shoot Kazumi in front of them.

He found just the right ones near the corner of First and Fremont. North Fremont at that time was an undersized avenue just beside a major downtown artery, the Harbor Freeway. It was an out-of-the-way place, with few pedestrians or through traffic. Because of the freeway's elevated roadbed, the only place to view this street was from the top floors of the Department of Water and Power Building, about a quarter of a mile away. It would have been very hard to find a more remote spot in the downtown area.

As Kazumi posed with her back to the camera, the door of a nearby green car flew open. Two men leaped out. As Miura later recalled the moment, they looked like Hispanics. They fired at Kazumi. They fired at Miura.

Kazumi went down, a .22-caliber bullet in her brain. Miura also went down, though his wound was very slight: another .22 grazed his leg. Screaming, "My wife! My wife!" he watched as the gunmen snatched some $1,200 from Kazumi's purse, then fled.

Oddly, the gunmen did not take Miura's high-priced camera or his wallet. And they left about a hundred dollars—money that fell from Kazumi's purse and was scattered on the sidewalk.

As Miura told it, after the shooting and robbery, the gunmen climbed into a car and roared away. The Hispanic behind the wheel had a long ponytail, he recalled.

Despite the isolation of its setting, there were several witnesses to this attack. Many employees of the Department of Water and Power parked their cars on Fremont Street, where it was cheaper to feed a meter than pay for an expensive monthly parking space in the DWP garage. These employees knew that parking enforcement usually hit that street about eleven, and so they kept glancing out their top-floor windows to see if it was time to move their cars or feed the meters. When Kazumi and Miura fell, two of the eyewitnesses called police. Minutes later, an ambulance arrived, and the couple was hurried to nearby County/USC Medical Center.

The bullet had pierced Kazumi's right cheek, just below the eye. She was on the operating table for four hours as physicians struggled to save her life. But after they had done everything possible and the young woman was out of immediate danger, she remained in a coma.

From his hospital bed Miura rallied his troops—the Japanese media, of whom there are many representatives in Los Angeles. He made a great show of his outrage and his anger, asking over and over, "To do this for a thousand dollars—what is this about?"

As days and then weeks passed Kazumi remained in her coma. Miura, living in a room provided free by the hospital, publicly bemoaned the $90,000 in medical bills and incidental expenses run up as a result of the shooting, and demanded compensation. The city of Los Angeles must pay, he said. The State of California must pay. The United States of America must pay. *Someone* must pay.

Miura pumped up the story, describing to anyone who would listen the dangers of walking the streets of Los Angeles. His assistant, Matsumoto, a Japanese national and a graduate of the University of Southern California, told the press that Miura had confided that although he had many friends in Southern California, he would never visit Los Angeles again.

Soon after the shooting, Kazumi's parents and sister rushed to her bedside, amid sizeable media coverage. With his in-laws at hand, Miura raged at the TV cameras. If his wife died, he would avenge her in the spirit of Bushido, the way of the warrior, Japan's ancient samurai code.

Miura's own way, however, was the media. Still on crutches, he led a correspondent from the Tokyo-based Fuji Network back to the crime scene, where he staged a reenactment of the crime for a television camera.

Miura's angry words did not fall on deaf ears. He became an instant celebrity in Japan, his picture flashed to the nation's most remote corners by all four networks. The Japanese consulate in Los Angeles issued a traveler's bulletin, warning Japanese tourists to beware, lest they also fall victim to the robbers prowling the city's streets.

Miura's fulminations were more than a minor annoyance to Los Angeles officials. Mayor Tom Bradley was a frequent visitor to Japan, promoting trade and tourism. Los Angeles has a large, prosperous, Japanese-American community, and more than 870,000 Japanese tourists visit the city every year, pumping tens of millions of dollars into the local economy.

The first police on the crime scene were in a patrol car. After giving first aid and securing the area, they turned the case over to Central Robbery, the detectives who work all robbery cases within the downtown district. Because the victims were Japanese, a Japanese-speaking officer from the LAPD's Asian Task Force was assigned to work with the robbery detectives.

Lieutenant Jimmy Sakoda was the godfather of the Asian Task Force. In 1975, he had conceived the idea of a special squad to help deal with the rising tide of crime involving Asians as victims or perpetrators. "Back in the Fifties, Sixties, and Seventies, the police department was reactive only," recalls Sakoda. "They didn't really become *pro*active. Somebody got killed or robbed, they went out and investigated. But [at the time] the Asian community was really starting to increase . . . there were things like organized crime that no one outside the Asian community knew about," he recalls.

Chief Ed Parker, then in the last days of his tenure, agreed. Seven officers were recruited for Sakoda.

A third-generation American, Sakoda was born in Washington State in 1935 but spent most of his early childhood in Los Angeles. In 1942, like hundreds of thousands of other Japanese-Americans, he was sent to a "relocation" camp to sit out the war. Afterward, he returned to Los Angeles. After high school he studied police science at City College and in 1958 he joined the Los Angeles Police Department. After he completed the LAPD's tough academy, his first job was undercover, as a narcotics officer. Later, he worked in a variety of assignments, including patrol, the juvenile and gang details, the vice squad, and several years as a detective, primarily in robbery.

After Miura and his wife were shot, Sakoda was called in to help the robbery detail. Speaking in Japanese, he interviewed Miura. While most of the robbery-squad detectives were inclined to believe him, there was something about Miura's demeanor, about the way he answered questions, that made Sakoda suspicious. He couldn't quite put his finger on it.

"He just wasn't reacting the way most Japanese would to having their wife shot. He was *too* aggressive, *too* angry, *too* loud," says Sakoda.

And then there was what Miura told police. He said that he had seen no one else on the street when the men jumped out of the car. But one of the Department of Water and Power witnesses said he saw Miura joined by somebody—it looked like a man—just before the shooting.

Sakoda, however, had little more than his gut to guide him. There was no physical evidence except the bullets removed from Miura and his wife, and they were worthless without a gun to match to them. Somewhere between the hospital and the police department, Miura's trousers got lost. There was no way to test them for gunshot residue, a lost clue that might have revealed whether Miura shot *himself* in the thigh.

Sakoda wanted Miura to take a polygraph examination. Miura agreed, but three weeks after the shooting, when he came to LAPD headquarters at Parker Center to take the test, he was edgy. Seated next to the polygraph machine, he argued with Sakoda in Japanese, accusing him of insulting his manhood. Suddenly, he jumped from his chair, waving his crutches, screaming, "Go ahead, you bastards! Just try!"

Miura stormed out of the building without taking the polygraph. That afternoon, with Kazumi still comatose, he flew back to Japan, where Sakoda and the LAPD could no longer question his manhood—or ask him to face a lie detector.

After Miura left the country, Sakoda found a bus driver who remembered seeing a white van pulling out of Fremont

Street about the time of the shooting. A security guard described a similar vehicle, which he thought was probably a Chevrolet van.

One of the Department of Water and Power witnesses, watching from two blocks away, also saw a white van driving away—and was also very sure Miura had been briefly joined by a man on the sidewalk while Kazumi had her back turned to the camera and was posing between the palms.

After more investigation, Sakoda discovered a city health-department parking lot a few blocks away. On any given day there were fifty white health-department vans coming and going on or near Fremont Street. So maybe the white van didn't have anything to do with the shootings.

Back in Japan, Miura became a major media celebrity. With aid from his father-in-law, who had connections to Japan's powerful, ruling Liberal Democratic Party, Miura distributed thousands of handbills bearing a photo of his daughter and a plaintive *Give me my mommy back* caption in a good facsimile of a child's scribbling. Thousands of donations for Kazumi's medical expenses poured in from warmhearted Japanese.

Miura wrote letters to President Ronald Reagan, California Governor Jerry Brown, Los Angeles Mayor Tom Bradley, and U.S. Ambassador to Japan Mike Mansfield, protesting their failure to ensure the safety of foreign visitors in America.

Through his father-in-law, Miura put diplomatic pressure on the U.S. government to have Kazumi returned to Japan at U.S. expense. Over the objections of her doctors, who feared the trip might kill her, a specially equipped U.S. Air-Force C-141 aerial ambulance flew the comatose young woman back to Japan.

Kazumi's arrival was another major media event, covered live by all four Japanese networks. Miura seized the spotlight again by limping out to a helicopter landing pad and using a smoke-signaling device to "help" guide the aircraft to a safe landing.

In the months that followed, as Kazumi lay unconscious in a Tokyo hospital, Miura found every possible occasion to rail against America as a turbulent, dangerously violent country where everyone carried guns and no one was safe in the street.

Violent crime is relatively rare in Japan, where handguns are outlawed for all but law enforcement and tightly controlled collectors. Miura's fulminations about the dangers of American cities reflected a view shared by many Japanese, especially the older generation. He became almost a national hero, the symbol of Japan's sufferings at America's hands.

A few months after Kazumi's return to Japan, Yoshikuni Matsumoto also went home. He took with him a .22-caliber rifle and some ammunition. In Japan, possession of such a weapon requires a license—and Matsumoto didn't have one. He hid the rifle very carefully in a secret compartment below the roof of his house.

On November 30, 1982, a little over a year from the day she was shot, Kazumi died without regaining consciousness.

Miura again seized the moment and called the media. Sobbing in inconsolable grief, he appeared over and over on Japanese television.

Hundreds of mourners, but few actually acquainted with Kazumi or Miura, came to a Buddhist temple in one of Tokyo's more affluent neighborhoods, Shinjuku, to join in the funeral ceremonies.

Miura was there, of course, accompanied by Yoshie Fukuzawa, an elegant young model. Many in the press would later note that she had been Miura's live-in playmate for several months before Kazumi's death.

Again a swinging single, Japanese-style, Miura decided that raising his child was too much to expect of him. He turned his daughter over to his own parents to raise.

Not that Miura wasn't able to afford child care. Within weeks of Kazumi's death, three insurance companies paid Miura 155 million yen, the equivalent, at exchange rates than in effect, of about $767,000. Miura had purchased the policies in February 1981, six months before the New Otani Hotel hammer attack, nine months before the shooting that left Kazumi in a terminal coma.

Miura's sudden wealth did not go entirely unnoticed. Tokyo police and insurance investigators separately questioned him. He stonewalled them, sticking very closely to what he had told police in Los Angeles.

In March 1983, Miura announced his engagement to Yoshie. His former in-laws were shocked. By ancient Japanese custom, the ashes of the dead are buried a year after death. By the same custom, widows and widowers wait until sometime after the interment ceremony before remarriage. It was bad enough that Miura had offended the Sasakis by flaunting a girlfriend at his wife's funeral—what was his hurry to remarry?

Miura explained that he was breaking with one custom in the hope of preserving another: By marrying Yoshie, he said, his young daughter could be raised in a traditional household. He neglected to mention that his daughter was still living with his own parents.

But Miura was always persuasive. The Sasakis allowed him to take them out for dinner following the burial ceremony.

Miura had a magnificent new home thanks to the insurance money, a sexy, beautiful wife, a thriving business, some very healthy bank accounts, and the kind of sympathetic celebrity that in Japan opens many doors. He had committed the perfect crime.

But not everyone in Japan was convinced that Miura had told everything he knew about the events in Los Angeles. A few reporters had already begun to unravel his secret life.

In Japan, the practice of journalism is uniquely styled to accommodate Japanese mores and values. That is, while journalism in most industrialized nations serves to inform the populace, and certainly does so in Japan, in that country the welfare of the group is always more important than that of anyone in it.

That basic imperative has shaped the growth of Japan's modern media. The television networks and daily newspapers enjoy very cozy relationships with the Establishment. For example, journalists who nominally cover, say, the Ministry of Finance, are all members of an exclusive club.

This is a ministry press association, a place with office space where members can work, a dining room, and a bar. Many journalists' clubs even have a few hotel-style rooms where members can spend the night at a modest cost. Like all clubs, Japan's journalists' clubs have rules, both written and unwritten. The number-one unwritten rule in every press association is that any reporter who breaks a big story significantly before his peers do risks embarrassing his less enterprising clubmates. Since this isn't of benefit to the group, there are few scoops—everyone publishes or broadcasts at about the same time.

Another rule is that any reporter who learns of something the Ministry of Finance (or the Ministry of Education, or the Toyota Motor Company, or Sony, etc.) doesn't want publicly known, but who publishes it anyway, risks losing access to officials on his beat. If he's transferred to another beat, chances are he won't be allowed to join the requisite club. Either way, the penalty for being too far out in front of the pack, for making things difficult for the rest of the group, is virtual exclusion.

So, no one with a lick of sense embarrasses his or her colleagues. The daily papers and electronic media do not make a practice of investigative reporting. An Establishment medium breaking a story that embarrasses the Establishment is exceptionally rare.

On the other hand, once a story *has* been reported in some paper or on television, it's fair game for all. And if it's a hot story, hundreds of reporters will swarm all over it, eager to get even the tiniest new detail before their public.

All this aside, there is still a Japanese tradition of investigative reporting. Many small, offbeat publications very definitely are *not* Establishment. They are outsiders who can't ordinarily get access to Japan's captains and kings. They must dig for scandal.

So it was that *Weekly Bunshun*, circulation 800,000, was the only Japanese publication to probe the 1974 award of an enormous contract to Lockheed, the American aerospace company, by the Ministry of Defense. And it was *Bunshun* that pointed out that Lockheed had paid hundreds of thousands of dollars to Prime Minister Kakuei Tanaka just before that contract was signed. Tanaka resigned and was tried, convicted, and sentenced to a four-year prison term.

In 1983, *Bunshun* struck again. This time, their target was the Lone Wolf, Miura. Back in 1979, Miura's company, Fulham Road, had employed Chizuko Shiraishi, an attractive, thirty-four-year-old accountant. She had been married to the wealthy president of an important trading company, but their marriage ended with a bitter divorce. Among many charges flung by Chizuko's husband was that she had carried on a lengthy affair with Miura, who had not yet married Kazumi.

When their divorce was final, Chizuko lost custody of her son to her ex-husband. She did, however, win a handsome cash settlement from him, to be paid in installments.

In March 1979, Chizuko vanished. Months went by. No one among her family or friends heard from her. It was no secret that Chizuko and Miura had been lovers, so several people asked Miura if he knew what had happened to her.

Miura told some people that Chizuko, frustrated by living close by her son but unable to see him more than occasionally, had spoken of moving to some remote part of Japan, perhaps the northern island of Hokkaidō. But he told others that she had borrowed money from him and gone to live in Los Angeles until her divorce settlement came through.

*Bunshun* reporters confirmed that Chizuko had obtained an exit visa for Los Angeles and left Japan on March 29, 1979. The document listed the Hollywood Holiday Inn as her address in Los Angeles, but when reporters checked with the manager, he said he had no record of a guest with that name. He also noted, however, that on the day Chizuko flew into Los Angeles, his registered guests included a "Mr. and Mrs. Miura."

Interviewed for the *Bunshun* story, Miura denied that he had ever lived with Chizuko. When that claim was published, however, several former neighbors contacted the magazine. Sometime in April 1979, they said, they'd seen Miura putting out an unusual quantity of trash for the weekly pickup: twenty plastic bags. Curious, they had opened the bags to find cosmetics, women's shoes, and women's clothing.

*Bunshun* ran a story featuring the recollections of Miura's neighbors. Then editors assigned more reporters to the story and some weeks later learned that just before Chizuko's disappearance, her former husband had begun making his alimony payments directly to her bank account.

*Bunshun* compared withdrawal records from Chizuko's bank with deposits to Miura's and concluded that he had systematically taken sums from her account, apparently by using her ATM card and secret access number.

Confronted by reporters, Miura readily agreed that he'd taken the money. He said that he'd loaned Chizuko money before she left Japan and she had agreed that he would take repayment from her divorce settlement.

But where was Chizuko?

On May 4, 1979, a young boy in the San Fernando Valley community of Lake View Terrace was walking his puppy when it began sniffing and pawing at something half-hidden beneath an old wooden door. To his horror, the boy discovered a blackened, desiccated, animal-gnawed corpse, partly concealed by the remains of a plastic trash bag.

Medical examiners determined that the corpse was probably that of an Asian woman in her early thirties, but the remains were so decomposed that it was impossible to determine the cause of her death. "Oriental Jane Doe #88" went into a drawer in the coroner's freezer until she could be identified.

Early in 1984, after local Japanese-language newspapers began reporting stories based on the *Bunshun* series about Miura's connections with the vanished Chizuko, LAPD's Major Crimes Unit began to wonder if their unidentified corpse might not be the missing woman. They asked Fuji Television's Los Angeles correspondent to help get copies of Chizuko's dental records. After careful comparison, the coroner announced that Oriental Jane Doe #88 was indeed the missing Chizuko.

Miura responded to news of Chizuko's death by telling a Tokyo Broadcasting System reporter "I cannot but pray for her soul. . . . I express my deepest sorrow."

Smelling a bigger story, *Bunshun* kept several reporters on the Miura case, digging, sifting, fishing. Soon they discovered Miura's hidden criminal past. A classic overachiever in high school, he was chosen freshman student-body president after a rash of local publicity about his discovery of a house fire that he had helped put out. Five months later, however, Miura was charged with five counts of arson. Confessing to his crimes, he was sentenced to reform school. Over the next several years he racked up more convictions for assaulting a reform-school guard, forging driver's licenses, another count of arson, extortion, rape, robbery, assault, and violations of Japan's tough gun laws.

*Bunshun* disclosed that in July 1968, Miura began serving a ten-year prison sentence but was released four years early for good behavior. By interviewing prison officials, reporters discovered that he'd spent most of his time in the prison library, reading detective novels. By all accounts, his favorite book, checked out several times, was *Blindspot in the Afternoon*, which tells the story of a criminal genius who pulls off a complex swindle—a perfect crime.

Miura was not about to let *Bunshun* besmirch his hard-won celebrity. In 1984 he published *Unclear Times*, the first of three books he would write about his life. In it, Kazumi is set gently on an alabaster pedestal and treated with the reverence due a goddess. In contrast, Chizuko is depicted as a sex toy, an amusement, a passing fancy. Throughout this memoir, Miura claimed to know nothing about who had shot his girlfriend or killed his wife.

The book was an overnight sensation, Japan's number-one best-seller. Once again on top, Miura was courted by the Establishment media. In exchange for exclusive television rights, Tokyo Broadcasting System paid for Miura's mock-Hindu-style wedding to Yoshie, staged in Bali. Virtually every Japanese who owned a television set watched some or all of this glitzy spectacle. After that, Miura demanded and got as much as $10,000 for a single interview. TV crews staked out his house and followed him everywhere.

*Bunshun*, however, was still digging. They discovered that Miura had arrived in Los Angeles the day before Chizuko disappeared. He acknowledged being in Los Angeles, but denied that he had even seen Chizuko. He admitted taking five million yen—about $21,000—from her bank account, but it was, he reiterated, his own money, repayment of a loan. "Why should I harm her for such a small amount?"

Miura's second book, *My Fulham Road Story*, was another best-seller. All but rolling in money, he again broke with tradition by hiring lawyers and bringing libel suits against several periodicals, including *Bunshun*. Libel is somewhat easier to prove in Japan than in America—there is no legal protection for those who write about public figures.

Still riding high, Miura and Yoshie opened a bar and boutique, Fulham Road Yoshie, which almost immediately became one of Tokyo's hotspots. The couple enjoyed such a high profile that in a 1985 poll of Japanese television viewers, Yoshie was voted one of Japan's ten leading women. Miura's face was so well known that he was cast as himself for a cameo role in *Comic Magazine*, a hugely successful movie. Miura resumed his writing career with a sexual advice column for *Weekly Playboy Magazine*, then posed naked for *Brutus*, one of Japan's leading men's magazines.

But as 1984 ended, one of Japan's most famous men quietly put his house up for sale and flew to London with Yoshie and his daughter. The trip was paid for by TBS, in exchange for the promise of several exclusive interviews.

The revelations slowly percolating to the surface in the Japanese media eventually reached the LAPD. Jimmy Sakoda, as ordered, had turned the Kazumi case over to Major Crimes, the LAPD squad that handles most high-profile cases. But while he had had no official connection to the case since Miura left Los Angeles in 1981, on his own time and in his own way Sakoda had continued to investigate. When *Bunshun* revealed that Miura had been in Los Angeles when Chizuko was killed, Major Crimes decided he was a suspect and assigned the case to Detective William Sartuche. He also reopened the investigation into Kazumi's murder.

In 1985, the two Miura cases were reassigned to Detective Frank Garcia. Unlike many who worked the case before, Garcia was convinced from the start that Miura was the killer.

Now three proud, highly competent investigators had worked on the case, and none wanted to give up on it. But ego conflicts, including theirs, spawned bureaucratic infighting that over the next several years did little to help speed justice for the killer of Kazumi and Chizuko.

Early in 1985, Sakoda, on his own time and money, returned to Japan a third time to speak with Tokyo police and journalists familiar with Miura's background. Before leaving Tokyo, he participated in a press conference organized by a sensation-seeking Japanese television network—for which he was widely criticized by LAPD supervisors. Returning to Los Angeles, Sakoda ended twenty-six years of LAPD service and retired. He was hired immediately by the district attorney's office to work in a newly created Asian Criminal Investigation Unit with major responsibility for the Miura case.

Because the statute of limitations on assault was about to expire, the investigation of Kazumi's attack by a hammer-wielding seamstress in the New Otani Hotel was converted to "conspiracy to commit murder," a crime without a statute of limitations. Deputy DA Louis Ito was assigned as legal adviser to the ACIU with a mandate to build a case against Miura.

Not long after Miura arrived in London, *Weekly Sankei*, a Japanese magazine, made the most startling revelations about Miura yet. Michiko Yazawa, twenty-five, a sexy, doe-eyed, soft-core porn actress and sometime model, recalled meeting the "Lone Wolf" at a 1981 marijuana party. It was a time when she was particularly desperate for money and affection, and she found Miura intoxicating. On their first date, he took her to a Tokyo love hotel, replete with mirrored ceilings, kinky love toys, and scented unguents.

The next morning, Miura offered Michiko a job: kill his wife. She was incredulous until Miura explained that it would be easy to kill a tourist in Los Angeles. Unlike Tokyo, he had explained, where police have less than a hundred murders a year to solve, in L.A. there are over

1,500 murders annually—so many that police can't investigate them all. They would never get terribly concerned about one more, especially if it was a foreigner, a tourist.

The proof of that, said Miura, was that he had already killed there. "I had another person do the murder before my eyes," said Miura. "The victim is still buried in the desert."

Michiko told *Sankei* that Miura wanted her to shoot Kazumi from a car. But Plan A went nowhere, explained Michiko, because she didn't know how to drive and had never even touched a gun.

Plan B was for Michiko to stab Kazumi to death.

No good, said Michiko. The sight of blood made her sick.

Maybe, suggested Lone Wolf Miura, Michiko could drown his wife in the New Otani Hotel's pool.

"So sorry," said Michiko. "I don't know how to swim."

Finally, Miura suggested that she hit Kazumi over the head with a hammer, a task that took no special skills.

Michiko was still reluctant, so Miura turned on the charm. If she would kill Kazumi, he would give her half of the thirty-million-yen insurance payout—about $200,000—on Kazumi's life. And of course he would marry Michiko as soon as decently possible after his wife's ashes were interred.

That did it. Fifteen million yen sounded like big money to Michiko, and she very much wanted to be married. She came to Los Angeles with a tour group a few days before Miura and his wife flew over from Tokyo. Along with her fellow tourists, she saw Southern California's sights on August 12, 1981. The next day she passed on the trip to Disneyland, explaining that she had to go see a friend.

Instead, she stayed in her room until Miura, pretending to call a seamstress, called. Michiko knocked on the door and Kazumi let her in. She opened her cloth bag, took out a hammer Miura had given her, and swung at Kazumi's head.

But Michiko wasn't much better with hammers than she was with pistols, knives, swimming, or driving. Her blow raised a small bruise and made a little cut on

Kazumi's head. When her would-be victim fought back, Michiko flew from the room.

The actress spent the next day in terror, barricaded in her room. When nothing happened, she caught a plane back to Tokyo.

In London, Miura accepted another three million yen, about $13,000, for an exclusive TBS interview to respond to these latest charges. Michiko was nothing more than a woman scorned, he said, crushed and angry because he had rejected her. She had made up lies to damage his reputation and get revenge because he had refused to marry her. Wasn't it interesting, he added, that she had waited until now to come forward—exactly when she was attempting to make a comeback in her acting career?

Miura had only contempt for Japanese law. He probably believed that since he and Michiko were not suspected of committing crimes in Japan, authorities there could do nothing to him. Moreover, he had worked hard to create a glamorous public image of himself. He was the Lone Wolf, the incarnation of bold action. Determined to destroy his latest accuser, he caught a plane for Tokyo.

Miura was probably not aware that in the 1970s, the Diet, Japan's legislature, had with scant ceremony passed a rarely invoked law authorizing prosecution of Japanese nationals who committed crimes overseas. Like many Japanese laws, this statute, while officially part of the public record, was largely secret. Few copies of it were published and none distributed to the media. There had been virtually no publicity about it.

Police in Japan had also been quiet, but far from idle. Soon after *Bunshun* began its sensational reports, a task force of one hundred Tokyo detectives was organized. Several investigators visited Los Angeles in August 1985 to compare what Miura had told them with what they could learn locally. One discrepancy: Kazumi had sought medical treatment after the New Otani attack, telling an ambulance attendant that she had fallen. But after returning to Tokyo, she told a girlfriend that *Miura* had hit her with a hammer.

On September 11, 1985, the Japanese police felt they

had enough evidence to arrest Miura and Michiko. They were accused of Kazumi's *attempted* murder at the New Otani Hotel—the first Japanese to be charged in Japan for a crime committed in the United States. Their arrest at the posh Ginza Tokyo Hotel was carried live on Japanese television.

Japan's criminal justice system traces its roots to the Napoleonic Code of the late nineteenth century. Juries do not determine guilt or innocence. That is left to a trio of judges whose presumption, when a case comes before them, is that the accused are guilty until proven otherwise. Unlike America, however, Japan has no law against merely *conspiring* to commit a crime. Japanese courts put more weight on physical evidence than do American. No one in Japan, for example, has been convicted of murder without a body to prove that death occurred.* On the other hand, confession and sincere public repentance are considered strong mitigating factors in Japan—one reason why police, who often hold suspects in special police-station detention cells for extended periods, obtain an overwhelming number of confessions.

The judges heard Michiko's confession. Miura testified that while he'd known the actress was a guest in the New Otani during the attack, he'd had nothing to do with any attempt on his wife's life.

The court found both the accused guilty of attempted murder.

Michiko drew a thirty-month sentence. Miura, still denying any involvement and showing no repentance, received six years in prison.

Even before Miura's trial, on December 7, 1985, the anniversary of an infamous date in Japanese-American relations, Kazumi's father, Yoshitsugu Sasaki, had held a press conference in Los Angeles. On a previous trip to the city, he had presented L.A. County District Attorney Ira Reiner with petitions of concern from 92,000 Japanese. Although Reiner had named Miura as chief suspect in the murders of Kazumi and Chizuko, whoever actually

* See "No Body," p. 238 (L. Ewing Scott)

shot Kazumi remained at large. In Little Tokyo's Japanese-American Cultural Center, Sasaki announced a $10,000 reward for information leading to the conviction of the triggerman who had shot his daughter.

The money would come, Sasaki explained, from the proceeds of a book *he* was writing, *Yell! Kazumi, Yell the Truth!* The press conference was beamed back to Japan by Fuji Television, which had also helped raise the money for Sasaki's trip to Los Angeles by soliciting contributions from viewers.

In 1987, Yoshie, no longer one of Japan's top-ten women, sued Miura for divorce.

On May 5, 1988, more than two years after he was convicted of attempted murder, Los Angeles authorities finally brought conspiracy and murder charges against Miura. Just why this took so long has never been fully explained, but many involved in the case believe the main reason was bureaucratic infighting. Too many different agencies wanted a piece of Miura. The result was gridlock, with the principals unable to agree on how best to proceed.

The Japanese government, having received formal requests from its own police and prosecutorial organs, also wanted to try Miura for Kazumi's murder. In February 1988, Tokyo's tough-talking chief prosecutor took personal charge of the Miura case. He flew to Los Angeles, where, after a meeting with police and DA's officials, an agreement was reached to try Miura in Japan rather than in the United States.

Afterward, with full cooperation from the LAPD, Miura's version of the shooting on North Fremont Street was meticulously reenacted for Japanese police technicians manning video cameras. Subsequently, LAPD Detective Frank Garcia and several other officers went from room to room in the Department of Water and Power, interviewing anyone who might have been looking out the window toward North Fremont Street on the day Kazumi was shot.

It cost a lot of time and shoe leather, but eventually they found five witnesses who described a white van pulling up on the street near Miura, exactly as he had said. But they also described a burgundy sedan pulling up behind the van. After the shooting, both van and sedan sped away.

Neither Miura nor Matsumoto, his assistant, had owned a burgundy-colored car—but Matsumoto, who lived in Los Angeles, might have rented one. In November 1988, Matsumoto's wife was questioned in Tokyo. She recalled that her husband often rented cars for Miura's import-export business. She even recalled the name of an agency with whom he often did business.

Police checking records at Valley Rent-A-Car found that Matsumoto had rented a white van on November 17, the day before the shooting—and a burgundy sedan on November 18. Checking mileage logs, they determined that the distance the burgundy car traveled while it was in Matsumoto's possession matched the round-trip distance between the rental agency and North Fremont Street. According to time stamps on rental documents, Matsumoto had left the agency just long enough before the time of the shooting to allow him to drive to the scene. The amount of time that elapsed between the shooting and the return of the vehicle almost exactly matched the time required at that hour to drive back from North Fremont.

Matsumoto was arrested in Tokyo on November 10, 1988. A search of his house turned up a .22 rifle—but ballistics tests proved it was *not* the weapon that shot either Miura or Kazumi.

Matsumoto said he kept the rifle, even though mere possession was a felony, precisely because it was *not* the murder weapon. Friends knew he owned a .22, he explained, and if he was arrested for the shooting, he didn't want to be accused of dumping the murder weapon.

Japanese police are very patient questioners. They do not always obey the most enlightened standards of behavior toward criminal suspects. Marathon interrogation sessions run by relays of questioners and deprivation of food, water, and sleep are normal police procedure. Less often, exquisitely brutal torture is applied until the subject confesses.

Under torture, Matsumoto admitted renting the white van and the burgundy sedan, but steadfastly denied shooting Kazumi.

Early in 1989, Miura and Matsumoto went on trial for Kazumi's murder. Evidence included bullet fragments taken from Kazumi's head. In opening statements, prosecutors argued that Miura's motive for murder was money: he'd suffered huge business losses and hoped to recoup them from his wife's life insurance. Prosecutors also believe that Matsumoto was the triggerman. A Los Angeles Department of Water and Power employee testified that he had seen Matsumoto shooting the rifle near the burgundy sedan.

In November 1988, L.A. County Deputy DA Louis Ito announced that regardless of the trial's outcome, because of double-jeopardy provisions in the U.S.–Japan extradition treaties, neither Miura nor Matsumoto would be tried in America.

Japan has relatively few courts and judges. To give all accused of crimes an equal chance, after each day of a trial, a recess is declared until all other cases before the court have been dealt with. Thus, a complex trial can last months or years.

On March 30, 1994, Miura was found guilty of murder. He was later sentenced to life in prison. Matsumoto was acquitted of the murder charge, leaving open the question of who actually fired the shots that killed Kazumi. Matsumoto was convicted of smuggling a rifle and ammunition into Japan and sentenced to eighteen months in prison. Ironically, these convictions came within days of the murders of two Japanese students in a carjacking on a Los Angeles street. Their deaths sparked an international furor over public safety on Los Angeles streets. In Japan there was an enormous outcry about America's "society of guns."

Since there is no physical evidence, it is highly unlikely that Miura will ever be tried for the murder of Chizuko. And so, had he contented himself with the modest spoils of that murder—the $21,000 siphoned from

Chizuko's bank account—he might well have remained unpunished.

Miura styled himself the Lone Wolf and conducted his personal affairs as an individual, eschewing, in a most un-Japanese manner, the responsibilities of a group. He preyed, wolflike, on vulnerable women. But the major flaw in his attempt at a perfect crime was that he ultimately depended on others, less ruthless and capable than himself, to kill Kazumi.

Even so, Miura was so bold and audacious in his choice of victim, time, and place that he almost succeeded. What brought him to justice was an unprecedented and unexpected event: the solution by Japan's news media of a major crime of violence. Ironically, it is likely that the only reason that *Bunshun* reporters went searching for the scent of Miura's crimes was because the Lone Wolf howled too often, too long, and too loud.

# Chop Chop Man
## (1991)

**M**OST HOMICIDES INVOLVE PEOPLE WHO KNOW EACH *other. The hardest murders to solve are those with no obvious link between victim and perpetrator. And where there is no link at all, where the killer chooses a victim at random, unless there is a witness, chances are excellent that the killer will never be found.*

*Having committed one perfect crime, such killers often feel tremendous satisfaction. Seeking to duplicate that singular thrill, they often kill again. And again. And again.*

An expensive security system guarded the front door of the seedy, second-floor, one-bedroom unit in the Oxford Apartments.

Inside, a severed human head lay in the refrigerator. In the freezer compartment, a plastic bag held a human heart. Next to it, neatly wrapped in plastic, were two other human organs. In a separate, waist-high freezer were three human heads, gray waxen horrors staring sightlessly through plastic bags. More freezer bags contained human biceps and other body parts. On a black table near a window was a large tank. Colorful tropical fish swam near the glass, their fins moving in a slow, primal rhythm. Bare-chested men in skimpy briefs smiled suggestively from wall posters. A lava lamp oozed silently in the living room.

A sickeningly overpowering—yet somehow familiar—

stench filled the tiny apartment. After the two police officers arrested Jeffrey Dahmer, the master of this chamber of horrors, they pushed open the sliding door to his bedroom and bath.

A personal computer sat on a table against the wall. Under it were two human skulls in a cardboard box. Three more skulls, painted in a smooth, plasticlike gray, crowded the top drawer of a steel filing cabinet.

Near the bedroom window was a large steel drum painted bright enamel blue. After prying the lid off, police discovered the headless torsos of three young men. The closet concealed two more skulls, bottles of a powerful acid, and a copper kettle containing decomposing hands and male genitalia. The bedspread was crusted with dried human blood.

In the chest of drawers were stacks of Polaroid photos. A smiling Jeffrey Dahmer posing with a limbless human torso, knife in hand, gore everywhere. A blissful Dahmer using a power saw to cut off a head. A jolly Dahmer with knife, hacking off hands, hewing feet, harvesting genitalia. It was a snapshot archive of casual horror beyond anyone's worst nightmare.

By the time Dahmer was led away in handcuffs, more than fifty police vehicles filled the streets and sidewalks around his two-story apartment building, blue-and-red lights flashing a silent message of shock that would rebound through every corner of Milwaukee—and the world.

Dahmer's neighbors in the Oxford Apartments shook in anger, fear, and disbelief. Now they knew what had caused the unholy stench that for months had wafted from Apartment 213.

When someone is found murdered, law enforcement in nearly every Western society adheres to the same, basic, time-tested routine. After identifying the victim—a critical first step, because most homicides are committed by someone known to the victim—police make a list of the victim's associates and family. Usually, this is a matter of routine: searching address books, telephone records, correspondence, and interviewing family and friends. By investigating everyone on this list, dropping those without motive, means, and opportunity to kill the victim, a roster of suspects meriting further inquiry is assembled. Those without an alibi become the subject of scrutiny. From there it is often simple to determine the perpetrator, although sometimes more difficult to prove his guilt. But most often, when police are willing and able to invest enough resources to uncover evidence, a conviction results.

But with no prior link between victim and murderer, it is very hard to find the killer. A man who kills a stranger, selected at random, stands an excellent chance of getting away with it.

But *why* murder a complete stranger?

Usually, it is a way to satisfy some desperate inner urge. Many who kill anonymous victims experience sexual gratification at the moment of death. For this reason, strangulation is the preferred method; the killer revels in watching and feeling his victim suffer. Stabbing is a distant second as a method of choice. Guns are relatively rare instruments of this type of murder. When such a killing goes unpunished, the killer is tempted to repeat the experience. When a murderer, driven by ritualistic need, sex, or power, kills for the fourth time, he—females who kill several strangers are exceedingly rare—fits the FBI's definition of a serial killer.

Serial crime has been around for centuries. Long before Jack the Ripper terrorized Victorian London, serial killers were a rare but recognized phenomenon. But since the 1970s, serial murder in America has multiplied at unprecedented rates. Between 1900 and 1970, according to a study by the University of Louisville's Southern Police Institute, there were 742 U.S. victims of twenty-eight serial murderers. But in the decade 1970 to 1979, at least twenty-nine identified serial killers accounted for 906 victims. In the next decade, no fewer than forty-seven serial killers claimed 670 victims. Some in law enforcement think the growing number of perpetrators and smaller number of victims suggest that police are becoming more efficient in identifying and apprehending serial killers. But while most pre-1970 serial killers slew their victims in pursuit of financial gain, most recent serial murder victims died to satisfy the sexual desires of their killers.

Along with the increase in sexually motivated killings has come a mind-boggling variety of American serial killers, a few of whom, encouraged by enormous media attention, have seemed to elevate their brutal crimes almost to an obscene art form. After capture, many serial killers have in strange, perverted ways become America's oddest celebrities, folk heroes glorified by sensationalized media coverage. Many of the most celebrated are even depicted on "mass murderer" trading cards sold in trendy novelty shops.

On one card is John Wayne Gacy, a wealthy, rotund, jovial Chicago contractor. Transformed by a few ounces of bourbon into a heartless monster, Gacy had, by 1978, strangled thirty-three young men, concealing their bodies in shallow graves beneath the crawl space under his home.

In the 1980s, Texas drifter Henry Lee Lucas was convicted of thirteen murders, nationwide. For a time, Lucas claimed upward of three hundred victims. Police later came to believe that number grossly inflated, as Lucas, desperate for celebrity of any sort, sought to magnify his own importance. Other law-enforcement agencies, anxious to "clear" unsolved homicides, were more than willing to let Lucas take responsibility.

In the late 1980s, Richard Ramirez, transformed by lurid media accounts into the "Night Stalker," terrorized suburban Southern California, brazenly invading homes and apartments to commit more than a dozen rapes and murders. Then he took his Satan-worshiping act to Northern California and killed still more. He was caught attempting yet another Southern California murder when alarmed citizens on neighborhood watch recognized him from a police artist's "wanted" poster.

Between 1985 and 1987, Cincinnati-area "Angel of Death" Donald Harvey poisoned or suffocated at least twenty-four hospital patients, most of whom were terminally ill. He joked about their deaths with coworkers for months before authorities began to investigate.

Wayne Williams may have murdered as many as twenty young Georgia boys, disposing of their bodies in the

Chattahoochee River. His sensational and controversial trial left many in Atlanta feeling police had the wrong man—but the child murders stopped as soon as he was behind bars.

In the late 1970s and early 1980s, Ted Bundy, a slick-talking law student, strangled as many as one hundred girls and women from Washington State to Idaho to Colorado to Florida. His method of operation was to charm them with his good looks and lure them into his car by asking for help while displaying a bogus "handicap," including arm casts and crutches.

Randy Steven Kraft, a mild-mannered computer consultant, may have killed upward of forty young men—he was convicted of eleven murders in one county alone—and left their strangled bodies alongside Southern California freeways. When he was stopped for a minor traffic violation, police found Kraft's latest victim's still-warm body in his van.

And between 1982 and 1984, a mysterious killer stalked and slew at least forty-nine prostitutes, leaving carefully camouflaged corpses in the Green River area between Tacoma and Seattle. The "Green River Killer" remains at large. Some in law enforcement suspect he may be in prison for some other crime, or has moved to another part of the country. In 1991 and 1992, however, new bodies began to turn up. The latest victims were, like the earlier ones, mostly prostitutes.

These are only a few of America's most notorious serial killers. The FBI estimates that in any given year, between thirty and fifty such monsters are in action somewhere in the country. Some thirteen or fourteen were identified or apprehended in each year of the last decade.

Law enforcement and the psychiatric community cannot agree on the causes of this enormous increase in serial killings. Some sociologists argue that the higher number of serial killers is linked to widespread juvenile drug and alcohol abuse, the breakdown of the American family, and the constant glorification of violence in the mass media. They point to the pervasiveness of blood-and-gore-filled "exploitation" movies like *Friday the 13th, Nightmare on Elm Street, Halloween,* and *The Texas Chainsaw Massacre,* aimed at juvenile audiences. Far more violent pornography is also widely available to young adults. Violence-glorifying music produced by such heavy-metal groups as Black Sabbath and Metallica or nihilistic punk-rock groups like Dead Kennedys, Social Distortion, and Tupelo Chainsex may also contribute.

Other experts speculate that most of the increase in serial murder comes from law enforcement's growing perception of the phenomenon, and that in a media-saturated age, more disturbed killers seek the notoriety that accompanies confession to lurid crimes. Whatever the causes, homicides of all types are increasing rapidly in America, from a little under 19,000 in 1985, to 23,440 in 1990. While serial killings still represent only a tiny fraction of all homicides, they are also increasing at a faster rate than other kinds of murder.

To deal with this epidemic, the FBI has set up a special unit to deal with serial killers, a synergy of forensic psychologists, pathologists, ballistics, handwriting, hair, fiber, insect, and serology experts, and highly skilled field investigators. The National Center for the Analysis of Violent Crime, established in 1985 at the FBI Academy in Quantico, Virginia, became world famous when it was featured in *The Silence of the Lambs*, a widely viewed 1991 film dramatization of the Thomas Harris novel.

Through in-depth interviews with thirty-six convicted serial killers, the FBI built a computerized database of case studies. From this has come several generalizations, starting with the fact that most serial killers are white males in their twenties or early thirties. Many have some impairment to their central nervous system, manifested in such symptoms as dyslexia or epilepsy. Most have been psychologically, physically, emotionally, or sexually abused as children.

They tend to be obsessive, deliberate, and cleverly practiced in their highly individualized rituals. Contrary to some popular notions that they really want to be caught, most experts believe that serial killers go to extraordinary lengths to elude capture, and once captured, many will do almost anything to escape punishment.

Since serial killers rarely kill those close to them, they

make things tough on police trying to link a victim to a killer. In the Bundy case, for example, a list of people who might have had contact with one of his victims—names culled from their address books, from teachers and class-mates, and employees at parks where victims disappeared—contained 300,000 names. A computer sort trimmed the list to names appearing three times or more. That still left al-most a thousand suspects. Only when the computer sorted the list to four appearances was the number cut to twenty-five. One of those names was Ted Bundy—but he didn't top the list.

Victims of serial killers are usually vulnerable individu-als, smaller and weaker than their killers. As one noted criminologist observed, serial killers don't go after NFL football players or masters of the martial arts. Instead they prefer to stalk children or young women. Others pursue transients, denizens of a seamy world where few care about them, and fewer still want to deal with police. Transients' disappearances often go unreported for weeks or months. By the time their bodies are found, any evidence has disap-peared. The head of the Green River Task Force tells of one victim whose body rotted for two years in the woods. It sat two more years in a morgue before the family reported their daughter missing.

And in crime-ridden urban areas where murders number in the hundreds annually, unless a killer leaves an especially bizarre "trademark" on his prey, police rarely suspect a se-rial murderer is on the loose until they have at least three victims to compare. This usually means that by the time po-lice have any idea that a serial killer may be on the loose, the murderer has already taken several lives.

From the FBI studies, police tracking a serial killer now know what kind of man to look for: men who hate the women in their lives—their mothers or sisters—and who hate what they think these women did to them. They are men who want to hurt women, to control them, to possess them. This is usually true even for the comparatively rare serial murderer who preys on men. John Wayne Gacy, who hated but also feared women so much that he couldn't attack them, selected homosexual or effeminate men and boys.

Serial killers are almost invariably psychopaths—but rarely insane in the legal sense of being unable to distinguish right from wrong. Instead, psychopaths know the rules but ignore them—they are for others to follow. They lack the ability to empathize with their victims, whom they perceive as objects to be used for their own gratification. Psychopaths consider themselves special; others exist only to serve their needs. They find it very easy to inflict pain and they never suffer remorse.

And yet, disturbingly, these killers usually appear completely normal. They blend into their surroundings, acting, dressing, and seeming totally unremarkable. Most are smarter than the average criminal. A few are near geniuses. As they continue killing they learn to correct their mistakes. Soon they can perform their own peculiar, individualized ritual of death with great efficiency.

Serial murderers act from internal compulsions. But these are not irresistible urges; most can control their behavior for as long as they want. That is part of what makes them so hard to catch. Most kill to complete a cycle that begins with a fantasy. As time goes on, the fantasy becomes more detailed and complex—but simultaneously less and less satisfying. In search of that ultimate satisfaction, they act out their fantasy ritual on a live victim. Satisfying for a short while, the previous act serves as the starting point for their next cycle of fantasies.

All this may lead to an addiction to the fantasy and the acts that fuel it. Like any addiction, ever-more-frequent doses of death are needed to give killers the high they seek. Some start by killing once every few months, but soon need to kill every few weeks, then every few days. This is often the time when, as they begin to spiral out of control, their waking hours increasingly preoccupied with frantic fantasies of their killing ritual, they become careless and are caught.

Beginning in the 1980s, Jeffrey Lionel Dahmer entered just such a cycle of death. If he does not entirely fit the

FBI's profile for serial killers, if his trail of murder and cannibalism is singularly repugnant, it may be because society has studied the phenomenon for only a comparatively short time.

Dahmer was born on May 21, 1960, in Milwaukee, the first child of Lionel Dahmer, a chemistry student at Marquette University, and Joyce Flint, of Chippewa Falls, Wisconsin. Lionel Dahmer received a master's degree in 1962, then took his family to Iowa State to complete his doctorate. By 1967, the elder Dahmer had a good job as an industrial chemist. The family had bought a home in upscale, suburban Bath Township, about halfway between Akron and Cleveland, Ohio.

Young Jeff grew up in an affluent, nearly all-white community. He did not have an easy childhood, however. His mother apparently suffered recurring bouts of mental illness, a condition alluded to in the 1977–1978 divorce proceedings that freed his parents to go their separate ways after years of bitter feuding. After the birth of his younger brother, in 1966, Jeffrey's mother seemed to have little time for him. Even before that, by most accounts, he got little physical affection. With his parents' constant battling, few schoolmates chose to visit. Jeffrey became a loner, and by the time he was in elementary school, he shunned physical contact, refusing to be touched by anyone.

So noisy and public were his parents' battles that neighbors often called the police. Jeffrey watched and learned as his parents turned away lawmen with soft-spoken denials of any serious problem. No matter how viciously his parents had fought, when police tried to intervene, the Dahmers presented a calm, low-key, united front.

There is a strong probability that at age eight, Jeffrey was sexually molested by a neighbor boy, an event his father would later describe to police, but that Jeffrey would always deny.

Young Jeffrey took refuge in the leafy glens and hidden places in the woods surrounding his home. He collected insects, small animals, and birds, either alive or from roadkills, and used a chemistry set—his father's gift—to strip the flesh from their bones. In some cases he kept the corpses in formaldehyde-filled jars. In others, he buried the bones in a small cemetery he made beneath the trees. And in a shed near the edge of the family property he stored jars of the foul-smelling sludge that was all that remained of flesh leached from the bones by caustic chemicals. As he grew older he turned his attention to neighborhood cats and dogs, often leaving their skulls impaled on stakes near his "cemetery."

Bright but desperate for attention, Jeff began, well before puberty, to drink, usually Scotch, gin, or beer. He sipped whiskey in class, daring his teachers to stop him, or drank from beer cans cleverly concealed in the loose folds of a customized jacket. He often swilled beer openly in shopping malls. No one, not even his parents, ever seriously challenged his drinking, or questioned how a juvenile regularly got liquor and beer.

In school Jeffrey became the class clown, pulling off one outrageous stunt after another, to the delight of classmates and the consternation of teachers. He regularly chalked crime-scene-like outlines of imaginary corpses on schoolyard sidewalks. He made faces and bleated like a sheep in class. He shouted in the library. He faked epileptic fits in the corridors. And in his junior year, Jeffrey sneaked into his high-school honor-society yearbook photo, despite—or perhaps because of—grades ranging from F's to A's. When Dahmer snuck into the photo a second time in his senior year, yearbook editors caught on. Unable to reshoot the picture, they blacked out his likeness, leaving a spooky outline that every student immediately knew was Jeffrey Dahmer.

So pervasive were Jeff's stunts at Revere High that any kind of zany behavior came to be known as "doing a Dahmer." Once, in exchange for beer money contributed by classmates, he put on a show in a local mall, knocking merchandise off counters, poking drink-filled cups off tables with an umbrella, accepting a sample of alfalfa sprouts, then spitting them out, screaming, "I'm allergic, I'm allergic, I'm going to die!"

In high school Dahmer had few friends, and fewer still were girls. He went on a date, but seemed fearful that the girl would want to touch him or, worse, kiss him. Nevertheless he asked her out again. She accompanied him to a "geeky sort of party," where Jeffrey participated in a séance, an attempt to contact the devil. The frightened girl left immediately, alone.

Despite his loneliness, Jeffrey was from his youngest years a glib and facile talker. On a school field trip to Washington, D.C., he called the office of Walter Mondale from a phone booth and persuaded an aide to show his classmates through the Vice-President's office. As the group strolled through the White House Dahmer fell to the floor, faking a seizure. "I like to shake people up," he told classmate Martha Schmidt, who today is a professor of sociology.

"He seemed to cry out for help, but nobody paid attention to him at all," recalled Schmidt. "He would come to class with a cup of Scotch—not coffee with something in it, just Scotch. If a sixteen-year-old drinking in an eight A.M. class isn't calling out for help, I don't know who is," opined Schmidt. "The Jeff that was my friend was, at sixteen years old, lost. I feel sad for that."

A few months before his high-school graduation, Jeffrey's parents finally split up. His mother got custody of his twelve-year-old brother, but Jeff, now eighteen, was considered an adult. Very soon after the divorce, his father moved in with a somewhat younger woman, Shari Jordan. Jeff's mother packed her clothes, bundled his brother into her car, and left the state, leaving Jeffrey alone in an empty house with no money, no food, and a refrigerator that worked only occasionally. It was several weeks before Lionel Dahmer learned what had happened. He moved back into the house with Jordan, by then his fiancée.

But before he did, Jeffrey Dahmer claimed his first victim, nineteen-year-old Stephen Mark Hicks. Hicks was hitchhiking back from a rock concert on June 18, 1978, when Dahmer picked him up and invited him over for a few beers. After a few hours of hanging out, sipping beer and swapping lies, Hicks decided it was time to proceed on his journey home, fifteen miles away.

"Don't go," pleaded Dahmer. Hicks had people to see, things to do. He got up to leave. Dahmer had been deserted by everyone. His father was gone, living with his new girlfriend. His mother and brother had abandoned him. Now his new friend wanted to leave, too. It was suddenly intolerable, too much for him to bear.

So Dahmer smashed Hicks's head with a barbell. Hicks went down, stunned, and Dahmer used the steel bar of the barbell to strangle the tall, skinny young man. He found unexpected pleasure in Hicks's gasps, gurgles, and wildly racing heartbeat. As life ebbed from his first victim Jeffrey Dahmer discovered he had an almost godlike power. It was a thrill he would never forget. Years later, when Dahmer confessed, his description of this murder was tinged with pride.

Dahmer initially concealed Hicks's body in the enclosed cavity between the house foundation and bedrock below, a crawl space where as a youngster he'd hidden dead raccoons, squirrels, and chipmunks. Then he returned to the crawl space and used a large butcher knife to dismember the body. He stuffed the parts in plastic trash bags, then scratched a shallow grave from the thin soil in the woods behind the house and dropped the body parts in it.

Almost immediately, he began to worry. Neighborhood children often played in these woods, as he himself had. So over the next two weeks, Dahmer dug up the body parts and dissolved them in acid to remove the flesh—just as he had disposed of small animals years ago.

Then he used a sledgehammer to break up the skull, ribs, spine, arm, and thigh bones, smashing each into pieces smaller than his hand. He scattered the bone fragments in a circle beneath the trees, where, in time, the soil would reclaim them. He dropped his bloody butcher's knife into the nearby Cuyahoga River, burned Hicks's wallet, and threw his victim's necklace in the trash. He did a very thorough job: beyond bloodstains in the crawl space, invisible to the naked eye, and some six hundred bone fragments scattered over acres of forest, nothing remained of young Stephen Mark Hicks. It would be thirteen awful, puzzling, fearful years before the Hicks family would learn what had happened to their son.

In the autumn of 1978, Jeff Dahmer enrolled as a freshman at Ohio State, declaring his major as business. He got little mail and few callers, but on one of his infrequent visits, Jeffrey's father noticed the empty liquor bottles lining the walls and windows of his son's dormitory room. By that time, early in his first and only semester, his roommate knew that Jeff often brought a bottle to class. Before long, he was selling his blood to a Columbus blood bank to get money for liquor. He made no friends, and was occasionally seen sleeping off a weekend bender on the streets of Columbus.

If he wasn't cut out to be a college man, decided Jeff, maybe he could find what he was looking for in uniform. Two days before the end of 1978, he was sworn in as a private in the U.S. Army. Dahmer wanted to be a military policeman, but after basic training and several weeks of MP school at Ft. McClellan, Alabama, the army decided he might do better as a medic and reassigned him to Ft. Houston, Texas. By July 1979, Jeff was an aid-station corpsman in the 8th Infantry Division at Baumholder, West Germany.

As before, Dahmer focused nearly his entire attention on imbibing as much alcohol as he could buy. He was in one of the few places in the world where he could legally buy untaxed liquor—quarts of good Scotch cost as little as four dollars. Even on a private's pay, he could afford lots of booze. When he wasn't on duty, he spent most of his time supine in his bunk, sipping martinis from a portable bar artfully concealed in a briefcase and listening to Black Sabbath tapes through headphones. On weekends he drank himself into oblivion, often skipping food entirely.

The volunteer army of that era had more than its share of alcoholics. Even so, Dahmer was such an exceptional boozer that by March 1981, nine months short of the three years he'd signed on for, the army decided he'd never make a suitable soldier. He was given an administrative discharge.

German authorities in and around Baumholder would later wonder if Dahmer had anything to do with a series of unsolved prostitute murder/mutilations that began after he came to Germany and ended just before he left. All of

Dahmer's known victims, however, were men and boys, not women.

After discharge, Dahmer took his mustering-out pay and drifted down to Miami Beach, where he slept on the sand at night and worked in a sandwich shop by day. While he lived in Miami Beach, six-year-old Adam Walsh of nearby Hollywood, Florida, was abducted from a shopping mall. His severed head turned up two weeks later, over a hundred miles away in Vero Beach. Police were baffled.

After six months Dahmer returned to live with his father and stepmother in Ohio. Jeff spent his days sleeping and his nights drinking. He closed bars, turned nasty when asked to leave, and woke up unable to recall where he'd parked the family car.

Perhaps thinking a new environment might encourage him to make a fresh start—or merely sick of his son's shenanigans—Lionel Dahmer arranged for Jeff to move in with his paternal grandmother. Catherine Dahmer had a cozy, well-tended home in a Milwaukee suburb. But the change of scene did nothing to change Jeff's behavior. After moving in, early in 1982, he continued his boozing and carousing. Milwaukee's saloon keepers were tough—when Jeff refused to leave at closing time, they rarely called the police. Instead, Dahmer went home with blackened eyes, cracked ribs, and assorted cuts and bruises.

But, at least when sober, Jeff seemed to have a warm relationship with his grandmother. He mowed the grass, trimmed shrubs, dug and weeded in the rose garden, and did other chores around the two-story house. His grandmother always had time to talk. He even accepted her hugs, and sometimes her grandmotherly kisses as well. In return, she gave him money and a room. Jeff usually came and went via a side entrance that gave private access to the basement as well as the kitchen. Thus he could bring visitors in and out without disturbing Catherine Dahmer.

It was during this homey interlude that Dahmer began to acknowledge his homosexuality. But while he eventually discovered Milwaukee's small but flourishing gay-bar and bathhouse scene, he remained deep in the closet, refusing to assume a gay identity.

Meanwhile, sexual frustration was boiling inside. In August 1982, he was arrested for disorderly conduct after lowering his pants in a park in view of about twenty-five people, including women and children. He pleaded guilty and paid the fifty-dollar fine. Four years later he was arrested for lewd and lascivious behavior when two twelve-year-old boys saw him masturbating in the woods near a park. Dahmer claimed he was drunk and only urinating. A judge gave him the benefit of the doubt, finding him guilty of disorderly conduct and disposing of the case with a small fine.

In this period, before the AIDS epidemic swept across America, Dahmer began frequenting gay bathhouses. These were establishments where men strolled around in little more than bath towels, and where in private cubicles, rented by the hour, casual solo and group sex between total strangers was the norm.

There were few restrictions on individual behavior in the gay baths; Dahmer nevertheless found a way to go beyond the pale. In the summer of 1986, he was banned from Milwaukee's Club Baths after drugging several patrons, including one who was taken, unconscious, to a hospital, where he remained in a coma for over a week.

Still living with his grandmother, Jeffrey picked up men, most often African Americans, and brought them to his basement. In 1987 he met Ronald Flowers in a gay bar. Flowers went home with Dahmer, but woke up the next day in a county medical facility, minus his cash and a gold wristwatch. Police questioned Dahmer, who claimed he and Flowers got drunk together and passed out. When he woke up, said Dahmer, he gave the man a dollar for the bus and left him, still drunk, at a bus stop.

Many, if not most, Milwaukee police officers thought of gay men as perverts and outlaws and were not inclined to spend much time safeguarding their rights. With no evidence, police dropped the matter.

Flowers was very fortunate, because by that time, Dahmer had resumed his career in murder. By the time he picked up Flowers, he'd killed three more times.

The first man he killed in Milwaukee was Steven Tuomi,

twenty-four. Tuomi met Dahmer at Club 219, a well-known gay pickup bar. They checked into a room at the Ambassador Hotel. Dahmer would later claim he didn't remember killing Tuomi, only waking up next to his bloody body after a night of drinking. Dahmer left the body, went out to buy a large suitcase, and returned to stuff Tuomi's body inside. An unsuspecting taxi driver helped him load the suitcase into his hack then carry it into his grandmother's house. In the basement, Dahmer chopped the body to pieces, used acid to remove the flesh from the bones, and put the rest in plastic trash bags for the city sanitation department to remove. No trace of Tuomi's body was ever found.

Not long after that, Catherine Dahmer called her son in Ohio and asked him to come to Milwaukee to investigate an unholy stench emanating from her garage. By the time Lionel Dahmer got there, Jeffrey had disposed of most of what was in the garage. All Lionel found was a slimy black substance on the floor. Jeffrey told his father he'd found a dead raccoon on the highway and used acids to dissolve the flesh. He'd later bought a chicken and again used acid to get rid of the meat.

"God, Jeff, this is strange. This is weird," said the bewildered father.

What Jeff had actually dissolved in his grandmother's garage were human bodies.

After Tuomi came James Doxtator, a fourteen-year-old Native American. He was a runaway who lived on the streets, surviving by selling the only thing he had. His marketplace was a bus stop outside Club 219 where he joined men who came cruising by in their cars. In January 1988, Dahmer invited the boy to his grandmother's house for a drink. Doxtator seemed uninterested, so Dahmer said they could watch some videos—and he'd pay him to pose for pictures.

In the basement, Dahmer and Doxtator had sex. Then Dahmer gave the boy a drugged drink. As he slipped into unconsciousness Dahmer strangled him. He dismembered the body, removed the flesh from his bones with acid, and pulverized the bones with a sledgehammer. What was left of the boy was carted away with the trash.

Two months later, Dahmer picked up Richard Guerrero, a Chicano, at the Phoenix Bar, just down the street from Club 219. Again, the bait was videos and nude pictures for pay. Again, Dahmer had sex with, then drugged and strangled his victim, chopped up the body, and got rid of it.

By then Dahmer had a new job, stirring vats of chocolate in a candy factory. He made $8.50 an hour and worked the graveyard shift, which left him most of the day to sleep off the booze he sucked down before and during work.

Dahmer moved out of his grandmother's house after she almost caught him having sex with a man in the basement. He found a small place at 808 North Twenty-fourth Street on Milwaukee's west side. The very day he moved in, he lured a thirteen-year-old Laotian schoolboy to his apartment with the promise of fifty dollars to pose for pictures. Dahmer gave the boy coffee spiked with Halcion, a controversial prescription tranquilizer readily available from Milwaukee drug dealers. As the boy faded into groggy semiconsciousness, Dahmer fondled his genitals. Then he left the apartment for a few minutes to go to a nearby store.

Miraculously, the boy escaped before Dahmer could return to kill him. After he collapsed in the street outside, passersby took him, semiconscious, to a hospital emergency room. When the child could walk again, he led police back to Dahmer's apartment. Jeffrey Dahmer was arrested for second-degree sexual assault and enticing a child for immoral purposes. Two months after his conviction on those charges and free on bail while awaiting sentencing, Dahmer went looking for another victim.

He found Anthony Sears, twenty-six and black, a restaurant manager. Dahmer took him to his grandmother's house, where they had sex. Then he drugged him, strangled him, and dismembered his body for disposal.

This time Dahmer decided to keep a souvenir: Sears's skull. He removed the flesh and brain with acid, then painted the bone gray so it would resemble the plastic skulls sold by medical-supply stores.

On May 23, 1989, Dahmer stood before Judge William

Gardner for sentencing on his sexual-assault conviction. Veteran prosecutor Gale Shelton, especially disturbed by evidence suggesting that Dahmer's victim had been drugged, and infuriated because Dahmer showed no repentance, argued for a long prison sentence. "It's really a miracle that [the victim] made it out of there," she said, unaware of how much truth she spoke. Shelton argued that Dahmer was manipulative, uncooperative, and evasive, that he showed no willingness to change his ways.

Dahmer's family hired a lawyer, Gerald Boyle, who argued for leniency. He told the judge that this was his client's first serious offense, that although he had received no treatment for alcoholism or his other psychological problems, he had continued to function in society.

Of course, no one knew that while awaiting sentencing, Dahmer had drugged and slaughtered Anthony Sears, the fifth man he'd murdered.

After Lionel Dahmer submitted a soulful letter requesting treatment, not incarceration, and after Jeffrey, "confessing" that he had problems with alcohol and in dealing with his homosexuality, begged for another chance, Judge Gardner decided to be lenient.

That leniency would cost a dozen lives.

Noting that Dahmer's night-shift job at Ambrosia Chocolate was the first well-paid, steady work he had ever done, the judge put him in a work-release program. He also ordered Dahmer to enroll in psychological counseling for alcohol abuse and his other mental problems. So instead of two consecutive ten-year sentences, the maximum allowed for the two felony counts on which Dahmer was convicted, he was sentenced to a year in a city jail and five years in prison—the latter suspended so long as Dahmer kept his job and remained on good behavior. Since one of his convictions was for enticing a child, Jeffrey was forbidden to have contact with anyone under age eighteen. Under the work-release program, however, he was free to visit the bathhouses and roam the streets of Milwaukee to and from his job.

Jeffrey's year in Milwaukee's jail ended short, with two months off for "good behavior." Except for once returning late—drunk—from a twelve-hour pass to celebrate Thanksgiving with his family, he presented few problems to his jailers.

Both his corrections officer and his father opposed the early release, however, noting that he had received no treatment for his sexual anxieties or his alcoholism.

Dahmer was placed on supervised parole in March 1990. His parole officer, Donna Chester, had been in contact with him since February 1989, while Dahmer was still in the work-release program. Chester noted that Dahmer usually seemed greatly disturbed and that he was experiencing great difficulty in dealing with his homosexuality. She recommended very strict parole supervision, including regular visits to Dahmer's apartment.

Soon after leaving the work-release program, Dahmer moved into Apartment 213 of the Oxford Apartments, at 924 North Twenty-fifth Street. This was very near his first apartment, on Milwaukee's west side, in one of the city's most dangerous neighborhoods. At night, most people in this community lock themselves in their homes, venturing out only for necessities. They leave the streets to legions of drug dealers and ruthless enforcers who control the area. So dangerous is this neighborhood that police patrols often include *three* officers. Donna Chester, quite understandably, followed her agency's guidelines and refused to visit Dahmer in his apartment without a male probation officer as escort. And since virtually all Milwaukee probation officers must cope with overwhelming caseloads, there was never a time when she could arrange a suitable escort. For seventeen months, Chester saw Dahmer at two-week intervals, always in her office. Never did she pay a visit to the apartment where he butchered victim after victim.

And so, as Milwaukee's trees began to show their first buds of 1990, Dahmer resumed cruising the city's gay bars. In late May, he picked up Raymond Smith, a twenty-two-year-old ex-con, at Club 219. Dahmer lured him to his apartment with the promise of money to pose for nude photos. As with his previous Milwaukee victims, he drugged and strangled Smith. Then he performed an act of oral sex on the corpse. Finally, he cut the body into pieces, put them in plastic garbage bags, and left them with the trash. He again kept the skull, however, removing the flesh with acid and painting it gray.

Smith's family—eight siblings, a ten-year-old daughter, and his grandmother—was accustomed to his frequent absences for weeks or months. No one took his disappearance seriously. Even when a rumor circulated that he'd been shot during a quarrel with a drug dealer, no one reported him as a missing person.

Dahmer's next victim was a very tall, thin black man who wore a trademark turban. Few knew his real name, Eddie Smith, or any of his aliases. He was known in the gay bars as the Sheik. He vanished June 14, 1990, into Jeffrey Dahmer's apartment of horrors. When his sister, Carolyn, reported him missing on June 23, Milwaukee police seemed not to care after learning he was gay. Carolyn would later learn that the missing-person report an officer took from her was either not filed or lost. "I think that once the officer left, he tore up the report," she later said.

Many months later, in March 1991, Carolyn's phone rang. It was around midnight, and she was sleeping. She woke right up when the caller told her she ought not to bother looking for her brother. "Why not?" asked Carolyn Smith.

"Because he's dead," said a strange male voice.

"How do you know he's dead?"

"I killed him."

Dahmer would never admit having made this call.

Four months later, in Dahmer's apartment, police would find grisly Polaroid mementos of Dahmer dismembering Smith's body.

While murdering victim after victim, Dahmer remained a curious nonentity to his neighbors at the Oxford Apartments. He usually kept to himself, only occasionally turning up at building barbecue parties, where he brought meat—sliced from one of his victims—cooked, and ate it without offering to share. He sat around quietly getting drunk.

From time to time, a ghastly smell would permeate Dahmer's part of the building. When neighbors knocked on his door to inquire, a soft-spoken Dahmer apologized profusely. His freezer sometimes worked intermittently, he said. It had malfunctioned, he added, and all the meat in it had spoiled. No one seemed to question this explanation the next time noxious odors emanated from Apartment 213.

Other neighbors heard the whine of a power saw late in the night, or early in the morning, and wondered what Jeffrey Dahmer could be building in his tiny apartment. No one inquired.

Not long after Eddie Smith died, Dahmer deviated from his usual ritual—and almost got caught. His would-be victim was a fifteen-year-old boy. Lured, as usual, by the promise of money to pose for nude photos, the boy refused Dahmer's drugged drink. So Dahmer smashed his head with a rubber mallet, then started to strangle him. Though momentarily stunned, the boy began to struggle and scream. Fearing discovery, Dahmer stopped. The boy promised not to tell police, and Dahmer took a chance and put him in a taxi. Since the boy, a Hispanic living in a foster home, didn't want his Anglo foster parents to know about his homosexuality, he said nothing until he left the foster home, months after Dahmer was arrested.

Meanwhile the murders continued. During the long Labor Day weekend of 1990, Ernest Miller, twenty-four, a Chicago dancer visiting Milwaukee relatives, ran into Dahmer in a bookstore and accompanied him home. Instead of strangling him, Dahmer cut his throat with a butcher knife. He dismembered the body, reducing the head to a skull by boiling it for days in a pot on his kitchen stove. He saved the skeleton and bleached it white. Dahmer wrapped up some of Miller's biceps and froze them. Later, he cooked and ate them. Sometimes he took sandwiches of human flesh to eat during a break at the chocolate factory.

Next, Dahmer killed David C. Thomas, whom he met in a downtown bar. But for reasons Dahmer never explained, Thomas, who died on September 24, 1990, wasn't his type. Disdaining sex with this victim, he merely drugged him, strangled him, dismembered the body, and disposed of it, keeping nothing as a reminder.

Thomas had a young daughter and a girlfriend, Chandra

Beanland. Although accustomed to Thomas being out of touch for weeks at a time, she reported him missing almost immediately after his death. Police could turn up no clues.

Dahmer did not kill again until March 1991, when he picked up eighteen-year-old Curtis Straughter, a gay youth who sometimes called himself "Demetra" and who desperately wanted to be a model. After drugging him, Dahmer had oral sex with the unconscious teen, strangled him with a leather strap, and dismembered his body. He saved the skull.

Next, Errol Lindsey, nineteen, the youngest of six children, was killed. On April 7, he left his mother's apartment to have a house key duplicated. Somewhere between the locksmith's shop and his mother's apartment, Lindsey ran into Dahmer, who offered him money to pose for photos. He was drugged, raped, strangled, dismembered. Dahmer saved his skull as a keepsake.

Anthony Hughes was thirty-one, deaf and mute, but he held down a good job and had a dazzling smile and an aura of goodness about him. Dahmer found him dancing, alone, to the vibrations at Club 219. He wrote a note with the usual offer: fifty dollars to pose for nude photos. He was drugged, strangled, dismembered, and disappeared but for his skull. Hughes's family noted him missing almost at once, and papered the city with flyers bearing his photo. They posted a reward. It went unclaimed.

Three days later, on May 26, while Hughes's strangled body lay on Dahmer's bed, Jeffrey went looking for another victim. He chose fourteen-year-old Konerak Sinthasomphone, a short, muscular Hmong refugee from Laos—and by incredible coincidence, the younger brother of the boy Dahmer had been convicted of molesting almost two years earlier. Like his sibling, Konerak was thoroughly Americanized and could barely remember the land of his birth. A budding athlete who hoped for a career as a professional soccer player, he was a freshman at Pulaski High.

It was the Sunday of the Memorial Day weekend, and Dahmer found Konerak hanging around the Grand Avenue Mall. He enticed the boy into his apartment in the usual way, then drugged, raped, and sodomized him. Afterward, he left the apartment to buy beer in a nearby bar.

Groggy and naked, Konerak awoke in Dahmer's apartment. He ran screaming, bleeding from his anus, into the street. It was past midnight when Konerak, staggering, unsure of his location, unable to speak, made it to what should have been safety. Two young women tried to help. Nicole Childress scurried to a pay phone to call 911. Sandra Smith, her cousin, went to help Konerak. Besides the blood on his buttocks, his body was covered with bruises and scrapes.

"I'm on Twenty-fifth and State, and there is this young man. He's butt-naked," Childress told the 911 operator. "He has been beaten up. He is very bruised up. He can't stand up. He has no clothes on. He is really hurt . . . he needs some help."

Operator 71 told Childress to stay on the line, then transferred the call to the fire department. Childress got to tell the whole story again to another operator. Eventually, an ambulance was dispatched.

In the meantime, Dahmer returned from the saloon with a six-pack. Konerak saw him and tried to flee. Dahmer caught up with him.

Moments later, Childress and Smith flagged down a squad car containing Officers John Balcerzak, Joseph Gabrish, and Richard Porubcan. Balcerzak, thirty-four, was a six-year veteran of Milwaukee's mean streets, an experienced cop with an excellent record and many citations for bravery. Gabrish, with seven years of service, also had several merit and bravery awards in his file. Porubcan, at twenty-five, had only fifteen months on the job.

Nevertheless, they did not do their jobs. After giving Konerak a blanket and dismissing the ambulance when it arrived, the police listened to Dahmer's tale. Konerak was his nineteen-year-old lover. They'd had a little quarrel, but everything was okay now, said Dahmer. He spoke in the disarming, low-key way he'd learned as a child watching his parents turn away inquisitive police called by neighbors.

Had police radioed Dahmer's name in for a records check, they would have known instantly that he was a paroled sex offender, forbidden to have contact with anyone under eighteen. That might have prompted further investigation into Dahmer's apartment. There they would have found a decomposing body in the bedroom and a human head in the kitchen.

Instead they bought Dahmer's calm and steady act, choosing to believe that a high-school freshman named Sinthasomphone was an adult gay named "Butch," and that the incident was simply a lovers' quarrel. Konerak, drugged, presumably in shock, and unable to speak, walked back to the apartment with Dahmer and the officers. He sat mute while Dahmer soothed away the police. And minutes after they left, Dahmer again forced Konerak to drink a powerful tranquilizer that rendered him unconscious.

As he had done with three other victims, Dahmer used a power drill to bore a hole through Konerak's skull. What Jeffrey Dahmer wanted most was not a dead body he could use only briefly to satisfy his lust before having to dispose of it, but a living, breathing sex slave that would never leave him. On previous attempts he had used boiling water; this time he injected acid into a still-living brain. As with previous attempts, Dahmer's crude lobotomy was a failure and Konerak died. After using the body as a sex toy for a few days, he disposed of it, saving the skull as a remembrance.

Not privy to the evil horrors of Dahmer's apartment but mightily alarmed and concerned about Konerak's safety, Childress and Smith, the two young women who had found the boy in the street, tried to tell police what they knew: the dazed youngster was a boy, not a man. But the police were white, the women black—as were most people in this neighborhood—and they ignored their repeated requests to make statements. One of them told Smith to "butt out . . . I've been investigating for seven years and I don't need an amateur telling me what to do." While Dahmer was drilling into Konerak's brain in Apartment 213, the police radioed the station to report "Intoxicated Asian, naked male. Was returned to his sober boyfriend." Amid laughter, the senior officer added that he could not return to patrol just yet.

"It'll be a minute. My partner is going to get deloused at the station."

Glenda Cleveland, the thirty-seven-year-old mother of Sandra Smith, didn't believe a word of Jeffrey Dahmer's story. When her daughter ran back to her apartment to recount the evening's bizarre occurrences, she telephoned police. She wanted to know what had happened.

"A moment ago, ten minutes, my daughter and my niece flagged down a policeman when they walked up on a young child being molested by a male guy," she told an officer who answered the phone at the district police station. "And no information or anything was being taken . . . I mean, I'm sure further information must be needed. The boy was naked and bleeding."

Her call was transferred to another policeman, and Cleveland started over. This time the officer said he was in the car the young women had flagged down.

"What happened?" she asked. "I mean, my daughter and niece witnessed what was going on. Was there anything done about the situation? Do you need their names, or information or anything from them?"

"No, not at all," said the officer.

"You don't?"

"Nope. It's an intoxicated boyfriend of another boyfriend."

"Well, how old was this child?"

"It wasn't a child. It was an adult."

"Are you sure?"

"Yup."

"Are you positive? Because this child doesn't even speak English. My daughter had . . . dealt with him before and seen him on the street catching earthworms."

"Ma'am, ma'am. Like I explained to you, it is all taken care of. It's as positive as it can be . . . I can't do anything about anybody's sexual preferences in life."

Cleveland tried again. "Well, no. I'm not saying anything about that. But it appeared to have been a *child* That is my concern."

"No. No. He's not."

"He's not a child?"

"No, he's not. Okay? And that's a boyfriend-boyfriend thing. And he's got belongings at the house where he came from."

"Oh. I see."

"Okay?"

"Okay. Well . . . I am just, you know, it appeared to have been a child. That was my concern."

"I understand. No, he is not. Nope."

Cleveland hung up, still worried. But she knew that the police would file a report, and if there was anything wrong, they still had a chance to follow up.

In fact, the officers did not make a formal report. They did not enter the name of Jeffrey Dahmer in their computer. Had they done so, they would have learned of his criminal record.

And so by the time police learned Dahmer was a convicted child molester on parole, it was much too late for Konerak Sinthasomphone. The day after he vanished into Dahmer's apartment for the second time, his parents told police he was missing. Since Dahmer had been convicted of molesting his older brother, one might expect that police would at least have paid a call on him. They did nothing of the sort, a fact that begs for explanation.

A small story reporting Konerak's disappearance ran in a Milwaukee newspaper. One person who noted it was Glenda Cleveland. She phoned police to tell them she had some information about the missing Laotian boy.

"They told me someone would come out and talk to me, take the information," said Cleveland.

No one ever came.

Dahmer was a pitiless killer. He was an alcoholic. He was also smart enough to know that he couldn't continue to prey exclusively on Milwaukee gays and stray children. But if Milwaukee was a small city, with only a handful of gay bars, Chicago, ninety miles south, had several dozen bars, lounges, and clubs catering exclusively to gays.

So next to die in his abattoir was Matthew Turner, twenty, and striving for a career in modeling or show business. Dahmer picked him up on June 30, 1991, Chicago's annual Gay Pride Parade day, at the Greyhound terminal, and offered him money to come back to Milwaukee and pose for pictures. He was drugged, strangled with a leather strap, dismembered. His head went into Dahmer's cooking pot, his torso into the blue fifty-seven-gallon drum he kept in the bedroom.

A week later, on July 5, Dahmer went back to Chicago. At Carol's Speakeasy, a flashy Old Town saloon featuring male strippers, he picked up Jeremiah Weinberger, twenty-three and from Puerto Rico. Once again, he offered money and Weinberger joined him. But after two days of consenting sex, Weinberger decided it was time to get back to Chicago.

Dahmer didn't like anyone leaving him. Weinberger was drugged, strangled by hand, dismembered. As he went along Dahmer used his Polaroid's self-timer to take pictures of his handiwork. The head went into the refrigerator, the torso into the drum.

Weinberger's disappearance did not go entirely unnoticed. He had told a friend that he was going with Dahmer. Missing-person notices ran in Chicago's gay publications, the *Windy City Times* and *Gay Chicago*. And rumors floated through the gay community that a killer was on the loose, stalking victims in the gay bars. Warnings about "stranger danger" were posted.

Oliver Lacy, twenty-three, moved to Milwaukee to be with his fiancée and their two-year-old son. He found work as a janitor. On July 15, he went into an ice-cream parlor on Twenty-seventh Street, where he ran across Jeffrey Dahmer. Dahmer invited him over to pose for photos. First he and Dahmer took their clothes off and exchanged rubdown massages. Then Lacy sipped something cold. Something laced with Halcion. Something that knocked him out.

Dahmer strangled, sodomized, and dismembered Lacy. The head went into his freezer, the torso into the drum, and the heart into a plastic bag so he could "eat it later."

Four days after this, Joseph Bradehoft, just arrived in town to look for a job while his wife and two toddlers remained in St. Paul, Minnesota, was standing at a bus stop with a six-pack of beer under his arm. Dahmer spotted him from the back of the bus and got off. Twenty minutes later they were in Apartment 213. He was victim number seventeen.

On the evening of July 22, Dahmer focused his charms on Tracy Edwards. After a chance meeting at the Grand Avenue Mall, Dahmer invited Edwards back to his apartment for a beer. As a further inducement, Dahmer said he had a video he thought Edwards would like to watch—and if that wasn't enough, he'd pay him fifty dollars to pose for some nude Polaroids.

As they sat on Dahmer's bed, watching the video, Dahmer put his arm around Edwards, but was rebuffed. Dahmer had picked the wrong man.

So instead of drugging Edwards, Dahmer whipped out a pair of steel handcuffs. After cuffing him, he put Edwards on the floor. He went into the kitchen and returned with a razor-sharp, six-inch knife. He put the tip of the blade near Edward's crotch. A strange look came over his face.

"I'm going to cut out your heart and eat it," said Dahmer.

But first he would watch a video, *The Exorcist III*. During a scene depicting a priest possessed by the devil, Dahmer began to rock back and forth, chanting with religious fervor.

On the floor, Tracy Edwards took advantage of Dahmer's momentary distraction to wriggle one cuff loose. Rolling to his feet, he hit Dahmer as hard as he could. Then he bolted from the apartment. Two blocks away, breathless, he flagged down a passing police car and asked the officers if they could help him get the other cuff off.

Officers Rolf Mueller and Robert Rauth were much more interested in knowing how those cuffs got on Edwards than how to get them off. Edwards told them only the barest details of his brush with death. He said Dahmer, a tall, thin, sandy-haired man, had made sexual advances, then cuffed him and threatened to cut his heart out.

"I have six kids. I love women. I ain't no fag," said Edwards.

Officers Mueller and Rauth rang every bell on the door panel. Tenant John Batchelor, just nodding off to sleep, was the first to answer. It was almost midnight, and he was annoyed.

"Who is it?" said Batchelor over the intercom.

"Police. Let us in."

Batchelor buzzed them in, then struggled into his clothes and opened his door. The police ignored him, rapping on the door of Apartment 213 down the hall. Calmly, Dahmer invited them to come in.

Inside the apartment, the police fought back the impulse to gag. Something smelled terrible. But the matter at hand was Edwards. Why did Dahmer put handcuffs on him? asked Officer Rauth, a thirteen-year veteran.

"I just lost my job and I wanted to drink some fucking beer," said Dahmer. It was true. He'd been late or absent once too often, and a few days earlier Ambrosia Chocolate, after several warnings, had fired him.

Both Rauth and Mueller had walkie-talkies on their belts. Mueller took Dahmer's ID and called it in. Minutes later their radios squawked. Jeffrey Dahmer's criminal record and parole status had come up in the station's computer, and as the information came over the air one of the officers decided he didn't like Dahmer. Across the hall, John Batchelor heard somebody shout, "Faggot." The sound of crashing and thumping came through the closed door. "Oh God, he's going into one of those homo modes again," said the same voice.

Edwards, cuffs still dangling from a wrist, was escorted from the building by one of the officers. Passing by his door, the cop told Batchelor to get back inside his apartment and close the door.

And just about then, the other officer opened Dahmer's refrigerator. His shriek of surprise echoed throughout the building. "Oh my God! There's a goddamn head in here! This is one sick son of a bitch!"

Dahmer tried to overpower the policeman, but it was too late. Jeffrey Dahmer's long, murderous career was over. From his gore-strewn apartment, police would remove body parts belonging to eleven men and boys.

Once in custody, Dahmer made a full confession. Awaiting trial, he was held without bail in a maximum-security facility where fellow inmates, mixing awe with loathing, labeled him "the chop-chop man."

Dahmer's arrest unleashed a torrent of criticism on the Milwaukee Police Department. All but four of Dahmer's seventeen admitted victims were black. When it was revealed that police failed to run an identity check on Dahmer the night he'd killed Konerak Sinthasomphone, that they didn't respond to Glenda Cleveland's repeated assertions that the bleeding youngster handed back to Dahmer was a juvenile, and that they failed to follow up even when Cleveland called to say she had information about the boy who had disappeared, the city's black community was outraged.

"If a black man was chasing a white boy down the street, they would have shot him," opined the Milwaukee Alderman Michael McGee, speaking for many of his constituents.

After an internal investigation, police chief Philip Arreola fired Officers John Balcerzak and Joseph Gabrish, two of the officers who failed to report their encounter with Dahmer. The third officer, rookie Richard Porubcan, was also fired, but his termination was "held in abeyance" for a year to give him a chance to prove himself as a police officer. The Milwaukee Police Association voiced strong support for all three officers and appealed the firings.

Despite repeated inquiries from police in Florida and Germany, who sought to tie Dahmer to unsolved murder/ dismemberments in their jurisdictions, he has maintained that he knows nothing about any but the seventeen murders he has confessed to.

Using information provided by Dahmer, Bath Township police were able to recover over five hundred bone fragments from the woods behind the onetime Dahmer residence. DNA tests conclusively determined that these were the remains of Stephen Mark Hicks, Dahmer's first victim.

Based on his confession, and the human remains and other victims' property found in his apartment, Milwaukee prosecutors charged Dahmer with fifteen counts of homicide. Despite his confession, he was not charged in the death of David C. Thomas because no trace of his body or personal belongings was found in Dahmer's nightmarish apartment.

Six months after his arrest, Dahmer changed his plea from "not guilty" to "guilty, but insane." Through his defense counsel, Gerald Boyle, Dahmer claimed to believe that he was the devil. "He became enamored, overwhelmed, caught up in the character in [the horror film] *Exorcist III*," said Boyle in his opening statement at Dahmer's sanity trial. "The character was Satan because he was the personification of evil."

Boyle went on to depict Dahmer's fascination with necrophilia and cannibalism as an attempt to continue deriving pleasure from the bodies of his victims. He would have preferred continued sex with a live partner, said Boyle, but the men and boys he lured to his apartment always wanted to leave. "He enjoys the bodies for a day or two but then he becomes tired of them. It then becomes a disposal problem," said Boyle.

Wisconsin does not have the death penalty. Since Dahmer had pleaded guilty but insane, the only issue to be decided by a jury was Dahmer's sanity. By pleading insanity, the burden of proof rested on Dahmer's attorney. Five of the seven psychologists and psychiatrists who testified said that Dahmer was insane. Under the state's rules of evidence, the jury was required to base their verdict on the less rigid standard of civil law—"the greater weight of the evidence"—rather than standard criminal law—"beyond a reasonable doubt."

After twelve days of grisly testimony, the jury deliberated only ten hours before returning a verdict: Jeffrey Dahmer had been sane, aware that his actions were wrong, and able to control his impulses, when he murdered each of his victims. Although two of the jurors disagreed and believed Dahmer was insane, under Wisconsin law the votes of only ten of the twelve jurors were needed to decide the issue.

While they did not discuss their decision in public, Milwaukee's media speculated that it was Dahmer's low-key, innocuous appearance and apparent sincerity that made jurors believe that he was twisted but sane. Had they decided otherwise, he would have been sent to a mental hospital, leaving open the possibility that he might some day be released. Instead, Judge Laurence C. Gram Jr. sentenced Dahmer to fifteen consecutive life terms, one for each of the murders.

Facing over nine hundred years behind bars before he would be eligible for parole, Dahmer was imprisoned in Wisconsin's Columbia Correctional Institute, where he was initially confined to an isolated cell block with only ninety-six inmates. He lived in an eight-by-ten-foot cell and was permitted to leave it only in shackles.

Unlike most serial killers, Dahmer seemed willing, even anxious, to talk about his crimes—and to take responsibility for them. He repeatedly denied that childhood alienation was the root of his evil ways. In confessing to every murder, including those where authorities lacked evidence to prosecute him, Dahmer often seemed to be searching for his own murderous motives. Trying to explain why he killed, he said, "I could completely control a person—a person that I found physically attractive—and keep them with me as long as possible, even if it meant just keeping a part of them."

Dahmer also denied that the prescription drugs his mother took while she was pregnant with him or his parents' rancorous divorce were factors in his behavior. He told a television reporter, "The person to blame [for the murders] is the person sitting across from you. Not parents, not society, not pornography. Those are just excuses."

After about a year in confinement, Dahmer was rewarded for good behavior by being transferred to a less controlled part of the prison and given such privileges as reading material, a radio and television set in his cell, and regular visitors and phone calls. He was also permitted to take part in sports and to work as a prison janitor for twenty-four cents an hour.

Seemingly possessed of a death wish, he ignored threats from other inmates and told his parents and other inmates that he preferred to die rather than spend the rest of his life behind bars. For the next year, Dahmer passed his days mostly in solitude, chain-smoking, reading Christian literature, and listening to tapes of humpback whales, Gregorian chants, and classical music.

After his father, a born-again Christian, sent him several magazine articles discussing creationism, Dahmer contacted the Reverend Roy Ratcliff, pastor of a small Church of Christ congregation in nearby Madison. Ratcliff, impressed with his sincerity, agreed to baptize his first confessed cannibal. On May 10, 1994, under the watchful gaze of the prison chaplain and two guards, Dahmer was dunked in a whirlpool bath as Ratcliff told him, "Welcome to the family of God."

In the prison chapel a few weeks later, Dahmer was attacked by another inmate who tried to slash his throat with a razor blade embedded in a toothbrush. Not seriously injured, he refused to testify against his assailant. While his parents were alarmed by this, Dahmer seemed unconcerned. "I don't care if something happens to me," he told his mother by telephone soon afterward.

The day before Thanksgiving 1994, Dahmer met with Ratcliff for Bible study. At one point he read aloud from the Book of Revelations. "In those days shall men seek death and shall not find it and shall desire to die and death shall flee from them."

Several days later, on the morning of November 28, Dahmer was found on the floor of a prison latrine, his head beaten into a gory pulp. Another inmate lay unconscious nearby in the showers. Dahmer died en route to a hospital; the other victim, murderer Jesse Anderson, lingered two days before dying. A third inmate, Christopher Scarver, a black man who was on antipsychotic drugs, was charged with their murders. Court records indicate that his psychosis seemed to manifest itself in the belief that he was Jesus Christ.

Much has been written—most of it speculative—about the demons that drove Dahmer to ritual murder and cannibalism. In the end we can only theorize that he somehow grew up without a conscience. He never learned to accept civilization's strictures and taboos; instead, he learned to manipulate authority, to ignore all needs but his own, and to survive as a nearly invisible predator among society's equally invisible prey.

In the end we can only wonder how any parents could, through ignorance or apathy, allow their child to become a notorious alcoholic while still in adolescence. And wonder how Jeffrey Dahmer's teachers and school counselors failed to step in where his parents did not.

Jeffrey Dahmer committed his first murder at age eighteen. Aided by a certain amount of luck, he pulled off the perfect crime: had he not killed again, the homicide of Stephen Hicks could well have remained unsolved. When Dahmer resumed killing, older and wiser, he substituted cunning for luck, selecting victims met during random encounters, people who, he must surely have known, might not be missed until long after he'd had time to dispose of their bodies. As he grew more arrogant and careless while he grew more practiced, Dahmer's string of perfect crimes was abetted by police incompetence. They caught him all but red-handed, then let him go. Had Jeffrey Dahmer taken that astonishingly unforeseeable event as a clue to move his nightmarish avocation to another part of the country, he might well be among the thirty to fifty serial killers still stalking America, committing perfect crimes as they snuff out the lives of perfect strangers.

# One-Way Ticket
# (1968)

**J**URISDICTION IS *"THE RIGHT AND POWER TO INTERPRET AND apply the law." In most Western nations, until the late 1980s, jurisdiction over crimes was limited to those committed within their individual political boundaries.*

*So, for example, no Indiana court would concern itself with matters that happened in Illinois, Ohio, Kentucky, or, say, Spain—unless some key component of the crime occurred in Indiana.*

*Of course, crimes involving acts committed in several states may fall under federal jurisdiction. But what if a killer lures a victim to a death trap in a foreign country? What if, en route to that terminal appointment, a clever, patient, devilishly devious killer accompanies his victim to another U.S. state and several foreign countries and so makes it impossible to determine exactly where the murder was planned?*

*And finally, what if the government of the country where the murder actually occurred, for reasons of its own, declines to prosecute the killer?*

*In such a case, the assassin would have committed a perfect crime.*

Thomas Edward Utter Jr. was born into an impoverished, alcoholic family in Fordyce, Arkansas, in July 1940. When Tom was seven, his parents and their five children moved to a small town in Northern California. Three years later they moved south to Los Angeles.

At fourteen, Tom dropped out of school without completing the eighth grade. Two years later he left home and struck out on his own, determined to get rich. By his late teens he was parking cars at a glitzy Sunset Strip saloon. He was a smart kid, good-looking in his slender, dark way, and he oozed personality from every pore. Many of the Cadillacs and Lincolns he parked belonged to wealthy men—among them more than a sprinkling of hustlers, high-living hoods, and con artists—who enjoyed passing along investment tips to a hip, self-assured teenager.

Utter lived leanly on meager wages while investing his tips in the stock market. He didn't get rich, but he did make enough money to dress as well as he looked and sounded. And by the early 1960s, Tom Utter had discovered California's perpetual mother lode: real estate.

Along the way, however, Utter dabbled in crime. When he was apprehended for an unpaid traffic ticket, police found a concealed weapon. But Tom was young and the courts were lenient, even though by his early twenties he had a multipage rap sheet that included busts for both residential and auto burglary, breaking and entering, theft, and several warrants for unresolved traffic offenses. To escape the stigma of that record, Thomas E. Utter Jr., in classic California style, simply reinvented himself. He became Thomas Devins and went to work for Archer Realty, a prominent Hollywood brokerage, while studying for a real estate license.

Thus, in 1964, when he was twenty-four years old, Thomas Devins met Norma Bell Carty Wilson.

Norma was leggy, full-figured, and blond, with a creamy complexion, generous mouth, high cheekbones, and an aristocrat's perfect nose. She was regal in dress and demeanor. She was worth millions—and she was fifty-three years old.

Norma Bell had grown up in a large, happy, Washington, D.C., family. Her father was a prosperous engineer. She married Roy Carty, a businessman several years her senior. When Carty died in 1959, Norma emerged from the grief and shock of her loss with a new determination to enjoy life.

Always very conscious of her appearance, Norma became almost frantically devoted to recapturing her youth. She spent hours every week in beauty salons and more hours daily applying elaborate makeup and dealing with the subtleties of coiffure and manicure. She shopped for clothes that flattered her figure and gave her a more youthful appearance. She affected a teenager's lilting giggle and adopted the flirtatious mannerism of a far younger woman. She allowed men young enough to be her sons to court her.

Among them was William Wilson, a sometime car salesman, Arthur Murray dance instructor, and "aspiring writer." He was a tall, fair-haired, well-scrubbed, boy-next-door type who was twenty-seven when he and Norma got married in 1964.

The marriage was not everything Norma had hoped for. For one thing, once they were wedded, William seemed reluctant to fulfill his conjugal responsibilities. For another, he seemed, on closer inspection, to be far more interested in her fortune than he was in her person.

Norma wasn't quite ready to give up on her second husband, but she soon realized that she was the brains of the family. She occupied herself with her appearance and her investments.

And so, looking for real estate opportunities, she paid a visit to Archer Realty. Tom Devins's boss, Frank Archer, was on vacation, and Tom had a long chat with the wealthy, flirtatious Mrs. Wilson.

Devins's fast-buck instincts resonated with the sudden realization that Norma was the chance he'd been waiting for since quitting school in the eighth grade. Seeing no sense in sharing what promised to be a large commission with his boss, Devins never mentioned Norma to Archer. Instead, he arranged to pick her up at her apartment or meet her at various restaurants while showing her suitable properties. Tom stalled any purchase decisions as he frantically studied for his broker's license.

When, at length, Tom Devins became a licensed real estate broker, legally able to handle transactions in his own name, he no longer needed Archer. He quit, opened his own brokerage—and took Norma with him as his first and best customer. By then they were handling more than business together. Norma found Devins's dark good looks, glib tongue, and quick intelligence irresistible.

Devins could have tried to ease young William Wilson out of the way, but that was not his style. Devins already had a young and beautiful wife. He gave Norma just enough sex and affection to keep her interested and distracted.

Devins was not totally inept; he knew or quickly learned enough about real estate to help make Norma an even wealthier woman. Out of gratitude, she made him her personal investment counselor, giving him free office space for his brokerage in return for managing her office building on busy La Cienega Boulevard in Los Angeles.

By 1968, the former parking attendant was driving a new Cadillac, living in a spacious Laurel Canyon home, and apparently banking big bucks.

Actually, he was not doing well financially. Devins was leveraged to the hilt, living on credit as he traded houses and lots like so many Monopoly pieces. He was impatient to be rich and playing fast and loose with some of his clients' assets. One of these was Cecile Jay, an elderly woman whom he had helped buy a vacant lot in Malibu. In September 1967, Devins, acting as broker, opened escrow for sale of a Los Angeles house owned by Cecile and her husband. Devins told the Jays that the purchaser, whom they never met, was "Jack Shitmeyer."

First, Devins convinced the Jays to allow the buyer, the alleged Shitmeyer, to give them only a small down payment. When they had agreed to this, Devins explained that Shitmeyer was having a tough time getting a bank loan, but if the Jays would take his note, secured by the property, they would not only sell their house but also get monthly interest and principal payments from the buyer. Since this was at a rate higher than banks would pay on deposit accounts, the elderly couple agreed. Such arrangements are not unusual in Los Angeles, where "creative financing" has long been a useful tool for eager buyers with little cash and no credit. But in this instance, the offer was purely a scam.

Soon after accepting the Shitmeyer offer, Mrs. Jay became anxious when he failed to keep successive appointments. She went looking for him, only to discover that the address listed on his offer of purchase didn't exist. When Jay complained to Devins that something stank about the deal, he offered to buy the house himself, on the same terms, and to reduce his sales commission.

Mrs. Jay agreed. She and her husband accepted a token down payment and Devins's promissory note—in effect, his IOU. After recording the sale and becoming the legal owner, Devins took out first and second mortgages secured by the house. His plan was to buy the property below market value with next to nothing down, collect a sales commission, and a few months later, in a rising market, sell it for a fat profit. When the market remained flat, however, Devins kept the loan money and walked away without ever making a loan payment. It cost the Jays over $12,000 to repay the mortgages before they could reclaim the property. Cecile Jay would eventually learn that the elusive Jack Shitmeyer was merely one of many aliases used by Devins—but by then the statute of limitations on fraud had expired.

By 1968, Devins had left a tangled trail of broken promises, forgeries, and double-dealing. Of all his clients, however, no one had been cheated as much as Norma. Among her real estate investments were apartment buildings in Santa Monica, an office building on San Vicente, and the Brentwood Convalescent Hospital on San Vicente Boulevard.

Early in 1968, Devins suggested that Norma buy another parcel on San Vicente from the Atlantic Richfield Corporation and develop it into a medical-office center. On its face, this was an attractive proposition, because the property was close to the new site of Cedars-Sinai, one of the nation's leading hospitals, and thus very desirable to doctors who held staff privileges there.

But, cautioned Devins, to avoid tax complications, it was best to avoid an outright sale and purchase. Instead, he recommended a swap: the La Cienega office building for several residential parcels in Malibu, which would then be traded to Atlantic Richfield for their San Vicente parcel. Instead of taking a commission on multiple sales, Devins said, he and his real estate partner, Glen Gould, would become 50 percent owners of the property. With Mrs. Wilson's financial statement and the San Vicente lot as collateral, there would be no difficulty in arranging bank financing to build a medical center.

After giving Devins power of attorney to dispose of the office building, Norma consulted her lawyer, Phillip Horrigan. Horrigan was worried because the power of attorney allowed Devins to sell the property as though it were his own. He called Devins, explained his concerns, and asked him to come by and modify the agreement. Devins, however, said he'd already traded the building for the Malibu properties and was in the midst of negotiations with Atlantic Richfield's real estate people. Nevertheless, he agreed to come by Horrigan's office and sign a modified agreement.

But Devins stalled. He hadn't expected Norma to consult her attorney. So he broke several appointments and finally showed up hours late, after Horrigan had left for the day. By now he was too deeply into a complex shell game, too far down a road paved by his own greed, to turn back. He had no intention of meeting Horrigan or anyone who would demand proof of what he was telling Norma.

After failing to convince Atlantic Richfield of the merits of a swap, Devins instead sold the La Cienega office complex to a building contractor for some cash and several Malibu properties. He pocketed the cash and transferred one house to his mother, who immediately conveyed it to Lawrence Kates, a partner in Standard Investment Company. Since Devins had little credit, Kates arranged a bank loan in his own name and gave Devins the proceeds: $46,000. Kates and Devins agreed that if the house wasn't resold by a specific date, Kates would keep it. If it was sold, they would share in any profit. Either way, Devins kept the $46,000.

Several other Malibu lots were conveyed to the wife of

another Standard Investment partner. To obfuscate matters, the transactions were recorded in her maiden name; her husband kept another of the lots as "payment for professional services"—mostly his efforts to help camouflage true ownership of the properties.

Somehow, Devins got Standard Investment's notary public, Rochelle Cohen, to notarize signatures on land-transfer documents without having the people appear personally before her—a violation of state law. Among the documents Cohen notarized were a power of attorney from "Okuma Aikba" to Devins and a real estate quit-claim deed ostensibly signed by Devins's wife.

But Okuma Aikba was merely another of Devins's aliases. He used Aikba's power of attorney to obtain a mortgage on another of the Malibu lots.

Norma, of course, had no idea that Devins had sold, mortgaged, or transferred title on the Malibu lots that he had swapped for her office building. When she pressed him for details, he said he had traded the lots for sixty-one undeveloped acres in San Bernardino County, east of Los Angeles.

This wasn't the only scam Devins had going against Norma. Some months before the Malibu lots disappeared behind Devins's veil of smoke and mirrors, he had suggested that Norma transfer her Brentwood Convalescent Hospital's title to him so he could sell it to Dr. Samuel Abraham, the ophthalmologist who leased and operated the property. Norma agreed, but in June 1968, Dr. Abraham filed a lawsuit against Norma, demanding that she conclude sale of the hospital or that the down payment he'd given Devins—$5,000—be returned, plus damages. Devins assured Norma that it was just a misunderstanding, that he'd go to the office of her attorney and straighten everything out. As before, Devins canceled or ignored almost a dozen appointments. He never met with the attorney.

In November 1968, Norma told Horrigan that she was almost ready to begin development of the medical center on San Vicente. She said that Devins had negotiated a swap of the San Bernardino County land for the San Vicente property. But, she added, after seeking construction financing at several local banks on her behalf, Devins had struck out. Instead, he had found private investors willing to back the enterprise. They were in Montreal, however, and so she was flying up to meet them. These people, she told her lawyer, were from Biafra.

Like Norma, Horrigan had no idea that the San Bernardino acreage didn't exist. Nor did he know that Devins had diverted to himself all the Malibu lots Norma thought had been swapped to obtain this property. Even so—Biafran investors? Biafra, one of the poorest places on earth, was a province of Nigeria, with whom it was fighting a war of independence. Conceivably there were a few rich Biafrans—but why would they be living in Montreal? And why would they want to invest in Los Angeles? It all sounded improbable to Horrigan, who had long mistrusted Devins. The attorney didn't know what to think.

But none of this seemed to trouble Norma; she had absolute faith in Devins. She resisted all efforts to initiate a lawsuit against him and she ignored her friends' and family's repeated suggestions that she fire Devins and force him to give a full accounting.

So on November 8, 1968, Norma bought a round-trip ticket at Los Angeles International Airport and boarded a plane for Montreal, where she was expecting to meet Okuma Aikba, a wealthy Biafran, who would put up the money to develop the medical center on San Vicente. Tom Devins and his wife would catch a later plane and meet Aikba and Norma at her hotel.

The next day, November 9, Norma called Los Angeles from Montreal to tell husband William that there had been a complication. She would have to go to Lisbon, Portugal, to meet Mr. Aikba. But, said Norma, not to worry. She would be traveling with Devins, and a young French-Canadian whom she had hired as a bodyguard. His name was Robert Forget (pronounced "four-jay"), and she knew him: he'd been the maintenance man at her La Cienega office building. As for Mrs. Devins, said Norma, she had fallen ill just before her scheduled departure and so had remained in Los Angeles.

William Wilson was a little surprised by all this unplanned globe hopping, but he knew the medical center was important to his wife. Several days later Wilson received a flight-insurance policy. The policy showed that Norma had left on a round-trip flight from Montreal to Madrid. After a few more days, he received a postcard from Norma, postmarked Madrid. It indicated that she had arrived safely and was headed for Malaga, on the Costa del Sol. A week passed until the arrival of a card dated November 14 and postmarked Tangiers, Morocco. In her usual telegraphic style, Norma wrote of being ill in Spain, visiting the Tangiers Casbah, and going on to Lisbon.

William Wilson never heard from his wife again.

Nearly three months went by, however, before he reported Norma's disappearance to Los Angeles authorities. In that interval, Devins and Forget returned, separately, to Los Angeles. Forget went to a new home in a small Washington State town called Sedro Woolley.

In December, Devins sold the Brentwood Convalescent Hospital to Dr. Abraham for $147,000. Abraham gave Devins two personal, interest-bearing notes, one for $10,000—the sales commission—and another for $137,000, representing the purchase price. The larger note was immediately assigned to "Sandra Lynn Bell," who signed it over to Okuma Aikba. A few weeks later Aikba assigned the note to Thomas Devins, who somewhere found a couple of credulous gentlemen to buy it for $75,000 in cash. Devins traded the $10,000 note to an auto dealer and drove off in a new car.

Now Dr. Abraham had his building and Devins had *all* the money.

But where was Norma? By late November, her friends and family had begun to ask this question. William Wilson called Devins, who explained that he'd last seen her in Geneva, Switzerland. He'd had to return to conclude some urgent business in Los Angeles, but, he said, Norma said she was heading for a health spa in Sweden, then might rendezvous with an old flame, a gentleman now living in Spain with his wife. So, said Devins, there was nothing to worry about.

Wilson waited through the Christmas holidays, which he

spent, as was Norma's long-standing custom, at their usual hotel on Waikiki Beach, half expecting his wife to turn up at any moment. But by February 1969, the letters and calls from Norma's friends and family could no longer be ignored and he went to the Los Angeles Police Department to report that his wife was missing. He was surprised to learn that the LAPD didn't care—Norma wasn't missing from Los Angeles, she was missing from Spain or maybe Morocco or Portugal. Since there was no evidence that someone within their jurisdiction had committed a crime, it wasn't an LAPD problem. They lacked jurisdiction—"the right and power to interpret and apply the law" over criminals outside Los Angeles.

So Wilson went to the FBI, only to hear an overworked agent tell him that if Norma had disappeared from any of the fifty states, then a possible crime would fall under their jurisdiction. But the FBI had no legal right to investigate someone missing from a foreign country, just as, for example, Spain would have no right to investigate the disappearance of one of its citizens in Los Angeles. Moreover, suggested the agent, based on the couple's relative ages and Norma's net worth, perhaps Norma wasn't so much missing as wandering.

In desperation, Wilson went to the Santa Monica offices of the Los Angeles County district attorney. Perhaps because this was one of several "satellite" offices, a smaller, less formal place, Wilson was finally allowed to have a conversation with an investigator.

Bill Burnett was in his early thirties, a lanky, rawboned pipe-smoking coal miner's son from rural Illinois. As a marine, he had seen combat in Korea, embassy guard duty in Ethiopia, and had served as a boot-camp drill instructor. As a deputy sheriff, he had guarded inmates in the county jail. Bored, in the early 1960s he wangled an investigator's job in the DA's office. On the day he met William Wilson, Burnett was anything but bored. His caseload, like those of his peers, was heavy, and he was less than overjoyed to hear a vague story of how Wilson's rich, older wife seemed to have disappeared on the other side of the world.

Burnett agreed to see Wilson only because his boss insisted on it. The young investigator's first question was how finding Norma Wilson fell within the jurisdiction of Los Angeles County. After listening to Wilson's vague answers, Burnett decided that the husband might actually be far more interested in having his wife declared dead than in finding her: under the terms of her will, Wilson would inherit most of her estate, valued at something over $10 million.

*That* piqued Burnett's interest.

Maybe, he supposed to himself, Norma hadn't actually disappeared in Europe at all. Maybe Wilson had killed her right here in Los Angeles County, disposed of her body, and was now constructing both an alibi and a scenario to lead authorities away from himself. Maybe Wilson was trying to commit the perfect crime—and trying to get Burnett to follow a scent he knew would lead nowhere. Maybe the young husband of the rich older woman was trying to play him for a sucker.

With these unspoken thoughts in mind, the investigator made up his mind: He had plenty of other cases to pursue, but he would make the time to follow Wilson's lead for a bit and see where it led. Maybe Wilson needed just enough rope to hang himself.

Burnett then met with several of Norma's family and friends. What emerged from his interviews were two portraits: one of a beautiful, rich widow desperately clinging to her vanished youth, and one of a young fortune-hunter named William Wilson, who was despised by his wife's kin.

From these interviews, and further conversations with Wilson, Burnette learned that while Norma had not taken many clothes to Montreal, she had taken several valuable items of jewelry, including a huge emerald ring, an expensive strand of pearls always worn to conceal a scar on her throat, a diamond-encrusted watch, and a full-length white mink coat. Norma's relatives also said that Tom Devins reported that Norma's destination in Sweden was an exclusive clinic, favored by sueh film stars as Sophia Loren, where she would discreetly have her face lifted.

There were three more interesting facts gleaned from

Burnett's interviews: William Wilson had, more than once, beaten or kicked his wife; Norma had discussed divorce, though papers had never been filed; and finally, under the provisions of her will, if a divorce action was pending when Norma died, William would get only $30,000.

Burnett found these facts so interesting that he decided a polygraph test was in order for Mr. William Wilson. After initially waffling, Wilson agreed to be tested.

As a matter of routine, Burnett had sent the flight-insurance policy and postcards Wilson had received from Norma to a "questioned documents examiner" to determine if the handwriting was Norma's and then on to the U.S. Postal Inspector's Office to verify that the postmarks were not forgeries. While that was being done, he dispatched letters and cables to law enforcement in Montreal, Madrid, and Geneva, as well as to Interpol. And he had asked the LAPD to check on Wilson, Devins, and Robert Forget, the onetime maintenance man who had accompanied Devins to Canada and Spain.

Days went by before answers to Burnett's inquiries trickled in. One of the more alarming was a note from the Royal Canadian Mounted Police: Robert Forget had a criminal record. He had entered the United States illegally in 1959 and had been arrested and deported. Later he married an American citizen and immigrated legally. (In that era, before millions of undocumented workers made a mockery of American immigration law, illegal entry was considered a serious matter.)

Devins also had a criminal record, although this did not become apparent until the FBI report came in, listing his aliases and the burglary and weapons convictions he had under his real name, Thomas Utter.

The Royal Canadian Mounted Police verified that Norma Wilson had stayed overnight at the Montreal Hilton before leaving the country on an Air Canada flight to New York City. Hotel records showed that she had called home from her room, and that calls from a room shared by Devins and Forget had been made to Ottawa. The RCMP were thorough: they also reported that Devins had rented a car and driven it from Ottawa to Montreal and back to Ottawa.

Burnett next contacted Air Canada and learned that in Montreal, Norma had purchased a one-way Air Canada ticket to New York. There she had booked another one-way flight to Madrid, this time on TWA.

Devins and Forget bought tickets on the same New York and Madrid flights. Oddly, however, there was no record of either man's name on TWA's passenger manifest to Madrid. Burnett wondered if they had used aliases—and if so, why.

But what bothered Burnett most was that on leaving Los Angeles for Montreal, Norma paid for round-trip fares, while her "bodyguard" and "financial adviser" took one-ways. She neither used the return portion of her ticket nor cashed it in for a refund. Did Devins and Forget know Montreal was only the first stop on a long, circuitous journey, and that Norma wasn't going to come back? This bothered Burnett so much that even after William Wilson's polygraph examination was deemed "inconclusive," the investigator decided that he was no longer a primary suspect.

Burnett wrestled with the urge to tackle Devins. But he knew that he ought to proceed with great caution. First there was the matter of jurisdiction: even if Devins suddenly confessed to killing Norma in, say, Spain or Morocco, Burnett wasn't sure he could make a case that would fall under the DA's jurisdiction. Then there was the fact that despite his criminal record, there was not one shred of evidence that Devins had done anything to harm Norma Wilson. Unless there was evidence that a plot to kill Norma had originated in California, Devins was immune from prosecution for murder in this state.

So Burnett decided to find out just what kind of financial work Devins had been doing for Norma. The place to start, he reasoned, was the hall of records, where the county recorder kept a copy of every transaction involving every piece of real estate in Los Angeles County.

It didn't take Burnett long to follow the paper trails left by Devins as he traded, deeded, or sold Norma's properties for the Malibu lots. From the deeds of trust and powers of attorney emerged a short list of names: Okuma Aikba, Sandra Lynn Bell, Louise Glantz, Mamie Elizabeth Utter, and Lawrence Kates. Armed with this information, Burnett con-

fronted Kates and his partners at Standard Investment. He
also questioned Rochelle Cohen, the notary public whose
seal was on many of Devins's documents.

Kates, who probably had no idea that Devins had acquired the property through fraud, immediately revealed
their arrangement. He had acted as owner of one of the
Malibu lots, he explained, and the property was recorded in
his name. Kates also said that Glantz was the maiden name
of his business partner's wife. Then, Rochelle Cohen
admitted to notarizing signatures she hadn't witnessed.

Suddenly, the scope of Devins's fraud was clear to Burnett: he had systematically looted Norma's choicest holdings. Now Burnett could understand why Devins would
want Norma Wilson dead. He thought he might be able to
prove that Devins had planned her death in Southern California to cover up his scheme to steal her real estate.

Burnett knew his supervisors were unhappy that he had
been taking time from his caseload to work on a missing-
person investigation. Now he believed he needed to devote
even more time to the case. He made an appointment to see
the chief of the DA's investigative unit, George Stoner.
When Stoner had been briefed, he transferred Burnett
downtown to work under his personal supervision and part-
nered him with George Murphy, an older, more experienced
investigator.

Not long after this, Tom Devins retained the services of
one of Southern California's leading criminal defense attorneys, Jerome Weber. Chief Stoner thought that was most interesting. He ordered round-the-clock shifts of detectives to
keep Tom Devins under continual surveillance.

Burnett contacted Devins and asked him to come downtown for a chat. Devins readily agreed—but as he had done
with Horrigan and others, he failed to show for three appointments, each time pleading a last-minute business con-
flict.

Just when Burnett was about to ask a deputy DA to issue
a subpoena for the grand jury, Devins called. He was breez-
ily informal, insisting that he and Burnett use first names.
He noted that Norma had been missing for several months
and he was concerned that something might have happened

to her. He suggested that the man behind her disappearance was her husband. William Wilson had hired an attorney, been appointed trustee of Norma's estate, and was now trying to push her will through probate so he could grab all of her holdings. Devins revealed that he'd filed court papers in an unsuccessful attempt to block Wilson's appointment as trustee.

From Devins's attacks on Wilson's character and his pointed recollections that Norma had told him she planned to divorce her husband, Burnett concluded that the only reason he'd called was to try to divert suspicion from himself.

But Burnett did get Devins to answer some specific questions about his dealings with Norma in Europe. Devins claimed that in Montreal he had given Norma $133,000—money from the sale of the Brentwood Convalescent Hospital, to be used to finance construction of the medical center. Forget was along as a bodyguard precisely because she was carrying so much cash.

Next, the trio had stopped in New York on the way to Spain to notarize the papers conveying the hospital to its buyer, Dr. Abraham. In Spain, said Devins, Norma had visited friends in Madrid and Malaga. They took the ferry to Tangiers, where Forget got sick and returned home. From Tangiers, he and Norma had flown to Zurich, where Norma put her money in a bank. Then they rented a car and drove to Geneva. Norma checked into the Intercontinental; Devins stayed at another hotel because Norma's "boyfriend" was flying in to be with her. Devins said he hadn't spoken to Norma again before flying back to Los Angeles on the twenty-third of November. However, several months later, he went on, he was so concerned about Norma that he had returned to Europe, stopped at the Intercontinental to interview the help, checked airlines, taxi companies, and the train depot, ran ads in the newspapers, and offered a reward. But, Devins concluded, no one had come forward. No one knew what had happened to Norma Wilson.

Then, pleading an urgent phone call, he hung up.

Burnett had nothing in the way of evidence, but as he put the phone down he had a strong feeling that Devins was a most accomplished liar.

A few days later Burnett and his new partner, George Murphy, flew to Seattle and rented a car for the eighty-mile drive to Sedro Woolley, population six thousand, thirty miles south of the Canadian border. A chat with the local police chief produced the opinion that Robert Forget was involved with smuggling guns into Canada, though there was no proof.

In the basement of Sedro Woolley's police station, Burnett and Murphy interrogated Forget, a dark, handsome man in his twenties. Forget said he had known Devins since 1960, when he was still parking cars for a living. After Devins hooked up with Norma Wilson, he hired Forget to do some carpentry work on his new office, and then kept him on as the building's maintenance man.

Forget described how Devins had become Norma's confidant, and how the older woman often cried on Devins's shoulder as she described her unhappy marriage to William Wilson.

By 1968, Forget had decided that Los Angeles was not the place for him and moved north to the tall timber country around Sedro Woolley. Then, the previous November, Devins had called and offered him $5,000, a thousand up front, to go along with Norma and himself to Europe as a bodyguard. Since he spoke French and some Spanish, he would also be their interpreter.

Eager to make some money, Forget had accepted. He was still a Canadian citizen and didn't have a passport, so during the day Norma spent in Montreal, he and Devins had driven to Ottawa, the capital, where it was possible to get a passport in a few hours. Then they returned to Montreal, flew to New York the next day to have some papers notarized, and then on to Spain.

In Spain and later in Morocco, said Forget, all he did was translate for Norma when she went shopping. He didn't much care for Europe or Africa, especially when he came down with a severe stomachache from eating bad food. Forget told Devins that his wife was sick and he wanted to go home.

Since they no longer seemed to need him, said Forget, Norma gave him the rest of the $5,000 and bought him a ticket for Los Angeles, where he had left his car. He flew via Paris, where he stopped off for a few days to do some sight-seeing before flying home.

When Devins and Murphy pressed him for details, Forget stated that Norma had made sexual advances, to which he did not respond. She had made eyes at handsome young men everywhere they went. So, said Forget, he wouldn't be surprised if Norma was seeing Europe from the inside of various hotel rooms in the company of some obliging young man.

Burnett was sure Forget was lying. Sure that he was concealing something.

Under intense pressure from the two investigators, Forget admitted that Devins had called some days earlier to tell him to expect Burnett and Murphy. Forget insisted he'd done nothing wrong, but he had a criminal record and had been with Norma. If Norma was dead, he might well be a suspect. Forget was worried.

Forget also admitted to having taken a gun to Spain, a caliber .380 automatic that he said had been stolen from his hotel room in Malaga. And he said that Devins had loaned him another $5,000 "to help build a house" he was hoping to sell at a profit. Forget said he had signed loan papers at a Los Angeles branch of Charter Bank of London, but was hazy on details like the term of the loan and the interest rate.

Burnett and Murphy kept pushing. Had Devins ever mentioned Biafra?

Well, said Forget, Devins had talked about going to Biafra and killing some government official who had kicked out all the American oil companies. There was big money to be made from the oil companies. But, continued Forget, he wasn't interested in that kind of action.

Before leaving Sedro Woolley, Burnett told Forget straight out that he was sure Norma Wilson had been murdered and that Forget was mixed up in it. If he didn't want to face the gas chamber—"the little green room," as Burnett put it—Forget would be well advised to cooperate.

Back in Los Angeles, Burnett decided it was time to meet Tom Devins. He wanted to see what he looked like, get a look inside his house, see how he lived, what his wife was like.

The problem was, Burnett could find no grounds for a search warrant. During his search of public records, however, he had discovered that Devins was building an addition to his home and had applied for a city construction permit. Masquerading as a building-inspector-in-training, Burnett accompanied a genuine inspector to Devins's hilltop home. He was breaking no laws, so any evidence he might find in this way would not be admissible in court.

Only two things of significance emerged from Burnett's visit. He came away with the impression of Devins as a man of overpowering intelligence. And he found a partially expended box of nine-millimeter pistol ammunition in the office.

Burnett decided that if he was going to learn what had happened to Norma, he would have to go to Europe and follow her trail, collecting evidence along the way. But before he could complete arrangements to do so, he found himself in the middle of a bizarre and almost unprecedented situation.

Jerome Weber, Devins's heavyweight defense attorney, apparently told Devins that for $35,000, his connections in the district attorney's office would make all of his legal problems go away. Instead, Devins went to the state attorney general and demanded they arrest Burnett, Murphy, and George Stoner, chief of the DA's investigation division, for attempted extortion.

Devins had worn a tape recorder during discussions with Weber and succeeded in getting his attorney to make the incriminating statements on tape. The charges were taken seriously.

For months the attorney general's office investigated the DA's office. The situation made for extra drama because the district attorney was contemplating running for California attorney general—and the man directing the investigation against him was his opponent. The two exchanged barbed comments in the newspapers. Insinuations of a cover-up and dirty politics were hurled back and forth.

Devins played this situation for all it was worth. He held

press conferences denouncing the district attorney and his investigators, claiming that he had been set up as a suspect in a murder investigation as a way to extort money. Now that this scheme had been exposed, the only reason the DA's office continued their investigation was to find some pretext to justify their original probe. He was an innocent man, Devins told the media, an honest businessman being railroaded for a crime he did not commit and that probably had not even occurred.

Burnett, Murphy, and Stoner were grilled repeatedly by the AG's investigators. Clearly, there was a leak in their office that had supplied inside information to Weber and Devins.

Very angry at this public assault on his integrity, Burnett redoubled his efforts to find evidence that would implicate Devins. But as the extortion investigation wore on, Devins continued his guerrilla warfare against Burnett and the DA's office. When he realized that detectives had staked out his home and office and were following him everywhere, Devins retaliated. He provoked a dangerous, high-speed chase on freeways and streets. His aim was to lay the ground for harassment charges.

According to police, Devins also shot up his own car, then showed police and reporters the bullet holes as "evidence" of an attempt on his life by the DA's men.

Eventually the AG would charge Jerome Weber with extortion, and a court would find him guilty. No one in the DA's office was ever charged.

While this sideshow played itself out, Burnett and Deputy DA Steve Trott planned the European phase of their investigation. If evidence could be obtained, Trott would be the man to actually prosecute Devins.

Steve Trott was thirty but looked much younger. Tall, dark, and slender, he dressed Ivy League. He spoke fluent Spanish and French and could get along in German, Italian, and Portuguese. Tough-minded, totally honest, he was such a straight arrow that few in public life could ever aspire to match his standards of personal conduct. Most of all, Steve Trott was a smart, tireless, and formidable prosecutor.

Yet Trott might easily have made a career in show business. He was a talented stage magician who could also sing and play the guitar. During his college years, he put together a folk-rock band, the Highwaymen—and went to law school on his share of royalties from their hit single, "Michael, Row the Boat Ashore."

Trott had worked with Burnett before. They shared a love of off-road motorcycling and had become friends. Armed with cash advances from the DA's travel funds, Trott and Burnett headed for Spain.

With his quick wit and excellent language skills, Trott made a favorable impression on law-enforcement authorities as they traveled in Europe. Chiefs of police and U.S. consular officials in Madrid, Malaga, Zurich, and Geneva were quick to offer whatever help the Los Angeles investigators requested.

In each country they visited, Trott and Burnett checked with local coroners to see if they had an unidentified body that might be Norma's. It was a dead end; no European "Jane Doe" matched her general description.

Relying on hotel registration cards, which in Europe are usually considered important documents and preserved for years in police archives, Trott and Burnett reconstructed Norma's journey.

With Devins and Forget, Norma had stayed at Madrid's Hotel Castellana. Norma had looked up her late husband's sister and told her that she was traveling with Devins and Forget to meet an investor from some African nation, who was traveling by yacht, in Tangiers. Norma quizzed her friends about opening a Swiss bank account. She also said her group would stop off in Malaga on the way to Morocco.

Hotel records confirmed the trio stayed at the Malaga Palacio on November 13. The next morning a chambermaid found a loaded caliber .380 automatic under the mattress in Forget's room. Spain's handgun-control laws are very strict, and all three were arrested. Norma paid several thousand dollars in fines, and they were released after a night in jail. Forget, recalled Burnett, had lied. He had said that the gun was *stolen* from his room.

On November 14, Norma, Devins, and Forget embarked

on the ferry *Ibn Fatouta* to Morocco. The next morning they were in Tangiers.

Trott and Burnett, fighting time constraints, did not go to Tangiers. Instead they satisfied themselves with telephone inquiries to the airlines, confirming Forget's route to Los Angeles, and Devins and Norma's flight to Zurich.

The investigators picked up Norma's trail again in Zurich, where she and Devins stayed at the Hotel Astor. Aided by the Kriminalpolizei's discreet, off-the-record inquiries, Trott and Burnett learned that despite Devins's claims, Norma had *not* opened an account in any Zurich bank.

From Zurich to Geneva there were several possible routes by automobile. After finding the Avis office where Devins rented a Volkswagen minibus, Trott and Burnett got a copy of the rental agreement, which showed the mileage Devins put on the vehicle and the times he had taken and returned it. With that information as a guide, it seemed clear that they had driven from Zurich to Lugano, stayed overnight, and then drove on to Geneva, via the Simplon Tunnel.

When Geneva police checked hotel registry cards, they found one for Devins at the Hotel Richemond, on the night of November 23. But there was no card for Norma at the Intercontinental, where Devins claimed she had stayed—or at any other hotel in the city or suburbs.

So Norma and Devins had left Lake Lugano together—but Devins alone arrived in Geneva.

The road from Lugano to Geneva is well traveled. But branching off the main road at intervals are many back roads, leading into high, frigid, sparsely populated alpine plateaus where few people venture in November. At that time of year there is little to see but ice and snow—thousands of square miles of magnificent desolation. It is an ideal location to kill someone and dispose of a body. Buried in even a shallow grave, it might be years—or centuries—before someone stumbled on it.

Burnett and Trott agreed that if Norma had been murdered, the most likely place was there, in some remote canyon or plateau a few kilometers off the main road. Now they had to prove that she was dead, Devins was responsible, and he had lured her to Switzerland from Los Angeles expressly for that purpose. Without a California tie-in, they had no jurisdiction in this murder.

Still searching for the mysterious Okuma Aikba, Trott and Burnett stopped in Lisbon on their way back to Los Angeles and paid a visit to the one-room Biafran "consulate," which Portuguese police suspected of being a front for the acquisition of arms by the Biafran rebels. The only person there confirmed the existence of Aikba, insisting he was a low-level clerk who had returned to his native country months earlier.

Back in Los Angeles, Burnett and Trott were contacted by some of the European law-enforcement officials they had met with on their trip. Police in Lugano tracked down the minibus that Devins had driven from Zurich to Geneva. It had been sold by Avis to a Lugano taxi driver, resold immediately to a local mechanic, and sold yet again, months later, to a local banker. At Burnett's request, Swiss police carefully checked the vehicle for traces of blood, hair, or skin.

They found traces of human blood on the passenger-side dashboard, door armrest, seat and on the driver's-side door. Each of the minibus's former owners denied that they had ever transported dead or wounded animals, and none could account for the presence of blood. While it was old blood, police experts concluded it was most likely human.

Trott and Burnett agreed that it was time to have another conversation with Robert Forget. And then they got lucky. One of Burnett's pals, whom he knew from his years as a county jail guard, relayed a fascinating tidbit from a jailhouse snitch. The snitch had overheard an inmate talking about a friend who had a lady's ring with a huge emerald, a ring that had belonged to a rich woman who disappeared in Switzerland. The man with the ring, said the snitch, was a French-Canadian who lived in Washington State and had flashed the ring at a bar.

Burnett knew from his interviews with Norma's family that the missing millionaire nearly always wore just such an emerald. Norma was wearing it the last time William Wilson saw her at the Los Angeles airport. Burnett spoke to the prisoner fingered by the snitch. He was released on reduced bail, flew to Sedro Woolley, and told Forget that Burnett knew about the emerald. If he didn't talk, Forget stood to take all the heat for Norma's murder.

After calling Burnett to say he had something to tell him, Forget drove down to Los Angeles and gave a long, detailed statement.

Early in November 1968, Forget said, Devins had called him to say that he had a plan to rescue former Congolese dictator Moise Tshombe from his jail in Algeria. Tshombe had lots of money in Switzerland and would pay Devins $50,000 after he was freed. Devins promised Forget half, $25,000, for helping with the jailbreak.

Forget was as dull as Devins was bright—but even he was not persuaded by this wild proposition. Nevertheless, when Devins wired him $1,000, Forget flew down to Los Angeles. He needed a passport to get to Africa, however, and so he and Devins boarded a plane for Montreal. Somewhere over Idaho or Montana, Devins told Forget that Norma Wilson was meeting them in Montreal.

After Forget had his passport, he and Devins met Norma at the airport. Devins told Norma that he had "just run into" Forget in Montreal and decided, on the spur of the moment, to invite him along. And, apparently without much thought, Norma agreed.

But, said Forget, she hadn't given him any money. He had lied about that, as Devins had told him to do.

In Spain, Devins kept spinning his plans for breaking Tshombe out of prison. He had been taking flying lessons and could do the job. They would come in low, under the radar, and land on a dirt strip. Forget almost believed him.

Their days in Spain were spent waiting for Norma's "investors" to clear customs with their stacks of cash. Forget had the feeling Devins was stalling. He was sure of it when Devins told him, before they flew to Malaga, that before breaking Tshombe out of jail, they had one little detail to attend to.

Norma had to die. And Devins wanted Forget to kill her. Norma had to die, said Forget, because Devins had been cheating her out of her real estate. If she was dead, she couldn't press charges.

Forget said he couldn't kill Norma. But now he was afraid of Devins, whom he knew was carrying a nine-millimeter Browning semiautomatic pistol. Forget took the .380 Star Devins had given him in Montreal out of his shaving kit and put it under his mattress. That was where the chambermaid found it, leading to their arrest by Spanish police.

They went on to Tangiers, said Forget, just to get out of Spain, where the police were surely watching them.

In Tangiers, Devins again asked Forget to kill Norma, and this time he agreed. They planned to take her out into the desert, shoot her, and bury her body in some isolated place. That plan was put on hold when a sudden sandstorm struck. After thinking it over, Forget said, he told Devins he couldn't kill Norma. So Devins bought him a plane ticket for Paris and sent him off with a few hundred dollars.

Several weeks later, Forget continued, Devins called from Los Angeles and told him to come down and get his money. Forget was suspicious, but Devins assured him that nothing was wrong, that "no crime had been committed in this country."

Broke and curious, Forget drove down to Los Angeles. There, Devins admitted he had killed Norma. He showed Forget her passport and gave him her nine-carat emerald ring, along with a string of pearls and a diamond-encrusted wristwatch.

Devins had taken a huge risk smuggling the jewelry back through U.S. Customs. The reason, concluded Trott and Burnett, was to frame Forget for the murder.

Forget hid the jewels in a beer can filled with caulking compound. But after his first encounter with Burnett, Forget decided he had to get rid of the incriminating evidence. He said he took the pearl necklace apart and pried the diamonds out of the watch setting and scattered them along a rural road. He tried to break the huge emerald by pounding it with a hammer, but all that did was leave a dent on the crescent wrench he'd put under the emerald. So he and his girlfriend threw the stone into a pond.

Forget admitted that Devins paid him $10,000, money he said came from a real estate deal.

Burnett pressed Forget for more details about Norma's murder. Forget said that Devins admitted to shooting her in the head and "she hadn't felt a thing." That had happened somewhere in the mountains between Lugano and Geneva, as Burnett and Trott had suspected. Next, according to Forget, Devins used a hunting knife to butcher Norma's body into pieces, which he scattered around in several shallow graves in remote locations.

Finally, said Forget, Devins said he had put all of Norma's clothes, including her full-length mink coat, into a box that he'd left in a train or bus station somewhere in Switzerland.

A few months later, when the money Devins had given him was gone, Forget asked for more. Devins gave him a look so menacing that it chilled him to the bone, said Forget. He went back to Washington and tried to forget about Tom Devins.

Later, Devins had called to tell him that Burnett and Murphy were coming up to see him. Forget was thoroughly coached on what to say.

Burnett and Trott had a long conference, discussing where they were with the case. They soon realized their case against Devins rested on Forget's testimony. Without effective corroboration, however, there was little chance of getting a conviction on what Forget alone could tell a jury.

Murphy went to Sedro Woolley with Forget to look for the emerald at the bottom of the pond. He also picked up a gun Devins had given to his wife's father, who lived in another Washington town.

On the basis of Forget's sworn statement, Trott and Burnett got a search warrant for Devins's safe-deposit box. When Burnett opened it, however, there was only a single piece of paper inside. It said, *Sorry . . . the Fox.* Obviously, Devins had anticipated that authorities would open his box. The signature might well have been a reference to one of the most famous cases in Los Angeles history—the mysterious 1927 kidnap-murder of twelve-year-old Marian Parker, a banker's daughter. The killer had communicated with authorities through notes, telegrams, and letters, all signed "The Fox." The subject of what was for decades Southern California's biggest and most arduous manhunt, that Fox was eventually caught, tried, and executed.

About the same time the box was opened, Trott questioned one of the AG agents who had worked with Devins trying to prove his extortion allegations. The AG agent said Devins had identified the elusive Okuma Aikba as a fictitious name he sometimes used in his real estate business.

Trott and Burnett, who had chased over half of Europe trying to find this character, were not amused. They could think of no explanation for the information they had received in Lisbon, that Aikba had been a clerk in the Biafran consulate. To this day, this detail remains a mystery.

Too many people had handled the nine-millimeter Browning that Murphy retrieved from Devins's father-in-law for useful fingerprints to be found. But the gun itself could easily be linked to Devins.

When he saw the gun, Forget remembered something else Devins had said: he'd bragged about replacing the barrel. Checks with Los Angeles-area gun shops turned up a bill of sale, and when Burnett checked with the Belgian manufacturer, he learned how to decode the manufacturer's markings on the barrel. They proved that the barrel on the gun was *not* the one on it when Devins bought the gun, just before leaving for Europe with Norma. If her body was ever found, Devins must have reasoned, the bullet in it could not be matched to the barrel of his gun.

The emerald Forget threw into a pond was not recovered. But in trying to shatter it with a hammer, he had left a shallow impression of the stone on the smooth surface of a wrench placed under the emerald. Burnett asked scientists at the world-famous Jet Propulsion Laboratory to photograph the impression under an electron microscope and use computer-enhanced imaging techniques to identify the shape, size, and proportions of whatever had made the dent. When matched with enlargements of insurance photos of Norma's hand-cut emerald, these scientists concluded that nothing on this planet except the emerald in question could have left that particular mark.

Shortly thereafter, Geneva police reported finding Norma's bloodstained clothing in a large box left at the main train station. Air-freighted to Los Angeles, the clothing was subjected to the scrutiny of DeWayne Wolfer, the LAPD's world-famous criminalist. The blood was identified as Type A, the same as the victim's. Examination of the blood-flow patterns on the mink coat and other clothing showed that the victim had been standing or sitting in an upright position when shot through the head. The bigger blood flow was in front, indicating an exit wound, which suggested very strongly that the shot was fired from behind the victim.

Devins had been very clever about switching gun barrels—but after the discovery of Norma's clothes, he stood revealed as *too* clever. The bullet he fired through Norma's head was never found, and probably never will be. In its absence, Devins's choice to replace the barrel of a nearly new gun provided prosecutors with one more bit of circumstantial evidence.

In further corroboration of Forget's statement (Devins had told Burnett about cutting up Norma's body with a hunting knife) microscopic examination of the small pieces of clothing suggested that this had been done with a sharp blade of a type common to hunting knives.

It was time, the DA decided, to arrest Devins.

Devins had been having marital problems and had moved out of his Hollywood Hills home to live with a beautiful young woman on a yacht he kept moored at Marina del Rey. Perhaps tipped off by his contact in the DA's office, he chose this time to shake his surveillance.

After hunting for hours, Burnett spotted a car he recognized as belonging to one of Devins's girlfriends. He nailed Devins at the checkout counter of a Marina del Rey grocery market.

Devins's trial for murder, conspiracy, fraud, and robbery began in mid-1970. If it didn't get the publicity it deserved, it was because just down the hall Charles Manson and his followers were being tried for murdering seven people.

Judge Malcolm Lucas ruled against Devins's motion for dismissal on grounds of jurisdiction. Lucas held that there was enough evidence to support the prosecution's argument that Devins had *planned* Norma's murder in Los Angeles. Therefore, his court had jurisdiction.

Robert Forget was given immunity for his role in Norma's murder. He testified at length about how Devins had tried to get him to kill Norma and, later, how Devins had bragged of killing her himself.

Devins's attorney, Joel Reichman, called no defense witnesses, introduced no evidence, and rested his case after arguing that Los Angeles had no jurisdiction to try his client.

On December 8, 1970, a jury found Devins guilty of murder in the first degree, conspiracy to commit murder, armed robbery, and real estate fraud. Guilty on all counts. He was sentenced to life in prison.

But on March 29, 1972, the California Court of Appeals reversed Judge Lucas on the issue of jurisdiction. If Devins was to be tried for this crime, said the appellate decision, it would have to be in Switzerland.

"If you kill someone on Mars, there's no jurisdiction" in California, said Joel Reichman, now a U.S. magistrate. "But Devins wasn't a lawyer. How would he know that this would happen?" he asked rhetorically.

Devins remained in prison to serve his sentence for real estate fraud. But in January 1974, Trott and Burnett learned that a Swiss mushroom picker had found a human jawbone, partly buried in a high meadow. Comparisons with Norma Wilson's dental X rays and a plaster impression of her jaw confirmed that this was indeed part of her body.

Trott began the process of convincing Swiss authorities to ask for Devins's extradition so he could be tried in Switzerland.

But before this could happen, Devins escaped from the minimum-security prison at Susanville. About two weeks later a Hollywood motorist reported picking up a hitchhiker who answered his description.

Several months later, Devins surfaced in Vichy, France, in the company of Beth Greenhouse, a wealthy young woman who had begun visiting him while he was in prison. Devins and Greenhouse stayed with her parents' friends until Devins reportedly stole some $700,000 worth of jewelry from his hostess, Michelle Chonac.

Devins was nabbed at the Sydney, Australia, airport as he tried to enter the country using an alias and a forged passport. His traveling companion, Greenhouse, hired one of Australia's most prominent attorneys, Bruce Miles, who argued to an Australian court that Devins should be granted political asylum. If he was returned to the United States, said Miles, he would be murdered because he knew too much about corruption in the district attorney's office. The court granted a brief postponement of extradition proceedings until they could ascertain the facts. While this was happening, Interpol learned that the Chonac jewelry had been fenced in the Sydney underworld. Some of the pieces were recovered, but not the money Devins had been paid for them.

The court ruled that since Devins was wanted in California for escaping prison, and this wasn't covered by Australia's extradition treaty with the United States, Australia wasn't required to turn him over to U.S. authorities. Devins, well aware of the treaty's provisions, thought he'd found a new home.

Until the next day, when several senior Sydney police, thumbing their noses at the court, simply picked up Devins and put him on a Qantas flight bound for Los Angeles. Tom Devins was arrested at the Los Angeles airport on October 11, 1974, and sent to maximum-security Folsom Prison.

Susanville Prison, from which Devins escaped, is in Lassen County, a sparsely populated, rural area. Lassen County authorities filed prison-escape charges against Devins, but the case was dismissed before coming to trial. The reason for this failure remains a mystery.

French authorities showed no interest in prosecuting Devins for stealing Madame Chonac's jewelry—after all, he was back in jail.

The U.S. Justice Department's office of International Affairs pressed Swiss authorities to ask for Devins's extradition, offering their full support to help prosecute the case. But in a move that shocked Burnett and Trott, the Swiss government, after lengthy secret discussions, chose to do nothing. Privately, officials told Trott that since no Swiss citizens were involved, a showy, sensational murder trial would only serve to discourage wealthy tourists like Norma from visiting their country.

"Devins structured the demise of his victim," says Trott, who has held several posts in the U.S. Department of Justice (including associate attorney general, the department's third-highest-ranking official) and is now a Ninth U.S. Circuit Court of Appeals judge. "He truly got away with the perfect crime."

Devins, who killed a woman in cold blood, was paroled on Valentine's Day, 1977, having served fewer than six years for theft of property.

It was not the last to be heard from Tom Devins. In the early-morning hours of June 21, 1986, he was the only one awake on the *West I*, a 167-foot fish-processing ship bound for the Philippines. At 3:30 A.M., when the ship was about six hundred miles northeast of the big island of Hawaii, Devins sounded the abandon-ship alarm.

The weather was calm and clear and the *West I*'s steel hull had been inspected only two weeks earlier. Nevertheless, Devins told the rest of the crew that the engine room was rapidly flooding. When crewmen started to go down for a look, Devins said he smelled smoke and tripped a firefighting device that filled the engine compartment with an inert gas, driving out all the oxygen. No one could enter. Only Devins claimed to have seen the sea pouring into the hull.

The eight people aboard hastily went over the side, then watched the ship wallow for more than three hours before sinking. Seven of the eight crew were left in a life raft without adequate food or water. The first mate navigated a battered, sixteen-foot skiff to landfall on Nihau, one of the Hawaiian Islands.

Before the crew was rescued on July 5 by a U.S. Navy spy ship, the *West I*'s captain died of exposure.

From the investigation that followed came a tangled tale. Those crewing the ship thought it had been sold and were delivering it to its new owners—but the "new owners" told authorities that they had merely agreed to look at the vessel before making an offer.

According to the crew, before sailing, Devins told them that he represented Land West, the ship's old owners—he had worked for Land West, a land developer, for seven years. But after the rescue, Devins insisted to authorities that he represented the *new* purchasers in the Philippines.

The ship's late captain had been paid just before sailing with Devins's personal postdated checks. They bounced after the ship was at sea.

In Hawaii, Devins wangled a mysterious personal audience with deposed Philippines dictator Ferdinand Marcos, reportedly to convey a deathbed message from the *West I*'s late captain, a Philippines national.

The captain's widow, however, later told reporters that her husband never knew Marcos and detested everything he stood for.

Devins repeatedly failed to come to Coast Guard headquarters with his report on the sinking. Then one of the crew members admitted that he had lied, at Devins's urging, about being on duty with Devins when he noted that the ship was sinking. Actually, said the crewman, Devins had told him to go to sleep at midnight, and he had done so.

The reason for all this chicanery surfaced with the insurance claim. The *West I* was insured for over $3 million, the declared purchase price by the "new" owners. But the ship was valued at under $1.4 million, the amount owed to a mortgage company.

Lloyd's of London, the insurer, settled the claim for about $1 million.

The only evidence of what actually caused the *West I* to sink lies beneath 14,000 feet of water in one of the deepest parts of the Pacific. No one was ever charged with a crime in the incident.

Could someone today do as Devins did in 1968? Probably not. New laws in many European states claim jurisdiction over their citizens in other countries, and since the mid-1980s U.S. courts have held that American citizens can be held responsible for acts outside this nation's borders.

And where is Tom Devins now? An attorney connected with the case said he heard that he was in Indonesia, working for a mining company.

Let Bill Burnett, now a semiretired private investigator, have the last word: "The Devins case kept me awake for a couple of years—and it made me aware that there are a lot of very smart crooks out there."

# Numbers Up
## (1980)

**G**AMBLING PREDATES HISTORY—AND CHEATING IS PROBABLY *only minutes younger. The essence of all gaming chicanery is to rig the contest so that only those who know about it can win. But if marking cards, weighting dice, fixing a fight, or doping a horse is not uncommon, the risk is usually far greater than any potential reward. The following case, however, illustrates how one fixer took advantage of modern communications technology to increase the possible payoff while minimizing the personal risk. Now, keep your eyes on the floating balls. . . .*

"Pete, what I'm going to tell you, I don't want you to tell no one. Not even your wife—I didn't even tell my wife."

His voice hushed, Nick Perry, also known as Nicholas Katsafanas, glanced around George Aiken's Delicatessen in Monroeville, a Pittsburgh suburb. The Maragos brothers, Peter and Jack, stopped chewing and leaned forward. Nick could be a big kidder. Sometimes it was hard to know when he was setting you up for a laugh or when he was on the square.

"What would you say if I told you the Daily Number could be fixed?" asked Perry. "Is that something you would be interested in?"

Pete Maragos was fifty-one; brother Jack was fifty-seven. They had known Nick Perry for over twenty years. Nick was choir director at St. Nicholas Cathedral, a Greek Orthodox church in Pittsburgh, and Pete sang in the choir. The three had been business partners since 1967, when Perry joined the brothers in Forbes Vending, a small but very profitable outfit that serviced food, beverage, and cigarette machines in prime Pittsburgh territory. The Maragoses spent most of their time at the business; Nick, who had several other interests, worked on the PR side. He was the front man, the one who made sure that their public image was good. And that was easy. A velvet-voiced, ruggedly handsome, wavy-haired man of sixty-four, Nick Perry was one of the best-known and best-liked men in western Pennsylvania.

Perry had been an announcer with Pittsburgh's WTAE-TV since 1958, when the station went on the air. For more than twenty years he'd hosted *Bowling for Dollars* and *Championship Bowling*, a local boy who had made good with two shows that drew a large audience from the region's predominantly blue-collar viewers. And in 1977, when the Pennsylvania Lottery added the Daily Number, a three-number-draw game in which a senior citizen selected the winning digits, Perry became host of the nightly drawing, a show seen in every corner of the state.

Now he was telling his partners the drawing could be fixed—and asking if they wanted in on it.

"Oh yeah," said Pete Maragos. "If you could really fix the lottery, I'd be interested."

Lotteries have been around for centuries. England used one to raise money for a kingdom-wide water supply system in 1680. In 1832 Philadelphia, tickets were hawked from some two hundred shops, paying out over $53 million—about $600 million in today's money. By 1890, U.S. lottery proceeds had erected hundreds of public buildings and supported myriad educational, charitable, and religious activities.

But many lotteries, public and private, were rigged. In 1818, for example, the manager of New York's Medical Science Lottery usually ignored numbers pulled from a wheel by a small boy, announcing instead a number of his own choosing—until he got caught. Counterfeit tickets were not uncommon, and the proceeds of many drawings vanished with their promoters.

Lotteries also funded a vast, illicit empire of graft, exploitation, and misery. By the late nineteenth century, most private lotteries, called "numbers" or "policy" games, were in the hands of organized crime. In 1894, New York City alone supported over six hundred policy shops, where a thousand-to-one chance could be purchased for as little as a penny or as much as one cared to wager. In the 1920s, most policy shops came under the control of ruthless goons like Dutch Schultz.

Lotteries were banned by an 1890 federal law, but in 1963, desperate for new funds, New Hampshire became the first state in modern times to reinstitute one. After watching huge sums of money flow to New Hampshire, other states followed with their own lotteries, including New York, Massachusetts, New Jersey—and, in 1971, Pennsylvania.

Pennsylvania launched the first of what would become several different lottery games with a half-dollar, winner-take-all drawing. In April 1972, six weeks after the first tickets were sold, the lottery created its first millionaire. Then the revenue department came up with Lucky Seven, a multidigit weekly drawing that sparked even wider interest. By March 1, 1977, when the first Daily Number game was offered to the public, the lottery had experimented with several different types of games—and had made twenty-eight people millionaires.

For more than three years, Perry had studied the system used to select the Daily Number. Under the supervision of a lottery manager, three machines were set up in a studio about an hour before the live broadcast. In much the same way that modern bingo-game numbers are chosen, each machine incorporated an air blower and a glass reservoir with a selection tube leading to a chute. Ten ordinary Ping-Pong balls, numbered zero through nine, were placed in each machine by the lottery supervisor. When the machines were turned on, the balls were whipped around the glass reservoir by the air blower, colliding with each other and with the walls. Within a few seconds, a ball from each machine bounced into the selection tube and rolled down the chute.

Since the proceeds of the Daily Number game were earmarked for senior-citizen programs, including housing and medical care, each evening a different senior citizen took the winning Ping-Pong balls out of the chute and announced the numbers. Perry finished the sixty-second show with a cheery salute: "If you got it, come and get it. If not . . . better luck tomorrow."

That minute of airtime brought Perry a hundred dollars a night, six hundred a week. But that was peanuts: most days, the lottery paid out over a half-million dollars. From his study of the system, Perry concluded that it could be fixed. And on a February morning at Aiken's Delicatessen, speaking in hushed tones, he explained the details to the Maragos brothers.

Although it was against lottery regulations for anyone even to touch the Daily Number selection machines unless a lottery supervisor was present, Perry was so highly regarded and had worked on the show so long that the Pennsylvania Lottery Bureau's western district manager, Edward Plevel, often allowed him to set up the machines. Despite this, Perry decided, Plevel had to be in on the fix if it was going to work.

Before talking to the Maragos brothers, Perry had spoken to Plevel. For $2,500, the lottery supervisor agreed to look the other way. As for rigging the game, Perry had it all worked out. All he had to arrange, Perry explained to the Maragos brothers, was a way to substitute heavier Ping-Pong balls for most of the real ones. The heavy balls would fail to rise atop the column of moving air and into the chute. Thus, only lighter balls—and their numbers—would be the winners.

All Perry had to do was create a set of bogus balls, identical in every respect but one to the state-sanctioned spheres, and substitute them just before airtime. After the drawing, the real balls would be replaced and the bogus ones destroyed. If everyone involved kept his mouth shut, it would be a perfect crime. And if they weren't too greedy, they could do it every six months or so. No one would ever know.

The only thing Perry couldn't do, he explained to his stunned partners, was buy lottery tickets. His face was far too well known. So the Maragos brothers, if they wanted in, would buy the tickets, cash in the winners, and share their take with Perry.

The Maragoses wanted in.

To carry off the scam, Perry needed two more accomplices, one to create the bogus Ping-Pong balls, the other to make the switch. For the latter job he chose Frederick Luman, a longtime WTAE stagehand. For the more difficult job of making acceptable substitutes for the state's Ping-Pong balls, Perry recruited Joseph Bock. Bock, a part-time stagehand, was a skilled artist, the television station's former art director. Each would profit from his role in the scheme by making several lottery bets on numbers they knew would win.

Bock bought ordinary Ping-Pong balls, the same brand used by the state, and number decals identical to those on the real balls. He used a hypodermic syringe and a can of white latex paint, both provided by Perry, to weight the balls. Injected through a tiny hole later hidden under the number decal, the paint diffused evenly, virtually invisible on the inner surface of the hollow ball.

Several weeks after agreeing to go forward with the fix, Perry and Peter Maragos met at St. Nicholas for choir practice. His voice obscured by a hymn sung to the accompaniment of the church's massive organ, Perry told Pete that Bock was having trouble weighing the balls. "No problem," said Pete. "My brother has a scale so sensitive it can weigh a single postage stamp." The scale, ordinarily used to apportion instant coffee for vending machines, was quietly borrowed. Bock then experimented to see how much paint was required to make a ball too heavy to be selected. By trial and error, he determined that 4.5 grams of paint was the exact amount needed. Finally, for extra luck in winning their own special lottery, the conspirators chose April 24, 1980, the fourth day of the fourth week of the fourth month as the date of the fix.

To confirm that the system would work, Perry wanted a trial run with one of the actual air-blowing machines. On Saturday, March 20, a day he usually didn't work at WTAE, Perry had stagehand Luman arrange to remove one of the machines from the station for "repairs." Perry and Bock tested all three sets of balls. It worked perfectly; no weighted ball could rise high enough in the glass reservoir to reach the selection tube.

To minimize the possibility that TV viewers might discover something amiss during the several seconds the bouncing balls were on screen, Perry decided to weight only eight balls in each set. The "4" and "6" balls in each set would be unweighted. That meant eight possible winning combinations: 6-6-6, 6-6-4, 6-4-4, 6-4-6, 4-4-4, 4-6-4, 4-4-6, and 4-6-6.

There were several ways to win at Daily Number. One, obviously, was to pick the numbers that came up on the television show in the order in which they appeared, say, 6-4-6. That paid five hundred to one. But one might also win by betting a "box," the same three numbers in any sequence, as, in the above example, 4-6-6 or 6-6-4. A box paid eighty to one. And if one played a box and two of the numbers picked were the same as the winning three, as in 6-4-X or X-4-6, the payoff was fifty to one.

So, since Nick Perry and his fellow conspirators knew that the winning numbers would be some combination of fours and sixes, they would not have to bet very heavily to clean up. A mere thousand dollars, carefully bet on all eight possible winning combinations and scattered around several lottery outlets in three or four cities, would bring a handsome return. And even $5,000, carefully bet by four people—Bock, Luman, and the Maragos brothers—would attract no undue attention. Since the conspirators planned to milk their scam again and again, they all agreed on this low-key approach.

There was another reason for the fixers to keep their betting profile low: they didn't want to attract the attention of the Pennsylvania mobsters who had horned in on the lottery almost as soon as it had become law in the state. When legal gambling returned to Pennsylvania, it didn't spell the end of illicit numbers games. On the contrary, organized crime welcomed the lottery. The number was chosen at random on live television and couldn't, in principle, be fixed. The media gave daily publicity to the lottery, as they did in more than a dozen other states with daily numbers. Shrewd bookmakers simply grafted their own game onto the legal lottery. The illegal operators hid behind mom-and-pop groceries, pool halls, newsstands, saloons, social clubs, gas stations, and a variety of other legitimate fronts. They attracted business because they paid immediately in sweet, untaxed cash, and offered slightly higher odds than did the state. The numbers bosses could afford bigger payouts because they had much less overhead than the Pennsylvania Lottery, which advertised heavily and paid a fixed portion of income to senior citizens' programs. The policy bosses also could buy "insurance": if any particular number was heavily bet, the racketeers "laid off" that number simply by buying legal lottery tickets. If the number came in, they would recover most of their losses.

Despite their agreement to limit the number of tickets they bet, the conspirators fell victim to their own greed. Instead of buying a few tickets in one neighborhood and a few in another, instead of dressing down and driving nondescript cars, the fixers displayed colossal stupidity.

On March 23, 1980, Pete Maragos went to Philadelphia, almost three hundred miles away at the opposite corner of the state. By nine the next morning, he, brother James, and James's wife, Jean Ella, were betting their way up Snyder Avenue in south Philadelphia. As they traveled in James's white Cadillac, their first stop on the clear and mild morning of March 24 was the Dew Drop Inn, a seedy saloon where Peter, dressed nicely in a good suit, bought 904 lottery tickets in various combinations of four and six. As the saloon's ticket printer, linked by phone lines to a computer at lottery headquarters in Harrisburg, noisily spit out the tickets, Pete dialed a Pittsburgh number.

When Perry answered on the other end, Pete spoke in Greek. He said, "Niko, do you hear the machine?"

"I hear," replied Perry, also in Greek. "Go big. Go big."

Those words would come back to haunt Perry and everyone in the conspiracy to bamboozle the Pennsylvania Lottery. By telling Maragos to "go big," Perry removed the scam's biggest safeguard, its invisibility.

A man in a white Caddy, speaking Greek, buying over nine hundred dollars in lottery tickets on two-number combinations at nine in the morning in a squalid south Philly bar was an event. Win or lose, the proprietor and his hardcore, early-morning tipplers at the Dew Drop Inn would remember the Maragos brothers for a long time. And when Pete went down the street to Herman's Cigar Store and bought $1,143 in tickets, he gave the proprietor the thrill of a lifetime. The well-dressed, middle-aged trio worked their way through south Philly's cigar stores, newsstands, barbershops, and meat markets, buying over ten thousand tickets on combinations of four and six. To the city's rackets bosses, that was like taking a full-page newspaper ad to brag about the fix.

Just in case there was anybody who didn't get the word, Jack Maragos gave a close friend "ten large" as a commission for spreading $4,000 around lottery outlets in and around Pittsburgh on combinations of four and six. And to keep peace in the family, Jack and Pete let brother James clue in his three children, residents of nearby Maryland. Each of them drove to different lottery sales points in Berks, Lancaster, and York counties in southeastern Pennsylvania and bought thousands of tickets. Even Pete's brother-in-law invested $4,400 on combinations of four and six, including a $1,600 bet with local bookmakers. Pete Maragos himself put down a few grand with some guys he knew in Pittsburgh who took bets on the Daily Number but weren't connected to the state of Pennsylvania, except insofar as they were obliged periodically to check in with their parole officers.

Long before noon, word was out in the City of Brotherly Love and neighboring burgs: the fix was in on the Daily Number, and the winning digits would be some combination of four and six. Hundreds flocked to lottery retailers to put down a dollar or two. And hundreds more went to see their local bookie and put a few bucks down with the fellows who paid cash and didn't forward names to the IRS.

Long before the game closed at seven P.M., Pennsylvania's racketeers were dispatching men to legal lottery sales points to buy "insurance."

Later that evening, Violet Lowery, sixty-eight, drew 6-6-6 from the forced-air machines on WTAE. Host Nick Perry closed with "If you got it, come and get it. . . ." The state of Pennsylvania was obliged to pay out some $3.5 million against only $1 million from that day's receipts.

When 6-6-6 came in, the reputed boss of Pennsylvania's numbers racket, Anthony M. "Tony" Grosso, said, "It was the Brinks job without a gun." Off the record, word went around that bets on 6-6-6 in Pennsylvania's back rooms would earn no payoffs. Which, of course, did not stop bookmakers from having their "layoff" men redeem an estimated $1 million in winning tickets at legal lottery outlets.

A few days after the drawing, Pete met Perry in a church cemetery and gave him a brown paper bag containing $35,000, the first installment on more than $1.2 million in winning tickets.

About the same time, the rumors of a lottery fix finally made the newspapers. Lottery District Manager Ed Plevel—not only Perry's co-conspirator but also a city councilman and street commissioner in tiny Monessen—met with his supervisors. He assured them that everything was completely kosher about the drawing of April 24, that the forced-air machine and the balls had never left his sight. He signed a statement declaring that there was no possibility the lottery could have been tampered with. Relying on that, Pennsylvania Revenue Secretary Howard Cohen issued a statement to the press, assuring anxious bettors there was no evidence of any improprieties with the Daily Number. "It was a totally honest pull," he said, adding, "we have looked into the matter as far as we are going to look."

And there the matter might have ended. But the rumors of a fix persisted. Reputed mob boss Tony Grosso, who had served time in Pennsylvania for running a $30 million gambling empire, flatly refused to pay out on the 6-6-6 winner, insisting that the number had been fixed. So widely known was the mob's connection to the legal lottery that Revenue Secretary Cohen told news reporters that Grosso was spreading rumors of a fix so that he could welsh on his payoffs.

In June, Pennsylvania Governor Dick Thornburgh—who, as state Attorney General, had prosecuted Grosso—ordered the Department of Justice to launch an investigation, and to bring their findings to the grand jury. With that public announcement, the revenue and justice departments and every other state agency connected to either the lottery or the investigation went mute. A few weeks later, the state senate created a special committee to investigate the possible fix. The Pennsylvania Senate was controlled by Democrats; the governor and most heads of state executive departments were Republicans. Suddenly the lottery was a political football.

One of the first things Assistant Attorney General Henry G. Barr did was to test the forced-air machines at WTAE. Ironically, the first three numbers drawn were 6-6-6. But that combination did not repeat during several dozen subsequent tests.

The first crack in the case appeared when Violet Lowery, the senior citizen who had drawn the winning numbers, contradicted Lottery Supervisor Ed Plevel's statement that he had never let the number-selection machine out of his sight. Lowery said that about half an hour before the drawing, Plevel escorted her and Theresa DeSanders, her designated alternate, into another studio to watch a news broadcast, leaving the lottery equipment unattended.

Not long afterward, investigators secretly brought in the vice-president of Metro Game Manufacturing, the New York maker of the bingo machine. He conducted an examination of the equipment and concluded that it was perfectly normal. But he also reported that ball selection *could* have been fixed if someone had weighted the Ping-Pong balls "with about five grams of water." To test that hypothesis, he was shown videotapes, obtained from the station, of Daily Number drawings on April 23, 24, and 25. In slow motion the tapes showed that on the twenty-fourth only numbers four and six ever rose high enough in the machine's reservoir to be selected. Barr knew that someone had tampered with the Ping-Pong balls—but he had only indirect evidence, videotapes. There was no hard evidence to incriminate Perry, the Maragos brothers, Plevel, and the rest. All they had to do was keep quiet.

The Mob, of course, doesn't use rules of evidence. It doesn't care about due process of law. Those who cross the Mob soon realize there are worse things than prison. Perhaps that was the reason that, within days of the investigation's launch, the Maragos brothers retained the services of attorney William C. Costopoulos. Dark-bearded and flashily dressed, Costopoulos lived in a huge estate on a mountainside near the state capital in Harrisburg. He was something of a mystery to the media covering the Pennsylvania underworld. His client list included several alleged heavyweight organized-crime figures, not only in Pennsylvania but also in New York and South Carolina, as well as members of the Pagans, a motorcycle gang reputedly hired as gangland enforcers. In 1976, Costopoulos himself was arrested, tried, and acquitted of fixing a murder case for a client found not guilty by a jury despite much damning evidence.

Costopoulos's sudden appearance as the Maragos brothers' representative raised media questions about their connections to organized crime. *Philadelphia* magazine suggested that the Maragos's exclusive vending-machine territory was virtually identical to the one once operated by an acknowledged underboss and consigliere to Pittsburgh's ruling "family." The Maragoses were forever silent on this subject.

For several weeks Costopoulos secretly shuttled back and forth between Pittsburgh and Harrisburg. In September 1980, the grand jury handed down indictments against Nick Perry, Ed Plevel, Frederick Luman, and Joseph Bock. The Maragos brothers had told investigators all they knew about Nick Perry and the lottery fix.

In exchange for their testimony and cooperation against Perry and Plevel, the Maragos family agreed to pay modest fines and serve five years probation. They returned some $600,000 collected from lottery tickets and about the same amount in uncashed tickets. The three children of brother James were not charged, even though they collected an estimated $125,000 in lottery winnings.

Confronted with the Maragoses' testimony, Bock and Luman pleaded guilty and accepted sentences of one to five years in state prison.

Plevel and Perry were tried on charges of criminal conspiracy, criminal mischief, theft by deception, and rigging a publicly exhibited contest. Perry was also charged with five counts of perjury; Plevel was charged with a single count of perjury and of "unsworn falsification." After a jury trial, Plevel was found guilty of all but "unsworn falsification." Perry, who did not testify, was found guilty on all counts.

Nick Perry was sentenced to three to seven years, fined $3,000, and ordered to repay the $35,000 he was given by Pete Maragos. Plevel, who lost his reelection bid to his hometown city council and was fired by the lottery, was sentenced to two to seven years in state prison, fined $1,000, and ordered to pay the state the $2,500 hush money he received. Perry and Plevel were also required to pay the cost of their trial.

Even before the trial of Perry and Plevel, rumors spread in Harrisburg, and were duly reported in the media, that the April 1980 fixing was not the first of its kind. Indeed, soon after Perry and Plevel's indictment, Tony Grosso told a grand jury that he was sure the Daily Number had been fixed on two previous occasions. At least two organized-crime figures testified before the grand jury under grants of immunity, detailing how "smart money" had been bet on the April 24 Daily Number, as it had on two previous occasions. A second, statewide rumor circulated that the attorney general had gone along with the Maragos family's plea bargain—which amounted to little more than a slap on the wrist—because William C. Costopoulos had intimated that if his clients were forced to do jail time, *someone* would fix the lottery again.

In the end, those that gained the most from rigging the lottery were the Maragos family and bookies. The Mob took in huge "smart money" bets but paid out next to nothing, while reaping almost $1 million from the state on "layoff" bets. The bookies and the Maragos family did all the talking and received immunity or token punishment. Virtually everything state authorities know, or think they know, came out of the mouths of those who had profited from the scam.

Is it more than a coincidence that these two groups were linked by reputed ties to organized crime and to the enigmatic William Costopoulos? Or that those who took the biggest risks, Luman and Bock, got almost nothing for their efforts and wound up doing hard time?

The rigging of the Pennsylvania Lottery was not a perfect crime for Nick Perry. But, perhaps, Perry's fall was merely an unpleasant but necessary detail for those who orchestrated the events of April 24, 1980, and who laid an evidence trail that led only to Perry. Of all those involved, only Perry maintained his innocence—which he has continued to do through three years in prison and all the years since his release on parole. He still refuses to discuss the incident publicly, except to say that because his attorney refused to let him testify or make a statement, his story has yet to be told. Perry also points out that except for the Maragoses, no one close to him won money from the April 24, 1980, drawing. "Why wouldn't I give [the fix number] to my family, who could have used the money?" he asks. Perry returned to broadcasting in 1988, host of a Pittsburgh-area cable show *KBL Jackpot Bowling*.

Many in Pittsburgh continue to believe that Perry was merely a tool for shadowy figures connecting organized crime with powerful politicians. If that is so, then perhaps a clue to the scope of their influence was unearthed in 1991, when Henry G. Barr came to trial. Barr was a top aide to Dick Thornburgh, former Pennsylvania governor, and U.S. Attorney General in the Bush administration. It was Barr, appointed by Thornburgh, who headed the investigation of the Daily Number fix. In June 1991, Barr was convicted in federal court of using cocaine and lying about his drug use on an employment application. In asking for a harsh sentence, federal prosecutors argued that Barr had sought to become a United States Attorney as a way to gain access to top-secret Justice Department documents, including dossiers on leading organized-crime figures in Pennsylvania.

# Airtight Alibi
# (1967)

**A**LIBI IS LATIN FOR "ELSEWHERE." ALIBI HAS LONG BEEN *a staple of detective fiction, where elaborate ruses are often constructed to confuse police—and readers— about a suspect's whereabouts when a crime is committed. In Dumas's* The Three Musketeers, *for example, d'Artagnan—in an era when portable timepieces were rare—sets a clock back thirty minutes, makes sure his commander notes the time, and relies upon that fiction to prove he couldn't have been present at a certain fight.*

*In real life, only in this century have alibis become important to those planning serious crimes. A notorious British serial killer, John Lloyd (c. 1914), who made a living killing his brides and collecting their estates, drowned Margaret Lofty in a bathtub. His alibi—that he was out buying tomatoes when she died—proved worthless when relatives of prior victims learned from newspaper accounts that yet another new wife had drowned in her tub while Lloyd was out buying tomatoes. A poor alibi, Lloyd found, was worse than none.*

*But a solid alibi is an almost irrefutable argument to protect an accused. An airtight alibi can often overcome, in a jury's collective mind, much circumstantial evidence.*

*Physical evidence, however, is a different matter. . . .*

The dining room table was set for two. A bowl of wilted salad lay in the center. A pair of glasses, three quarters full of now tepid red wine, stood to either side. On the patio, the hibachi's charcoal had long since become dull white ash, and what had once been a portion of a steak was now a charred lump. A jar of barbecue sauce lay nearby, drowned flies in its open neck.

In the bedroom, redheaded Elaine Terry Kirschke lay sprawled on a huge, ornate, circular bed, her lush body nude beneath an open black kimono with a delicate white flower design. A bullet hole marked the spot where the center of her right ear had been.

On the floor next to the bed lay the large, muscular body of Orville "Bill" Drankhan, clad in slacks, open-necked sport shirt, and shoes. The front of his trousers was unbuttoned and open. A bullet had nicked his left ear before entering his brain through the side of his head. He lay facedown in a coagulated pool of his own vomit.

Sheets, blankets, and mattress were drenched in blood. Waves of gore had splattered against the quilted headboard and the walls.

At about nine on Sunday morning, April 8, 1967, upstairs neighbor Frank Cornell, a commercial artist, thinking it was odd that on the previous evening there had been no activity in the ground-level apartment, sent his son-in-law, James A. Miller, down to check. Miller, a reserve deputy in the Los Angeles County Sheriff's Department, pounded on the door for several minutes. No one answered. Peering through a dusty window, Miller saw the blood, black in the dim window light of an overcast morning. Then he saw the pale and stiff bodies, and ran back upstairs to call the Long Beach Police Department.

The apartment building at 185 Rivo Alto Canal was in Naples, a wealthy bay-island community in Long Beach, California. A labyrinth of curving canals, dead-end streets, and almost-hidden walkways makes Naples difficult to navigate. But the officers who responded to Cornell's call had no difficulty finding the address. Like most Long Beach police, they knew very well who lived there: Jack Kirschke, deputy district attorney, the hard-driving lawyer in charge of the DA's Downey office—and one of the county's most effective criminal prosecutors.

A very youthful forty-five, Jack was slim, handsome, and intelligent, a social lion among the bayside set, and a popular member of the Long Beach Yacht Club, where he docked his thirty-three-foot sloop.

Practically everyone in Southern California knew of Kirschke's wife, Elaine Terry. In the Fifties and Sixties, she was one of a handful of fashion designers who collectively reinvented the pricey California look. Even after selling her Los Angeles boutique to a conglomerate, Elaine Terry labels continued to define upscale chic for tens of thousands of women. Elaine was forty-three, a slim, sexy, redhead with hazel eyes and alleycat ways.

The Kirschkes had a son in the Marine Corps and a married daughter to show for twenty-four years of marriage— but they no longer had what anyone would call a real marriage. Four years earlier they had sold their home and moved into the expensive apartment along a Naples canal. They lived together, but they had made a secret pact: they would eschew sex with each other for a year, and after that, each could quietly pursue other relationships. Meanwhile, each would respect the other's privacy.

Jack, a strong supporter of Governor Reagan, was in line for a judgeship, probably in the Superior Court. So while he had his share of brief romances and one-night stands, he remained ever mindful of scandal. Jack was fast from the lip with a come-on, but when it came to carrying through on a conquest, he was usually very discreet.

As time went on, however, Elaine seemed ready to abandon all pretense of a marriage. She developed a preference for wild men, sometimes young studs far beneath her income and social standing. Within the yacht-club circles she and Jack usually frequented, Elaine flaunted her affairs, bragging of them at parties. Once she threw a drink in Jack's face, trying to provoke him. But it was a public place, so Jack stayed cool. Jack was famous for his cool.

Now Elaine was dead, and with her Bill Drankhan, forty-one, bon vivant, well-known local aviator, businessman, and Casanova.

But where was Jack? Police issued an all-points bulletin. Near midday on Monday, April 10, Jack Kirschke, driving a notably dilapidated red Volkswagen Beetle owned by his married daughter, was speeding south and west through the magnificent desolation of California's Mojave Desert on Interstate 15. A San Bernardino County sheriff's deputy pulled him over near Victorville, a hundred miles from Long Beach.

In similar circumstances on previous occasions, Kirschke had flashed his DA's credential and tried to talk his way out of a ticket. This time he was strangely quiet.

The deputy sheriff wasn't interested in how fast Kirschke had been driving. Instead, after making Kirschke identify himself, the deputy said, "You're under arrest."

"What's the charge?" said Kirschke.

"One-eight-seven," said the deputy, citing the California Penal Code section dealing with homicide.

"No more words," replied Kirschke.

"Follow me to Victorville," instructed the deputy.

At the Victorville Sheriff's Station an old friend was waiting—Los Angeles County Chief Deputy DA Buck Compton, the DA's alter ego and chief troubleshooter.

"Elaine and Bill are dead," said Compton, with little preamble.

Kirschke showed no surprise. "I guess a burglar must have broken in and shot them."

Buck Compton's mouth almost dropped open. He had said nothing about a gun, or about where the deaths had taken place. Nevertheless, he knew Kirschke pretty well and was willing to give him the benefit of the doubt.

"Hell, I knew he didn't do it," recalled Compton, many years later. "I told him, 'Take a lie-detector test, and let's get this all cleaned up.' "

Kirschke refused to take the test.

He was charged with two counts of first-degree murder. A Long Beach PD detective apologetically put him in handcuffs and drove him back to Long Beach. Jack was all but silent the whole trip. The only thing he said was, "I guess there goes my judgeship."

If Kirschke had in fact killed his wife, speculated some in the district attorney's office who thought they knew what made him tick, it was because he had finally lost control of his legendary temper. Elaine's closest friends whispered that the couple fought often, that he frequently beat her—even that he had tortured her with lighted cigarettes.

Others advanced a different theory: Kirschke's motive was not jealousy but indignation—outrage over his wife's high-flying, low-life lover.

Elaine had taken flying lessons from Drankhan. Her friends knew she had been sleeping with him for months. They recalled February 22, when teacher and student took off from Long Beach airport in a small plane, Drankhan a little drunk. He flew over the Kirschkes' apartment at a few hundred feet, waggled the wings, jazzed the engine—and went back around for several encores.

A sheriff's helicopter went up after the miscreant flier and ordered him to land. Police arrested Drankhan minutes after he touched down. Curiously, Jack Kirschke, who until then had never met Drankhan, went himself to the jail to post bail. Then the odd trio went over to the yacht club and had a few drinks together. It was all terribly civilized.

Unfortunately, Drankhan's aerial exploit, along with his passenger's name, made all the local newspapers—it was the first time police had made a drunk-flying arrest. Jack Kirschke's friends ribbed him about it—"Hey Jack, where's Amelia Earhart?"—until it was apparent he didn't see the humor.

In Long Beach police custody, Kirschke denied that he had killed his wife. Homicide investigators were inclined to believe him: the coroner had placed the time of death as around two A.M., plus or minus a few hours. Jack Kirschke had an airtight alibi for that time frame.

Kirschke told police that early Friday evening he'd driven to Los Angeles International Airport in his daughter's Volkswagen—his own Karmann-Ghia was in the shop for repairs—arriving about 8:20. He was scheduled to speak at the Rotary convention in Las Vegas Saturday morning, but because of a very hectic schedule he had neglected to make reservations. Kirschke said he couldn't get on the 8:30 Bonanza Air flight because it was full. So he put his name on a standby list for the 9:30 flight. It, too, was full. Kirschke then tried the Western Airlines' 11:30

flight. But by eleven o'clock it was plain that there would be no room. So Kirschke decided to drive.

He climbed in the Volkswagen and headed east, stopping at a Denny's in San Bernardino for coffee just after midnight. He gassed up in Yermo between 3:30 and 4:00 in the morning, arriving in Las Vegas at dawn. After a few hours of gambling, he went to the Rotary convention.

Kirschke spoke to hundreds of Rotarians that Saturday morning. He was returning from Las Vegas when the deputy stopped him.

With no evidence to link Kirschke to the murders, the district attorney's office told Long Beach police to turn him loose. But bearing in mind Kirschke's position as an important deputy DA and wishing to avoid even the appearance of impropriety, Los Angeles DA Evelle Younger turned the case over to the California Attorney General's Office.

Murder in California, like most crimes of violence, is usually handled by county district attorneys. The attorney general's office normally prosecutes political corruption, large-scale fraud, civil rights infractions, and noncompliance with state regulatory laws. It's unusual, even rare, to find a deputy California AG with much experience with homicide.

Unlike many other big-city police, the Long Beach Police Department has rarely enjoyed good notices for its crime solving. Critics have often accused the department of sloppy investigations, political toadying, even outright corruption.

Miles Rubin, senior deputy AG in charge of the Southern California office, was not unfamiliar with the Long Beach PD's reputation. When the Kirschke case landed on his desk, he accompanied Keith Byram, the attorney general's chief investigator in Southern California, on a visit to Naples.

They were dismayed to find their worst fears confirmed. Long Beach investigators had made a terrible mess of the crime scene. They had used black-and-white film, not color, to record the scene, making it difficult to distinguish between bloodstains and dirt or even shadows. They took no photos that could help determine the trajectories of the fatal bullets and too many that leered at the female victim's genitals.

Worse, in photographing the crime scene, they had violated it, trampling everything, leaving footprints outside and fingerprints inside. They took no measurements and made no drawings, leaving the AG's investigators to painstakingly reconstruct the death scene as it had appeared when the first officers responded. Rubin and Byram also noted that someone, perhaps the killer, had removed a screen from the only window with a clear view of the deathbed.

The lead police investigator, long an admirer of Jack Kirschke's stiff, law-and-order attitudes and high conviction rate, had developed a theory about the murders. He was sure that one of the dozens of miscreants whom Kirschke had helped send to jail had come by for revenge and in the dark had mistaken Drankhan for Kirschke.

Strangely, when Kirschke held a press conference to announce his innocence, he advanced this same theory, adding that the killer was probably "dope-crazed."

Plainly, the Attorney General had been handed a hot potato. He had to move quickly, decisively, and fairly to establish Kirschke's guilt or innocence. There could be no hint of whitewash. That would be political suicide.

Accordingly, deputy AGs Robert Samoian and Albert Harris were given the task of preparing the state's case against Kirschke. Samoian was young, idealistic, and impressionable; he had, at that time, tried exactly three felony cases—and no murders. He told his boss that he doubted that Kirschke could have had any involvement in the murders.

Harris was the senior assistant AG in charge of trial-and-investigation sections all over the state. Not only was he the AG's most trusted trial lawyer, he was known as a man of such unbending rectitude that he would have cheerfully prosecuted his own mother, if she had broken the law. Nevertheless, Harris, like most AGs had little experience with felonies. He had tried only seven cases.

Police investigators had questioned Cornell, the neighbor who'd called police. Cornell said he'd heard what sounded like two shots coming from the Kirschke apartment around 2:30 A.M. Saturday morning. Another neighbor woke at about 4:00 A.M. to use the bathroom. He looked out the window and noticed a light on in Kirschke's bedroom. Suddenly it went out.

So maybe, thought Samoian and Harris, the murderer was still in the death room at four o'clock. How very odd, they thought. How very, very odd.

On a hunch, investigators checked every parked car in all the lots at Los Angeles International Airport. They found Kirschke's Karmann-Ghia roadster, covered with dust but in good running condition.

Suddenly Kirschke's alibi looked less airtight. What if he had driven to Las Vegas, flown back to Los Angeles—an hour's flight—then used his Karmann-Ghia to drive home and murder his wife and her lover, returning to the airport for a quick trip back to Las Vegas?

Through his own attorney, Kirschke told investigators that he had loaned his car to his mechanic, whom he'd known for years, because he needed to keep it several days while doing repairs and bodywork. The mechanic was located and confirmed that he had dropped the car at the airport lot on Sunday, when he'd been told to expect Kirschke's return from Las Vegas.

The murders took place early Saturday morning, so Kirschke couldn't have used the Karmann-Ghia. Once again his alibi was solid.

An AG's investigator named Barney Allen found a 1963 Volkswagen in about the same shape as the one Kirschke said he'd driven to Las Vegas. Allen drove the car from Naples to Las Vegas, timing the trip at four hours and thirty minutes. Plenty of time to kill Drankhan and his wife at 2:30 and make Las Vegas by early morning.

Kirschke's lawyer had hired a private investigator named Joe Carroll. Carroll, too, had found a Volkswagen similar to Kirschke's and drove it to Las Vegas, stopping at Yermo en route. The driving time to Yermo—155 miles from Naples—was two hours and forty minutes. Carroll had located two gas station attendants who said they clearly remembered Kirschke and his beat-up Volkswagen at the station between 3:30 and 4:00 A.M. If the killings took place at 2:30, when Cornell heard gunshots, then Kirschke was clearly not the killer. No one could have driven a beat-up Volkswagen 155 miles in ninety minutes—it would have required an *average* speed of 103 miles per hour in a car that wouldn't do much more than 80.

And then there was the bedroom light that went out at four in the morning. If Kirschke was in Yermo at 3:30 or 4:00, he couldn't have been in the Naples apartment.

Then investigators went through Kirschke's car again and found a sport shirt. Light tan in color, of knitted rayon, it was in the car when he was arrested in Victorville, but no one had considered it important. Under a button flap were tiny specks of what looked like blood.

The shirt was rushed to the Criminal Identification and Investigation (CII) Laboratory, where the spots were analyzed. They were human blood, Type O. Drankhan's blood was Type O. So was Elaine's.

Unfortunately, so was Jack Kirschke's. The blood, he said through his attorney, came from a finger he'd sliced open after dropping a bottle of aftershave in a Las Vegas hotel bathroom sink. And sure enough, there was a still-healing scar on Kirschke's index finger.

Once again, Kirschke's alibi was secure.

Gene Frice, a fair-haired, wiry man in his midforties, was a doctoral candidate, an Army-Reserve Green Beret major, and a senior CII investigator, one of the best detectives CII assigned to the Kirschke case. A few days after Kirschke was released for lack of evidence, Frice drove to Naples to look over the crime scene. Along the way he collected Detective Garold McIntyre of the Long Beach PD, one of the first officers to reach the scene of the crime.

McIntyre reached in his pocket and handed Frice a piece of paper he said he'd taken from a drawer in Elaine's bedroom on the morning the bodies were discovered.

It was a note, in Elaine's handwriting, confirming her and Jack's agreement about their unusual living arrangements. Among other provisions, the note said that until May 1, 1967, neither "would seek the companionship of the opposite sex in any manner." Elaine had been murdered on April 8—in bed with her lover.

Frice rushed back to downtown Los Angeles to show the note to Harris. But Detective McIntyre had not bothered to get a warrant to search the apartment and had carried the note around in his pocket for days. The "chain of custody" necessary to preserve the integrity of evidence was violated. Ultimately, a judge would rule that the note could not be used as evidence.

Nevertheless, Harris believed it proved that Kirschke, who had since his arrest maintained that he'd had a normal and loving relationship with his wife, had lied. And it revealed at least one motive for the murders: jealousy.

Frice went back for another look at the crime scene. He spent almost an hour looking and thinking. Just before he left, he glanced up at the bedroom ceiling light. He flipped the wall switch to turn it on.

Nothing happened.

Frice got a chair and stood on it. He removed the glass globe and unscrewed the lightbulb. He held it to his ear and shook it. The tinny sound of broken filament proved that the bulb had burned out. So when the neighbor woke at four A.M. to use the toilet and saw the Kirschkes' bedroom light suddenly go out, he had seen the bulb *burn* out. There wasn't necessarily anyone alive in the apartment.

Frice reasoned that if Kirschke was the killer, he had from 2:30 until about 9:00, when he checked into his hotel, to drive to Las Vegas. Plenty of time. Except, of course, there were two gas-station attendants who swore Kirschke was in Yermo between 3:30 and 4:00.

Perhaps they were mistaken about the time or the date. But that was a problem for Harris and Samoian.

More pressing, from Frice's point of view, was an explanation for an apparent anomaly: why was Elaine's body found on the bed, while Drankhan's was facedown on the floor?

The medical examiner had found semen matching Drankhan's in Elaine's body, traces of semen on Drankhan's clothes, and evidence that he had ejaculated soon before his death. The medical conclusion was that the victims had had intercourse just before they were shot to death.

So why was Drankhan on the floor?

The answer lay in the medical report. At death, the heart stops, and blood, no longer under pressure from the heart's pumping, comes under the influence of gravity and settles into the lowest parts of the body. This phenomenon is called *lividity*.

The medical report showed that although Drankhan was facedown on the floor, his blood had congealed in his back. Since, after death, blood cannot flow against gravity, the inescapable conclusion was that when Drankhan was shot, he was faceup.

Frice theorized that Drankhan must have been shot while lying near the edge of the circular bed. As blood began to collect in the lower half of his body, it made that part heavier. If his body was at the very edge of the bed, this shift in his center of gravity would have been enough to cause the body to roll off the bed and land, facedown, in the pool of vomit that had previously oozed from his mouth to the floor.

Frice went home and tested this theory by lying on his own bed, rolling off, over and over, usually winding up facedown on the floor. He was bruised from his effort and his wife openly questioned his sanity—but Frice didn't care. He had accounted for the position of the bodies at the moment of death.

Frice and the AG's prosecution team now turned their attention to the murder weapon.

The inside of modern gun barrels are "rifled" with "lands" and "grooves." The slightly raised portion of the barrel is a land; the spaces between lands are grooves. Lands and grooves twist around the inside of the barrel. Forced between lands and grooves at tremendous velocity, the bullet spins, thereby stabilizing its flight for added accuracy.

Most .38-caliber handguns have five lands and four grooves, but tests of the bullets retrieved from the victims' bodies told an interesting tale: each had been fired through a barrel with *six* lands and *five* grooves. By measuring the spacing between the grooves, ballistics experts concluded that the gun that killed Elaine Kirschke and Drankhan was a rare revolver, the Harrington & Richards Defender.

A few thousand H&R Defenders were manufactured under a single U.S. government contract and the gun was carried by postal inspectors until the late 1950s.

Keith Byram, the CII agent-in-charge, put his staff to work combing statewide police files for H&R Defenders that had been used in crimes. After several days, Agent Barney Allen discovered that a gun of this type had been used in a robbery and kidnapping in October 1961. The perpetrator, James Vernon Mitchell, had held up a Long Beach market—and the DA who put him behind bars was Jack Kirschke.

Following up, Allen pulled the DA's files on the Mitchell case. Buried amid reams of paper was a receipt: one H&R Defender, serial number 22068, had been removed from evidence, as per court order, after Mitchell's conviction. The gun had been given to Jack Kirschke as a souvenir—not an unusual disposition. So Kirschke owned a gun *like* the one used to kill his wife and her lover.

Questioned, Kirschke told police investigators that he kept the gun in a bedroom nightstand drawer—but that he hadn't seen it in months.

Merely owning a gun *similar* to the murder weapon was not much in the way of evidence. Before it could be used to implicate Kirschke, investigators needed to prove that the gun that killed Elaine and Drankhan was the *same* gun that Kirschke owned. This could only be established by finding the gun and test-firing it, then comparing the two sets of bullets under a microscope. They had to find the H&R Defender.

Whoever the killer, reasoned Byram, he or she wouldn't want to be caught with a murder weapon and would have gotten rid of it at the earliest opportunity.

Probably.

Under Byram's supervision, dozens of police and AG investigators searched virtually all the public areas of Naples, looking under bridges, in ivy beds alongside roads, even dragging the shallow canals.

Meanwhile, Frice took on the daunting job of tracing H&R Defender number 22068 from its sale by the postal inspector's office until it entered Kirschke's personal possession. Frice wasn't sure what he was looking for—but he was sure he would know it when he saw it.

Frice traced the gun from the postal inspector's office to a wholesaler who had bought all the obsolete revolvers. He had resold the guns in small lots to dealers all over the country. Number 22068 had gone to a Long Beach sporting-goods store owned by David Weinstein. Weinstein had sold it, but the customer returned weeks later and exchanged it for another pistol.

Then Weinstein's store was robbed and the robber made off with number 22068. Sometime later, the gun was recovered and returned to Weinstein. In February 1961, Weinstein sold it to Jack F. Norton. But neither Frice nor Weinstein had any idea how it had gotten from Norton to the kidnapper, James Vernon Mitchell. None of this left Frice any closer to finding the gun.

Frice put aside his quest temporarily to devote his attention to reconstructing the crime scene. It was important to know where the shooter was located when the shots were fired.

Some Long Beach police thought that the shots had come through the open window from which the screen had been removed. But Frice, studying the bloodstain patterns on the wall and the headboard, didn't agree. It seemed to him that the shots had come from the other side of the room.

After interviewing all police officers who had visited the Kirschkes' apartment, Frice finally found a rookie motorcycle officer who admitted removing the screen, placing it on the ground, and forgetting to mention this fact to anyone.

Another theory on the shooter's location involved a bedroom closet. Inspector McIntyre believed the killer had lain in wait in the closet, and when the couple on the bed had finished making love, threw open the door and fired.

Frice returned to the scene of the crime yet again and carefully looked through the one-bedroom apartment. Based on his experience, he thought that the bloodstains showed that the shots came from an area a few feet from the closet—but not from the closet itself. A few feet from the closet, in about the right spot, was a door that led to the living room. But this door was not used; instead, the Kirschkes used the other door, near the window. It opened onto a long hall.

The unused door was blocked by a pile of personal belongings—empty boxes, out-of-season clothes, framed paintings, rolled-up carpets, old phonograph records, books, etc. Behind this pile of junk was the living room couch. Frice crawled behind the couch and found a space where he could sit, resting his feet on a carpet roll. Easing a few things aside, he could reach the doorknob. He pushed the door open.

The door opened smoothly, silently. Through a three-inch gap Frice had a perfect view of the spot where the bed had been. Clearly, this was where the shots had come from—not from the window or the closet.

So the killer had been someone who knew every detail of the Kirschke apartment. He or she also knew Naples's confusing streets, walkways, and canals well enough to leave the island without getting lost. Frice himself got lost almost every time he went to Naples.

More and more the evidence pointed to Kirschke as the killer. His motive: Elaine's affair with Drankhan might have permanently damaged his chances for a judgeship. It was certainly reason enough for him to decide to kill his wife and her lover, Frice believed.

By now, virtually everyone connected with the AG's investigation was sure Kirschke was their man. He was a brilliant prosecutor, well versed in criminal law and in courtroom proceedings. Maybe, they thought, he had killed his wife and her lover in revenge for their jeopardizing his judgeship, thinking he was clever enough to avoid the consequences.

Looking for more witnesses who could testify about Kirschke's relationship with Elaine, Harris sent the task force into the field, ringing doorbells up and down Rivo Alto Canal. The group also questioned everyone they could identify with any ties to the couple, personal or professional. It was detailed, demanding, draining work.

But from these interviews emerged a stark portrait of a couple with serious marital difficulties. Kirschke, by all available evidence, had been brutally jealous of his wife's infidelities—and yet had tirelessly pursued many women, including his own secretary, Sharon Lyle. Lyle told investigators that Kirschke had repeatedly tried to seduce her, but she wanted no part of him. She also said that her boss had bragged of beating Elaine until she told him her boyfriend's name: Bill.

The interviews also revealed the existence of what was known as the Jolly Girls, an informal club of middle-aged women who enjoyed the relaxed morality of yacht-club living. They confided the juiciest details of their extramarital affairs to each other and furnished their sisters-in-swinging with alibis and cover stories to explain their absences while dallying with one or another of the men whose company they enjoyed. Elaine had been a member in good standing of the Jolly Girls.

Two of her cohorts told investigators that, just a week before her death, Jack beat Elaine, bruising her and deeply frightening her. She had hidden in bushes near a Jolly Girl's home, unwilling to come inside because, as she put it, "Jack knows every closet in your house and will find me."

One of the Jolly Girls said Elaine had confided that, during the beating, she had taunted Jack. "Why don't you just get a gun and shoot me?" she said. Another said that she often saw bruises on Elaine's arms and legs, and that not long before the shooting, Jack had bruised her ribs.

Harris now thought that he had enough circumstantial evidence against Kirschke to go into court. If he failed to win a conviction, however, the double-jeopardy statute meant Kirschke could never be tried on the same charges.

So Harris made a strategic decision. He decided to bring the evidence and witnesses he had, incomplete and perhaps flawed as they were, before the grand jury. This latter is a panel of citizens who are, in general, more affluent, more educated, and older than a typical trial jury. Their brief was to hear evidence and decide if sufficient cause existed to try the accused. If these jurors were convinced of Kirschke's culpability, they would hand down an indictment. Kirschke would then stand trial.

If the grand jury thought the evidence too weak, they would not indict Kirschke. But *that* wouldn't prevent Harris from trying to dig up further evidence and, if successful, seeking an indictment.

In preparation for the grand jury presentation, Harris set out to learn more about Dennis Baily and Gene Ledet, the gas station attendants who said Kirschke was in Yermo at 3:30 on the morning of April 8, 1967.

Frice drove out to Yermo, population 950, and talked to the two young men. He discovered that Baily, a strapping, apple-cheeked, blue-eyed blond, had become a local celebrity, with people—especially young women—driving from hundreds of miles around to get a look at him. He had started a scrapbook, filled with clippings on the Kirschke case from local and Los Angeles newspapers. And he had denounced to his friends such reporters as the *Los Angeles Times*'s Dial Torgerson, who had reported on the AG's slowly strengthening case against Kirschke. Ironically, while Torgerson, an excellent reporter, was faithful and dispassionate in his stories, privately he believed Kirschke innocent.

Very interesting, thought Harris and Samoian when they heard Frice's account. Maybe there was more to Baily's story than there seemed. Or less.

Harris called thirty-six witnesses before the grand jury. Kirschke was invited but not subpoenaed; under the Fifth Amendment, he could not be compelled to testify against himself. He declined to appear.

Baily and Ledet, the gas station attendants, testified at length. What they said gave Harris good cause to think they were mistaken about seeing Kirschke between 3:30 and 4:00 on the morning of April 8.

Human memory is still something of a mystery. But psychological experiments suggest that memories can be altered, even planted. A person shown a photo of a man, for example, may not recognize him at all. Yet if the same person is shown the same photo days or weeks later, he often finds it familiar. He thinks he remembers the man in the photo—but what he actually remembers is having seen the picture before. Often, people convince themselves that they have seen the *person* before.

Prosecutors and investigators have long known about this phenomenon. They are used to showing witnesses to crimes photo lineups of four or five pictures. If these lineups are carefully presented in certain ways, witnesses can be manipulated into believing they have seen one or more individuals on a previous occasion.

People with "implanted" memories are rarely aware that their recollection is untrue and will vociferously defend themselves. These people are not lying. They simply don't remember what they saw—they remember what they *thought* they saw.

Baily, squirming in the hard wooden seat, testified that he had seen Kirschke in a red Volkswagen between 2:30 and 4:00 in the morning. He admitted, however, that a week afterward, when Kirschke himself turned up at the gas station, he had not recognized him. Ledet essentially confirmed Baily's story. He said that Kirschke's face "looked familiar" when he came by the station with Joe Carroll, Kirschke's private detective.

Harris also called Carroll, who testified that Kirschke had first hired him in January to check out Bill Drankhan. "Mr. Kirschke wanted to make sure their affair wouldn't bring bad publicity" that might endanger his judgeship, said Carroll.

Three of the Jolly Girls testified about the tumultuous nature of the Kirschkes' marriage.

Harris then put on the witness stand a young neighbor of the Kirschkes, who had walked her dog about eleven o'clock Friday night, when Kirschke claimed to be at the airport. She said that she looked right into Kirschke's apartment and saw Elaine in the kitchen. In the living room, the young woman observed the back and lower half of a big, muscular man who answered Drankhan's description. She also saw a part of a third person, a man's bare arm, slender and sinewy, the rest of his body obscured by a kitchen cabinet. But she heard no voices and could not say if the arm belonged to Jack, whom she knew and had seen many times.

CII investigators had also turned up a Los Angeles International Airport parking lot attendant who testified that his records showed that *every* car entering after 8:26 P.M., when Kirschke said he got to the airport, had left the lot before 9:56 that evening. Kirschke had always claimed that he was at the airport until eleven.

Upstairs neighbor Christine Cornell, sixteen, testified that she had heard loud, angry voices coming from the Kirschke's apartment between 10:30 and 11:00 that night.

A waitress from the yacht club in Naples testified that Elaine and Bill Drankhan arrived at the club after eleven that night, downed several drinks, and left, arm in arm, about one in the morning.

Not more than ninety minutes later, testified a deputy medical examiner, both were dead.

The evidence that the grand jury saw and heard was far from compelling. Harris needed only fourteen of the twenty-three jurors to bring in an indictment, but he was worried because he still couldn't prove that the murder gun had been Kirschke's.

Fifteen grand jurors voted to indict.

"We barely snuck it by them," recalls Samoian, now a Los Angeles County deputy DA. As it was, several of the grand jurors who voted *for* indictment doubted that Kirschke could be convicted on the evidence they had seen.

Charged with two counts of first-degree murder, Kirschke was held without bond in the county jail. He was suspended without pay from his job in the DA's office.

While the AG's investigation continued, Harris and Samoian were forced to do without Gene Frice for a time. His Army Reserve unit was called up in June, and he was parachuted into Alaska's tundra country to spend weeks playing war games.

But when Frice returned, he was eager to get back to what had become almost an obsession: finding the gun that killed Elaine and Bill. He strongly believed that the whole case turned on it. If he could match it to the bullets in the two victims, the case against Kirschke was far stronger—

conviction was almost certain. But Frice felt stymied. He had checked everything twice. He'd searched long and hard for the gun in Naples, to no avail.

The trial began on August 14 with the usual flurry of pretrial motions. Kirschke's lawyer, Albert Ramsey, was one of Southern California's most successful criminal law practitioners. He nevertheless lost motions to exclude key evidence and change the trial venue to Long Beach. He won on two lesser motions: the note McIntyre took from the Kirschke apartment was thrown out, as was the blood-flecked sport shirt found in the car.

But Kirschke's admission that he had owned a Harrington & Richards Defender, made to police officers while he was en route to Long Beach from Victorville, was ruled admissible, even though Ramsey made a strong case that Kirschke's arrest was illegal because there had not been legal "probable cause" to justify it.

The first major surprise of the trial was the testimony of Sharon Lyle, Kirschke's secretary. She had not testified before the grand jury because Harris had worried about tipping his hand about just how deeply his staff had investigated Kirschke's past.

Lyle, a pretty young divorcée, testified at length about Kirschke's long-running attempt to seduce her. Without doubt, such conduct in the 1990s would have brought sexual-harassment charges. But this was 1967, when women were still putting up with lecherous bosses. So the real bombshell was Lyle's testimony about how angry and jealous Kirschke was about Elaine's infidelities. In the months before the murders, he repeatedly ranted and raved about Bill Drankhan, turning purple with rage as he told Lyle how much he hated his wife's indiscretion.

A very effective witness, Lyle established a clear motive for murder. Kirschke's lawyer, Ramsey, could not shake her on cross-examination.

With the trial under way, time was running out on finding the gun. If he couldn't find the murder weapon, thought Frice, maybe he could find something else to link Kirschke to it, or something more about the gun itself. Working at home one evening, he went through his notes again. This time, something caught his attention. Sporting-goods store owner David Weinstein had reported that the gun in question was briefly out of his store twice between 1956 and 1959. The first time a customer returned it. The second time it was stolen at gunpoint. After police arrested the robber in 1960, it was returned. Frice realized there was a good question he hadn't asked Weinstein.

He got in his car and drove to Long Beach, a distance of twenty-five miles, arriving just as Weinstein was closing the store. "Mr. Weinstein," he asked, "when that punk stole your gun, did he use it in another crime?"

"Oh yes," said Weinstein. "The police said he used it to shoot some woman in the ass."

Frice was astounded. If the gun had been fired in the commission of a crime, then police might have done a ballistics test. And if so, those records might still exist.

While Harris and Samoian presented the state's largely circumstantial case, Frice spent nearly every waking moment looking for some record that H&R number 22068 had been through a ballistics test. First, he went through police records in every Southern California jurisdiction, looking for a crime report that would provide a case number. With a number, he could learn if the gun had ever gone to the county crime lab. But Frice could find no record of a crime involving that particular gun.

Harris, knowing how important it was to his case, had been stalling on the gun issue for days, putting on witness after witness and hoping for a miracle. Now he could stall no longer. The judge had directed him to conclude the state's case on the following day.

"Find that gun," Harris said to Frice. "Our whole case comes down to the gun and how much the jury will believe the gas station attendants." Bailey and Ledet were to be called as defense alibi witnesses.

So Frice began sifting through the files of the Los Angeles County sheriff's crime lab. Eventually he tracked the "dead" 1960 cases to a basement where they were haphazardly stored in battered filing cabinets.

Resigning himself to another long search, Frice opened the first drawer of the cabinet. The first file was the one he was looking for. It contained a single envelope in which was listed the name of the victim, Toni White, the date the offense had occurred, a description of the gun, its serial number—and a cross-index number.

With the case number, Frice quickly tracked down the ballistics test results. In another file drawer was an envelope with bullets taken from the ballistics test, and the bullet taken from the victim's hip. That evening, Frice called Toni Harris.

Later, he and Harris called in DeWayne Wolfer, the LAPD's internationally renowned ballistics expert and criminologist.

Wolfer got out of bed and drove himself to the crime lab. He worked through the night making oversize photo enlargements of the bullets taken from the bodies of Elaine and Bill, and others of the bullet taken from Ms. White's buttock. By dawn, he had laboriously compared the tiny striations that marked each bullet.

When Wolfer brought these enlargements to court the next day, he testified that the gun that had wounded White, the very same gun that was later the property of Jack Kirschke, was the only gun in the world that could have killed Elaine Terry Kirschke and Orville "Bill" Drankhan.

Kirschke sat through Wolfer's damning testimony with an expression that conveyed belief in his alibi. Indeed, Kirschke's demeanor rarely changed during the trial. To most observers, he seemed arrogantly disinterested. But there were a few notable exceptions, one of them damaging. Early in the trial, while the jury was viewing police photos of Elaine's body, many of them seemingly calculated to appeal to prurient interests, Kirschke was seen at the defense table, joking with his eighteen-year-old son and pointing at one of the photos. The joke may have had nothing to do with the photos or, indeed, with the trial, but many in the courtroom were appalled at the unsympathetic juxtaposition. Now Kirschke's defense, stripped to its essentials, turned on his alibi.

Kirschke produced a surprise witness of his own. Mrs. Vera Judd, a comely divorcée with a three-year-old son nicknamed Squeak, testified that she had met Kirschke at the airport terminal when he prevented Squeak from running out of the building into the busy street. The time, she clearly remembered, was eleven o'clock.

This was precisely the time that Harris and Samoian had told the jury that Kirschke had returned to confront his wife and her lover.

On cross-examination, Judd explained that she had thought nothing at all about the brief encounter until, some six months later, Kirschke was arrested and his picture ran in all the papers. Judd said she put the paper aside but later that night realized that the man in the photo was Kirschke.

Harris also elicited from Judd that she had come to the airport with a man named Robert Johnson, but had discovered that he was married and decided not to go with him on a trip. She wasn't sure if Johnson was even his real name, said Judd, because he might have used an alias.

The next alibi witness was the bartender from the airport lounge, who testified to serving Kirschke three or four drinks between 8:30 and 11:30. He remembered Kirschke, said the witness, because of his deep tan. The bartender was followed by a waitress, who recalled that Kirschke had stopped at Denny's in San Bernardino between 12:30 and 2:00 A.M. He ordered wheat toast and sausages, two side orders, so she remembered him among the stream of patrons. And yes, Kirschke had stopped by, after his arrest, to refresh her memory about the time and date.

That left Dennis Baily and Gene Ledet, the gas station boys. Baily went first, describing, under defense counsel Ramsey's guiding questions, how he was cleaning the men's room when Kirschke came in. The time was between 2:30 and 3:30 on the morning of Saturday, April 8. Baily described the car, noting that the front license plate was fastened to the hood latch in such a way as to make closing the hood difficult.

Baily testified that Sergeant Castillo, a Long Beach officer, had showed him a photo of Kirschke, identifying it as someone who had been in the station on April 8. Sometime later, Kirschke and his detective, Joe Carroll, had come to the station themselves and talked to Baily.

On cross-examination, Harris asked Baily how he knew

what time it was when Kirschke came in. Baily said that when a carload of girls had come into the station about an hour earlier he had asked Ledet the time: 1:45 A.M.

Harris produced the transcript of the grand jury proceedings, where Baily had testified that the girls came in at 1:15. Later in the transcript, Baily had told the grand jury that Byram, the AG's investigator, had asked him what time the red Volkswagen came in, and he had said that he couldn't give him a definite time.

Baily agreed that he'd said that. Harris pressed further on the issue of time, pointing out that Baily had told the grand jury that the time he saw Kirschke could have been anywhere from fifteen to thirty minutes before or after the time frame 2:30 to 4:00. Bailey admitted that this was true.

So Kirschke could have reached the station as late as 4:30 in the morning. That meant he would have had to cover 155 miles in two hours—not impossible at that traffic-free time.

Next, Harris zeroed in on Baily's first memory of seeing Kirschke. Baily had learned from Ledet that two police officers were coming to see them about a man "wanted for murder."

According to Castillo, when he pulled into the station, Baily had rushed up to him and said, "That man was in here last Friday night."

Baily denied that he'd said that. "How could I identify a man without seeing his picture?" he complained.

"That's an excellent question," said Harris.

Baily began visibly perspiring.

Harris took Baily through his prior testimony again. He was in the gas station office on April 15, a week after Kirschke's first visit, talking to an officer, when Kirschke and Carroll came in.

"Did you recognize Mr. Kirschke as the man who had been in your gas station a week earlier?" asked Harris.

"No, I did not," said Baily.

"A week after the event you looked at a man and you didn't recognize him at all—isn't that correct?"

"That's right."

"No further questions," said Harris.

When Ledet took the stand the next day, he was obviously nervous.

With Ramsey's guidance, Ledet said he was emptying trash at 2:30 on the morning of April 8 when he noticed Baily pumping gas into a beat-up Volkswagen. He came over and struck up a conversation with Kirschke about the car seats, which were badly ripped. Ledet owned a 1960 Volkswagen and had found that the upholstery tore easily. Kirschke agreed with Ledet about the fabric, got back in his car, and drove off.

On cross, Harris reminded Ledet that seven days later he didn't recognize Kirschke in the photo Castillo showed him and suggested Castillo return when Baily was on duty. Ledet admitted alerting Baily that a police officer was coming by to show him a photo.

When Kirschke himself came to the station later that day, Ledet did not recognize him, even after he identified himself.

"I recognized him in the sense that he looked familiar to me," said Ledet.

Not until Kirschke asked Ledet about the Volkswagen seats did the young man remember meeting him. Sort of.

"I can't swear that it was the same man, but the resemblance is so great that it must have been his twin brother if it was not he," said Ledet.

Next, Harris tried to pin Ledet down on times. Ledet had told the grand jury that he could not state positively what time Kirschke came through the station, or even if it was in fact during the small hours of April 8. Reminded of this by Harris, Ledet agreed.

On redirect, Ramsey reminded Ledet that he had also told the Long Beach police that "we had a conversation about the upholstery that I'll swear to on fifteen thousand stacks of Bibles."

"I still will," said Ledet.

Harris jumped up and asked for recross. Did Ledet ever tell the grand jury or the police that if the man he'd spoken with wasn't Kirschke, he was his twin brother?

"No, sir," said Ledet.

After Ramsey had rested for the defense, Harris put on

his rebuttal witnesses. Among them was one of the Jolly Girls, Marma Herfter, who testified to a conversation she'd had with Ledet while waiting to be called to the grand jury.

"He said, 'I don't know what I'm doing here. I was asleep when Kirschke was supposed to have been there. . . . I'm just disgusted to have to come up here and waste time.' "

One of the jurors emitted a low whistle. It echoed clearly through the shocked courtroom.

Harris and Samoian took every opportunity during the trial to study the jury, hoping to divine from a gesture, a facial expression, a glance, how they were doing.

This is a custom of both prosecution and defense, even though there is no evidence to suggest that anything useful is ever learned in this manner. Nevertheless, the prosecution was heartened by the actions of one juror.

"She was a grandmother with white hair in a bun—looked just like the woman on Mrs. See's Candy boxes," recalls Samoian. "We worried that she'd be inclined to give Kirschke the benefit of the doubt, that she didn't have the gumption to vote for conviction.

"Then one day a spider appeared on the railing of the jury box, and very slowly walked across. When it got in front of this old woman, she smacked it dead with her bare hand.

"After that we didn't worry about her anymore."

It was a long, bitterly contested trial. The prosecution put on nearly 50 witnesses, plus 30 more in rebuttal, and Kirschke's defense included 122 witnesses. Kirschke himself did not testify.

On December 14, 121 days after the trial began, the case went to the jury. After six days of deliberation, the jury returned with a verdict: guilty of murder in the first degree.

During the penalty phase, Kirschke dismissed his defense counsel and went before the court, not to plead for his life, but for the death penalty. "I prefer death to spending the rest of my life in prison. I don't mind dying, if it's the will of the jury, and if courts all the way up the chain of command, including the nine men in Washington, say, 'Yeah Jack, that's it.' "

In a long, convoluted diatribe during which he quoted Abraham Lincoln and the New Testament, Kirschke complained to the jurors about an elderly woman who appeared in court for every session. Knitting silently, she had proclaimed his guilt "like Madame DeFarge" in the courthouse corridors. At the end, Kirschke, standing before the jury, extended his arms at shoulder level and let his head loll to one side, approximating the position of Christ on the cross. "Forgive them, Father, for they know not what they do," he said.

Judge Kathleen Parker, however, did not want Kirschke to get the death penalty—because if he did, there would be a mandatory appeal of the case, and the state would pay for it. "I took his automatic appeal away," she recalled. "I called the prosecutors in after the case and suggested that they not ask for the death penalty."

Jack Kirschke was sentenced to life in prison. He was one of several life inmates to benefit from changes in California's indeterminate sentencing laws. He served eleven and a half years and was paroled in February 1977. He remarried, and lives quietly with his new wife, Sara, on an island in Puget Sound, where he spends most of his time writing.

"It was an intriguing case," recalls Albert Ramsey. "I don't think this was a planned crime, but happenstance. When Jack got back from the airport he didn't expect to find his wife and her boyfriend waiting. So if he did it, then that must have flipped him out."

Kirschke has never admitted to or publicly expressed remorse for the murders. Whether he planned the crime days ahead, or if it was a crime of passion, once the victims had been shot, there was no looking back.

Experienced in criminal trials, Kirschke undoubtedly knew the fallibility of human memory, and the suggestibility of people when approached in a certain way. Undoubtedly he was in the Yermo gas station, but probably well after 2:30 to 3:30. By the time he rolled in, he was already building an alibi. He had dined at Denny's in San Bernardino, as the waitress recalled, and undoubtedly chatted with her, ordering something unusual that would cause her to remember him.

Kirschke was well versed in the law; he knew that without the murder weapon, there was much less chance of a conviction. But he was no gun expert and may not have known that his H&R .38 had a unique barrel rifling scheme. He could not have known that his souvenir had been used in an obscure crime, or that the results of a ballistics test still existed.

But in the end Kirschke's alibi was worthless. His perfect crime was foiled because the AG's investigators and prosecutors refused to let a killer walk away from his crimes. And because the jury, reasonable people, chose to believe the mute, unblinking testimony of a handful of lead slugs over the recollections of even the most sympathetic witnesses.

# The Kingdom of Brown
# (1986)

**T**AKING INTO ACCOUNT THEIR LESSER EXPERIENCE IN LIFE, and the increased probability of rehabilitation for younger offenders, laws in every state treat juveniles far more leniently than adults. In California, for example, an adult murderer who avoids the death penalty or life-without-parole can look forward to a harsh thirty years or more behind the bars in a bleak prison. On the other hand, juveniles convicted of homicide are usually sentenced to a relatively benign Youth Authority facility that is often cleaner, safer, and more comfortable than their own homes. With good behavior, nearly all juvenile offenders are free by their twenty-fifth birthday—and some far earlier. This difference in sentencing is not lost on older criminals. Many gang-related offenses, including murder, are "solved" through the "confession" of juveniles, sometimes as young as eight or nine. Too often, the juvenile has been tricked or coerced into confessing to a crime in which he or she had little or no involvement—while the real criminal remains free.

And sometimes, the killer isn't in the kind of organization most people would think of as a gang. The Brown case illustrates how a cunning and amoral adult manipulated a juvenile to take him off the hook for a vicious murder. For years, it looked like a perfect crime.

\* \* \*

David Arnold Brown liked his females naive and young. Very, very young. Early in his own teen years, David discovered that some juvenile girls, products of homes impoverished both by lack of material goods and loving parents, were emotional blank slates whom David could fill in as he wished. Applying native shrewdness and an untutored talent for manipulation, he learned to program such girls to please his selfish desires. Inevitably, each girl aged, learning in the process that there was more to the world than David—more than he wanted her to know. And so, when they passed from unqualified obedience to hesitant questioning of David's omnipotence, he rid himself of each one, moving on to the next blank slate.

David Brown was born in Phoenix, Arizona, on November 16, 1952, the sixth of eight children born to Arthur Quentin Brown and Manuela Estrada Brown. Arthur was an auto mechanic, a low-key, submissive, but industrious man who often held down two jobs to keep his family fed and housed. In 1960, the Browns moved to Needles, California, a tiny, arid, windswept border town in the vast Mojave Desert. As David grew up, his family moved again and again, following whatever work Arthur could find. They lived in Bakersfield, a dusty San Joaquin Valley oil-patch town, and in Wilmington, the grimy port of Los Angeles.

David had a hard childhood. He began working at age eleven, pulling weeds, washing dishes in a greasy-spoon café, then running, on his own, a small gas station at a remote crossroads. At fourteen, after completing the eighth grade, he left his parents' home. Perhaps, as he would later say, he left because he was subjected to severe beatings. Or maybe because he was tired of being poor and powerless. Or perhaps because he was molested by a male relative.

But David was a survivor. He had a quick mind and a facile tongue. He worked hard. Passing through puberty, he developed a surprisingly deep and mellifluous voice that commanded attention. Aside from his voice, however, at fifteen, with a face marred by acne and the beginnings of the pudgy, amorphous body he would later fill out, David was not exactly a winsome package when it came to attracting girls.

David's first girlfriend was Brenda Kurges. At fifteen she was a petite charmer with olive skin, long straight brown hair, fine features, and big, inviting brown eyes. Brenda was the oldest of eleven children, the one her mother leaned on for help with raising the younger ones, most of whom had different fathers. Brenda, who had almost nothing to wear but the clothes on her back, robbed of her childhood by immense responsibilities, was desperately unhappy. She ran away with David's sister, Susan, and got as far as Lawndale, ten miles up the freeway. Police brought her home; a few months later she ran away again, only to be caught and returned to her mother's home.

And then along came David.

David asked Brenda's boyfriend, Andy, if he might take Brenda out, just once. Andy, a pal, agreed. Before their date was over, David told her that she was his steady. She listened to his words, to the convincing timbre of his voice. She felt the confidence behind those words, and as many women and girls would do in years to come, she obeyed.

In David, Brenda found the first male who wanted to care for her. He wrote her mushy poetry, bought her clothes and food—and ran every minute of her life. Jealously possessive, he balked at letting her out of his sight. When he needed to use a public toilet, David insisted that Brenda remain just outside so he could speak to her through the door.

At sixteen Brenda ran away with David. They lived by his wit and charm. Even working intermittently at odd jobs, they had more to eat, more clothes to wear, and better places to sleep than she had ever before enjoyed.

After several weeks of working for room and board in a tiny cottage in a retirement development, however, David was stunned to discover that the management had, years earlier, installed listening devices in each cottage. Probably, as originally installed, these allowed elderly residents to summon aid. In any case, the system was no longer in use. But David and Brenda, thinking that the manager was eavesdropping on their intimate moments, became fearful. David called his parents. They allowed him and Brenda to move into their home.

As a teenager—and, by most accounts, until well into his

thirties—David was preoccupied with sex. Brenda would later confirm that he demanded it "at least three times a day." Small wonder that at seventeen she became pregnant. In May 1970, the two were married. Their daughter, Cinnamon Darlene, was born on July 3.

Cinnamon was a beautiful baby with thick hair, big brown eyes, and a sunny disposition. While delegating all disciplinary chores to Brenda, David seemed to enjoy fatherhood. He made himself the focus of Cinnamon's existence, tickling and teasing and playing with her every day, taking her for short rides on his motorcycle and on trips to amusement parks. Brenda was stuck with the hard work of parenting, the washing, changing, wee-hour feeding, and comforting that every child needs.

Throughout their three-year marriage, David worked to keep his wife under his thumb. When Brenda was anxious to get a driver's license, David refused to teach her to drive. He preferred her to remain totally dependent on him. When Brenda got a neighbor to teach her, David was surprised and angry.

Beyond the daily sexual demands David placed on her, Brenda could see that when he wasn't succumbing to one of his frequent bouts of anxiety-ridden depression, he was all but totally consumed with the *idea* of sex. He ogled women constantly, even in her presence. Young women, girls, even attractive older women—David was interested in them all. Few, however, seemed to reciprocate. The more David was refused, the more he tightened his possessive grip on Brenda. There came a time when he forbade her to join office coworkers on lunch excursions, insisting that she eat alone.

Living on food stamps and welfare, the young couple struggled. But David had lofty ambitions. In 1971, at age eighteen, he enrolled in a program to train welfare recipients in useful job skills. Based on better-than-average scores on the high school GED test, David was admitted to Control Data Institute to study the emerging technology of computers. After completing his studies, he worked at a succession of data-processing jobs in Orange County. Displaying his lifelong tendency to exaggerate his importance and inflate his accomplishments, he padded his résumé to get each new job.

By 1973, David, Brenda, and Cinnamon were living in Anaheim, California, and David was working at Cal Comp, a data-processing company. And he was constantly fooling around with other women, among them his coworker Lori Carpenter, a slender girl of nineteen. As her marriage dissolved, Brenda became fearful of David. Enlisting her employer's help while David was at work, she moved their furniture into a small apartment that she had rented for herself and Cinnamon. And she got a lawyer.

All this caught David off guard. The shy, submissive, fourteen-year-old he had so completely dominated had grown into a determined young woman who knew what she wanted. He appeared at her new apartment with a rifle, put it to her head, and made an impassioned speech: if he couldn't have her, then nobody would. "Go ahead and shoot," said Brenda. "You'll never get away. The police will come, and they'll lock you up forever." David wavered, then dropped the rifle. Because she was willing to risk everything for her freedom, Brenda won back her life.

Since his teen years, David had been morbidly concerned with his health. He told Brenda he had colitis, which, he explained, accounted for his frequent bouts of diarrhea and constant heavy perspiration. He was a heavy cigarette smoker—three to four packs a day was his normal consumption—and rarely exercised. He visited doctors frequently, complaining of hypertension, high blood pressure, and gastric problems. Nevertheless, in July 1971, Selective Service doctors classified him 1-A. David requested a hearing from his draft board and somehow persuaded them to reclassify him. He never again faced the draft.

From all this came another lesson. David learned to manipulate people by preying on their concerns for his health. And since he cared about no one but himself, he learned to get what he wanted from members of his family by threatening to end the relationship, a classic psychological ploy called "tyranny of the weak." David would ultimately develop this tactic to take control of everyone in his tightly constrained little kingdom.

After their divorce, David, then twenty-two, came to a tenuous peace with his ex-wife. Brenda got child support but no alimony but all of their furniture, and custody of Cinnamon. Under the divorce agreement, however, Cinnamon visited her father nearly every weekend. As she grew up Cinnamon learned to think of David as her fun parent, the one who always bought her things and took her places.

As soon as the divorce from Brenda was final, David married Lori Carpenter. Soon, however, he realized that his new wife was too mature for him. After four years they divorced. David had learned that he could never be happy with an adult woman. It was not merely that he could not fully enjoy sex unless his partner had the smooth, firm body of a teenager. It was that no grown woman would long put up with his smothering, infantile behavior, his incessant sexual demands, his abrupt mood swings—and his utter disregard for her emotional needs. So, decided David, from then on, the women in his life would be very, very young. He would mold their malleable minds to do his bidding.

During most of their brief marriage, David and Lori rented a small house in Riverside, a sleepy town an hour's drive east of Los Angeles. Their house on Randolph Street was not in one of the community's finer neighborhoods. Two doors down lived the Baileys, eleven children and their alcoholic mother. Despite dire poverty—they survived on welfare and food stamps—the children were attractive. Linda Bailey was about thirteen when David first cast a covetous eye on her. She was a very pretty girl, with long, ash-blond hair, pert features, and even in her early teens, a sensationally mature body that included long, slim legs, a tiny waist, and very full breasts.

David knew about growing up in poverty. From Brenda he had learned about the desperate vulnerability of young girls of welfare families. He told Ethel Bailey, the forty-two-year-old matriarch, that he had terminal colon cancer. His marriage was breaking up, he said, and since he had to work long hours to make a living, there was never enough time to keep up his house. If Ethel would allow some of her older daughters to do his housework, he would pay them well.

To Ethel Bailey, David must have seemed heaven-sent. Her kids found him a laughing, joking, affectionate man who took them on shopping trips. Ethel didn't know that he made a game of teaching her kids to steal anything left in unlocked cars and trucks.

Even before Lori and David separated, David was seeing Pam Bailey, then about sixteen. He also had his eye on Linda. And on Patti, then about five, a skinny towhead who idolized him.

David made himself indispensable to the Bailey family. Days before the next welfare check was due, when nothing was left to eat but cold cereal, he took the kids out for burgers or pizza. Noting that they had few clothes, he trucked them to Sears and Kmart and bought them jeans, T-shirts, blouses, and sneakers.

When Linda was fifteen, David dropped Pam. Not long after that, he announced his miraculous recovery from cancer. And since his marriage to Lori was over, he asked Ethel Bailey if he might marry her daughter Linda.

Ethel said no. Linda was too young. Too young, even, to use the birth-control pills she got from a free clinic. When she learned her daughter was having sex with David, she hit the ceiling. Linda moved in with her older brother Rick and his wife, Mary. When Linda turned seventeen a few months later, her mother gave in. Linda and David were married in Las Vegas in June 1979.

Less than two months later, David kicked her out of his rented house and sued for divorce, telling the Baileys and anyone who would listen that he couldn't be married to someone who abused drugs and alcohol.

Linda was devastated. The one man she wanted had told her she was "just too young" for marriage.

Perhaps she just didn't understand that David needed sex with many different women—like Cindy, the young mother of two who worked with him at Memorex Corp. David married Cindy in May 1980, but he continued to have sex with other women—including Linda Bailey.

David would later say that although his fourth wife was beautiful and sexy, she was too greedy. He made about $36,000 a year as a manager with Memorex, a very good salary at that time. Cindy liked to spend his money, he would later explain, and then complain that they were always broke. That may have been the reason their marriage foundered. Or perhaps it was because she was very protective of her own children, with whom David felt no parental bond. Whatever the reason, less than eight months after they were married, David served divorce papers on Cindy.

Long before California's mandatory six-month interlocutory period was over, David turned his attentions to the woman he had selected to be his next wife: Linda Bailey. He showered his ex-wife with gifts, wrote her poems, and begged her to marry him again, pledging that this time things would be different. What was a girl to do? She moved out of her brother Rick's home and back in with David just before the end of 1980, while he was still married to Cindy.

The Bailey clan was not entirely happy with this move. By now, some of Linda's siblings, not to mention her mother, had begun to take David's real measure. The man who had seemed like a Santa-for-all-seasons now seemed calculating, scheming, somehow sinister.

Others, however, saw him as an up-and-comer, a man with a bright financial future. Even if he was suffering from asthma, colitis, ulcers, anal bleeding, panic attacks, and a heart condition, David always seemed to have money. And there were those among the Baileys who harbored hopes that some of that money might come their way, a belief David carefully nurtured. Someday he was going to start his own company. There would be plenty of jobs for his in-laws. Someday, and maybe soon, they would all be, if not rich, comfortable.

Despite whatever compunctions she may have had, soon after Linda and David remarried, Ethel Bailey allowed eleven-year-old Patti to move in with them. Patti was ecstatic. At home she had to endure grinding poverty and an older brother's sexual advances. Living with David meant good food, her own room, plenty of clothes and toys, her own TV, Walkman, and other goodies.

In the late 1970s, before personal computers became as ubiquitous as adding machines and typewriters, comparatively few people understood the new technologies. As companies grew steadily more dependent on computers for payroll, inventory, personnel, accounts payable and receivable, marketing data, and other information-intensive operations, they rarely employed anyone who could do much more than *operate* a computer. So when something went wrong, not only did operations come to a screeching halt, but they often remained that way until a contractor could fix things.

Devices used for storing vast reams of data, when subjected to natural disasters like earthquakes or floods, or man-made problems like fire or power outages, usually failed. When a type of storage device known as a hard disk "crashed," the computer's owners were in deep trouble unless they had backup data. Too often they did not, and lost thousands of dollars every hour their system was down. They were willing to pay handsomely the expert who could recover even *some* of their irreplaceable data.

Repairing these early disk drives was the area in which David Brown began to specialize when he went to work for Randomex, a company based in Signal Hill, a suburb of Long Beach, California. Randomex used a variety of methods to recover 40 to 60 percent of the data from crashed hard disks and other storage media. A common source of disk failure was dirt and dust particles that had penetrated a damaged unit. If they could be removed, then most or even all of the data could be saved. The trick was to find a way to remove the dirt without scratching the delicate surface of a disk.

In addition to the cotton swabs and denatured alcohol commonly used to clean crashed disks, David discovered a substance with ideal cleaning properties. It was inexpensive and widely available, but since few people seemed to know it could be used for this particular purpose, he made it his secret, the heart of his data-recovery procedure. He called it "the Process."

With "the Process" in hand, and by concentrating on just one type of storage device, "minidisks," David could usually recover more data than companies like Randomex averaged. In 1980, while still working at Randomex, he started his own company, Data Recovery. He soon quit his job to concentrate on work subcontracted from Randomex.

He got rich—richer than anything in his previous experience. As demand for data recovery increased, Data Recovery's business boomed. Not counting whatever he could skim off the top—and by his own later accounts, this was quite a bit—within a few years Data Recovery was grossing hundreds of thousands of dollars. Many of the jobs they performed as Randomex subcontractors were for the largest American corporations and for various government agencies.

This success and affluence might have brought David Brown into contact with the upper strata of the still-young computer industry. It did not, because David dealt only with Randomex, which received the damaged equipment, invoiced the client, and collected the funds. All David—and later, his father, wife, and two of her brothers—did was clean disks and extract the data from them. It was tedious work that required close attention to detail. And it was work that did not require much education or understanding of computers. But only David knew how the Process worked.

Because of the success of the Process, David Brown became a minor media celebrity in certain sectors of the computer industry. He enjoyed reading stories in the trade press about the data-recovery "miracles" he worked. But David avoided contact with the industry's true superstars and its swelling legions of young technocrats. His knowledge of the business was limited and specialized. In the company of laymen he could drop buzzwords and seem learned. Conversing at length with any of his supposed peers, he ran the risk of exposing the vast gaps in his education and his limited grasp of advanced computer concepts. This was not a risk his ego would allow.

So David avoided social contact with his industry peers. He did much of his work from home, and by the mid-1980s, was devoting nearly all of his time to his extended family—his parents, wife, daughter Cinnamon, who had come to live with him in the fall of 1984, and Patti Bailey, just two years older than Cinnamon. These were the people he wowed with his stories of saving over a hundred people in the MGM-Grand Hotel fire and in unraveling the secrets of the space-shuttle Challenger disaster. They didn't know enough to realize that David's work came long after the MGM-Grand fire was out and that his Challenger work was peripheral to the mystery of the crash. They didn't challenge David's ridiculous assertion that his Data Recovery work was so valuable to the Coca-Cola Company that by contract he and his wife, Linda, were never allowed to fly on the same plane together. The only people David impressed were those easily swayed by his charm, by his casual but superficial use of unfamiliar computer terms. They were people who believed him when he boasted of designing computers and disk drives and of training engineers. David's family never challenged even his most outrageous falsehoods. They depended on him for virtually everything in their lives and wanted to believe almost anything he told them.

It was almost exactly 3:30 on the morning of March 19, 1985, when police arrived at David Brown's home in Garden Grove, a thoroughly middle-class Orange County suburb southeast of Los Angeles. A police dispatcher told Officer Darrow Halligan that there was a "possible one-eight-seven"—murder—at 12551 Ocean Breeze Drive.

Halligan was met at the door by David Brown, a short, chunky, hunched-over man who seemed far older than his thirty-two years. Inside the modest house the officer saw pretty seventeen-year-old Patti Bailey weeping nonstop and cradling a bawling infant in her arms. "I think my w-w-w-wife's been s-s-s-shot," stuttered David, adding that his wife was in their bedroom. And that he was afraid to go look.

Halligan thought that was an odd statement, but chalked

it up to shock. Parking David and Patti on the sofa, he went to check the bedroom. As he opened the door, Halligan heard a faint sound, perhaps a gurgle. Pointing his powerful flashlight toward the sound, the policeman saw a young woman lying on a bed. Bright red blood oozed from her chest. Halligan leaned over the bed and tried to find a pulse to match the soft choking sounds he heard coming from the victim's chest. There was no pulse, no trace of breathing.

Nevertheless, Halligan told paramedics who swarmed into the house minutes later that she might still be alive. The medics tried CPR. They performed an emergency tracheotomy to open an airway to her lungs. They pumped in fresh blood through an intravenous hookup. A physician arrived and tried, in desperation, to restart her pulse by carefully but swiftly carving open her chest and massaging her heart in his gloved hands.

Nothing worked. Linda Bailey Brown, twenty-three, died from the effects of two gunshots that had pierced her chest between her breasts. Police found the weapon that had fired those shots, a chrome-plated .38-caliber Smith & Wesson revolver, on the bedroom floor. It was bagged as evidence.

The homicide investigator was Fred McLean, a competent eighteen-year veteran of the Garden Grove PD. Awakened at 4:30 A.M., he was on the death scene with his partner, Detective Steve Sanders, shortly after five, well before first light. McLean did a quick once-around of the Brown house. Off the kitchen was a laundry room; peering inside he saw, atop a clothes dryer, three empty plastic prescription vials, lids off. Next to the pill bottles was an empty glass. According to their labels, the vials had contained Darvocet-N and Dyazide, prescribed for David Brown.

McLean bagged the vials and the glass as possible evidence. Then he began questioning David Brown. David said that after midnight the previous evening, after patching up an argument with his wife, Linda, and with a lot on his mind, he had gone alone for a long drive. He remembered stopping off at a local convenience store and later at a coffee shop as he made his way to the beach. When he returned, David said, it was about three in the morning, and

Patti, his wife's sister, had greeted him, hysterically shaking and crying, with the news that she thought his fourteen-year-old daughter, Cinnamon, had perhaps killed Linda—and that Cinnamon had taken a shot at her, too.

Why, asked McLean, would a teenage girl shoot her stepmother? And where was the girl now?

David Brown, sucking on cigarette after cigarette, told McLean how for months his daughter had been disturbed and disobedient. Cinnamon was insolent to her stepmother, to her mother, Brenda, and to Patti, with whom she had, until recently, shared a room and a sisterly relationship. He'd tried to get Cinnamon into counseling, said David, but she had stubbornly refused.

McLean turned his attention to Patti. She was a very grown-up seventeen, short of stature with a tiny waist, full, flaring hips, a very generous bustline, and long locks of light blond hair framing pale skin and well-defined features. Patti looked amazingly like her late sister, Linda. Patti confirmed that for months Cinnamon had been angry and moody, that she had fought with everyone in the house over domestic matters like dishwashing chores. Patti volunteered that while Cinnamon had been unwilling to talk about her problems, she had recently threatened to get a gun and shoot herself.

As McLean watched and listened a picture emerged of a troubled teen who had not responded to the care and loving concern of her family. "Where is Cinnamon now?" he asked.

Neither Patti nor David could say. His daughter no longer shared Patti's room, explained David, because they didn't get along. Cinnamon had so upset her stepmother that several weeks earlier she had been banished to a small trailer in the backyard. The police checked the trailer, but Cinnamon was not there.

McLean got Cinnamon's description: she was chubby, about 120 pounds, an inch or two under five feet tall, with medium-length light brown hair. McLean put out a citywide bulletin with her description. Other officers began calling her school friends. Surely, a fourteen-year-old girl wouldn't be hard to find.

Meanwhile, McLean questioned Patti about the events of the previous evening. Now Patti remembered that after eleven, Cinnamon had come into her room with "a small gray gun" and asked her how it worked. The gun described was not the revolver that police had already bagged and would ultimately prove was the murder weapon. Patti said she had asked Cinnamon why she wanted to know how the gun worked, and the younger girl had said something about being worried about a break-in. The house had an elaborate electronic security system, but Cinnamon's backyard trailer was not hooked into it.

So, Patti said, she had told Cinnamon about the gun. "I'm not positive how to work it. I've just seen it on TV— but you just cock it back and pull the trigger."

McLean wondered briefly why Patti would tell a youngster how to use a gun when the same kid had recently threatened to commit suicide. But he supposed that Patti might not have recalled the suicide threat at the time. He kept this question to himself.

At twenty-three minutes after two, said Patti, she had been sleeping in her room and was awakened by a gunshot to find Cinnamon standing next to her bed. When Patti opened her eyes, Cinnamon ran from the room.

From somewhere in the house, said Patti, she heard eight-month-old Krystal, Linda's daughter, crying. Then she heard another shot, farther away. And then, said Patti, as she lay on her bed, frozen with fear, she heard a third shot. After a few minutes she got up and forced herself to go into the nursery, where she picked up the screaming infant and walked around the room, wondering what to do and whom to call.

An hour later, said Patti, she heard a faint rapping at the front door. Afraid it might be Cinnamon—who didn't have a house key—Patti did nothing. Then she heard the knock again. This time she went to the door and waited, silently, in the entryway. Finally, she heard the scratching of a key in the lock. Moments later, David came in.

The investigator wondered why a man would knock to enter his own home. Why he would knock at three A.M.

when he had a key. But McLean said nothing about it at the time.

After blurting out in dismay that Cinnamon had shot Linda, said Patti, David walked through the house, checking every room. Except the one he shared with Linda. Patti said she begged David to check Linda's room, but he refused, saying he was terrified of blood. He told Patti to open the door and look, but she was equally frightened of what she might find.

So no one went to the bedroom where Linda lay bleeding to death. Instead, David told Patti to take the baby and see if Cinnamon was in her trailer. Then David got on the telephone and made a call. And, oddly, his first call was to his father, Arthur, who told him to call the police.

By the time David had made this second call, Patti had returned from the backyard to report that Cinnamon was not in her trailer and was nowhere to be found.

McLean ordered a gunshot residue test for David and Patti. This is accomplished by swabbing the hands and fingers with cotton, then bagging the cotton swabs for lab testing. If a person so swabbed has fired a gun, or even handled one that was fired recently, tests will show traces of the chemical compounds associated with gunpowder.

After this testing, McLean joined a pair of uniformed patrol officers to have a look at the Brown's backyard. Besides the trailer there were two doghouses for the family's pets. Just before seven o'clock, McLean saw that while all four dogs were temporarily confined to a fenced run, the larger doghouse was not empty. Looking inside, he found Cinnamon Brown, semiconscious, curled into a ball, resting in a pool of her own vomit. In the vomit, McLean noticed, were dozens of orange-tinted capsules.

Cold and woozy from the drugs she had swallowed, her muscles stiff from cramped sleep, Cinnamon crawled out of the little doghouse and into McLean's arms. A roll of pink construction paper was clutched in her right hand. McLean pried it loose. There was something on the paper, printed in the round, clear hand of a child. McLean unrolled it to read, *Dear God, please forgive me. I didn't mean to hurt her.*

At the police station, Cinnamon was taken to a holding

cell. One of the detectives who first questioned her was Steve Sanders, who, five months earlier, had spoken to the girl at her school about a flasher who had exposed himself to her. Though ill and drowsy, Cinnamon remembered meeting Sanders. Then, complaining of a terrible headache, she vomited.

Under questioning by paramedics, Cinnamon said she had taken the entire contents of three prescription drug vials. Dyazide, a diuretic, was usually prescribed to lower blood pressure by purging the body of excess water. A massive overdose almost always causes severe heart arrhythmia, which frequently leads to a heart attack. Darvocet-N, a compound of acetaminophen and propoxyphene napsylate, is a pain killer. In overdose, it depresses the central nervous system to the point where automatic functions— breathing and heartbeat, for example—cease. The paramedics concluded that if Cinnamon hadn't vomited up many of the estimated 260 pills she had swallowed, she would have been dead long before McLean found her. As it was, she was a very sick child.

After exchanging her vomit-stained sweatsuit for a prison jumpsuit, Cinnamon was read her Miranda rights and gently questioned by McLean and Sanders. While these police veterans may have known that in her condition, Cinnamon might not be capable of understanding her rights, they were anxious to find the truth. They pressed on with questions. Complaining of being very tired, and frequently drifting off, she seemed genuinely shocked and upset to learn that Linda was dead—and that she was under arrest.

Rambling, backtracking, responding haltingly, Cinnamon said that her stepmother had ordered her out of the house, adding that if Cinnamon wasn't gone by the time she awoke in the morning, Linda would kill her. Fading fast, Cinnamon rambled on about how Linda was jealous of her relationship with her father. She loved her father very, very much, said Cinnamon.

McLean continued his interrogation, but Cinnamon's answers often seemed to have nothing to do with the questions he asked. Sometimes she contradicted herself. But she did say that she had found the gun in her father's office—and *denied* asking Patti to show her how to use it.

And she said she had fired three shots. "One was in the room with Patti, and the other two were with Linda," she said.

"Why did you shoot . . . in Patti's room?" asked McLean.

"The gun got stuck," said Cinnamon. "Something in it . . . the thing you pull back . . . I couldn't turn on the light. . . ."

Twenty minutes after the questioning began, blood samples were taken from Cinnamon so doctors would have a better idea of what was in her system. Another twenty minutes later, with Cinnamon fading into unconsciousness, unable to focus her eyes, unable to respond to his questions with more than unintelligible sounds, McLean decided to stop.

Cinnamon was in very bad shape. Her blood pressure and pulse were so low that she was hooked to an IV and rushed to the hospital. For several hours, slipping in and out of consciousness and vomiting periodically, Cinnamon, with no prompting, mumbled several times to Officer Pamela French. French, sitting at her bedside, thought she sounded "robotlike" or programmed. "She was hurting me," said Cinnamon. "She hated me. . . . She wanted to kill me . . . wanted me out of the house. . . ."

About noon, Cinnamon slipped silently into unconsciousness.

As the comatose girl struggled for her life, police at the crime scene confirmed at least one element of her story: two .38-caliber bullets were in Linda Bailey's body and a third was dug from the wall above Patti Bailey's bed.

The autopsy of Linda Brown's body showed that the two shots that ended her life had come from very close range; one was fired from less than six inches, the other from between twelve and twenty inches. One shot pierced her right lung; the other nicked the lung but hit the vena cava, the large vein that returns blood to the heart. This second wound was the cause of her death. Even if she had been rushed to a hospital immediately, the Orange County medical examiner concluded, it was still very likely she would have died.

Soon after Cinnamon regained consciousness in the Garden Grove Medical Center, she gave a long, detailed statement to Kim Hicks, a third-year University of California, Irvine, medical student. It was Hicks's duty to write a complete medical history of each patient assigned to her supervision and to present a summary of that history to the supervising physician. The fourteen-year-old related, in detail, the events that had led to her taking three vials of her father's prescription medicine—and of the episodes that followed, including shooting Linda and putting a bullet into Patti's bedroom wall.

In Orange County, California, as in many places, police refer most cases to the county district attorney. It is a deputy DA who decides what crime or crimes the suspect will be charged with, if any. To obtain more evidence than provided by the police's initial investigation, the deputy is often paired with a detective from the DA's own investigative staff. The case of *California* v. *Cinnamon Brown* was assigned to Deputy DA Dick Fredrickson, probably the county's most experienced prosecutor of teenage killers.

Assigned to Fredrickson was investigator Jay Newell, thirty-nine, a ruggedly good-looking athlete and veteran of fourteen years in law enforcement. Newell is a very good detective, smart, subtle, and tough. His colleagues often kidded that once he'd fastened his teeth on a case, he became a pit bull, refusing to let go until his quarry was convicted.

To most initially involved in solving the murder of Linda Brown, the evidence against Cinnamon seemed so overwhelming that the case was deemed a "slam dunk." But Jay Newell was not convinced. It would be weeks before the results of the forensic tests were known, but the more Newell learned about Cinnamon and the Brown family, the more he was sure that something was missing. He went to the crime scene and walked around the empty house. He knocked on doors and talked to neighbors, but none seemed to know the Brown family or Cinnamon very well.

Some of Cinnamon's school friends, interviewed by Garden Grove investigators McLean and Sanders, said that she had always seemed a happy child who got along well with her stepmother. Her only problem, said her friends, seemed to be an overly strict father who continually grounded her for the most minor of infractions, such as returning a few minutes late from school or talking back. On weekends, said one friend, Cinnamon was often confined to her trailer and allowed into the house only for meals. She hadn't had telephone privileges in several months and had been denied visitors.

Detective McLean also interviewed Cinnamon's mother, Brenda Sands, who said that Cinnamon had moved in with her father after she and her daughter had quarreled. But they had patched things up and forgiven each other, said Brenda. Mother and daughter remained good friends, but Cinnamon continued to live with her father because David insisted that their daughter had threatened to run away if she was forced to move back in with Brenda.

Brenda had a few other things to report that interested McLean. A few weeks before the shooting, her daughter said Linda and David were not getting along. Cinnamon had also said David and Patti overheard Linda on the phone, plotting with her twin brother to "get rid of David."

"Something was going on," said Brenda. "Cinnamon told me that Linda was afraid David might leave her for Patti." And, added Brenda, Cinnamon said that David was thinking about hiring a private detective to keep an eye on Linda.

It all sounded so dramatic and bizarre. McLean wondered if Cinnamon hadn't made all this up, as adolescents sometimes will, to get a parent's attention.

Later, Steve Sanders discovered that Patti Bailey was no longer in school. A few weeks before the murder, David had pulled both her and Cinnamon out of Bolsa Grande High, telling school authorities that the school wasn't safe, that their lockers had been broken into, that students dealt drugs and carried weapons to class, that teachers were ineffective. David had said that Cinnamon would transfer to nearby Loara High and that Patti was moving to Nebraska.

When McLean went back to see David for a second interview, less than a day had gone by since the murder. Much of what he said appeared to contradict the story told by Patti just hours after the shooting. For instance, Patti had said that David, fearful of what he might find, refused to check Linda's room when he returned home from his drive. But now David reported that, as man of the house, he naturally wanted to check the room. But Patti had stopped him, keening, "Don't!"

Nevertheless, David continued, he'd opened the door and looked in to see his wife on the bed in "an unnatural position." Frightened, he went no farther.

McLean knew from his own death-scene visit that Linda was in a completely natural position, on her back. He made a mental note of David's statement.

In response to McLean's sudden and direct questions, David denied killing Linda. Then he volunteered that some two weeks earlier, Cinnamon had attempted suicide by taking an aspirin overdose. When McLean asked about taking Patti out of school, David said nothing about her moving to Nebraska. Instead, he said, Patti wasn't doing well in Bolsa Grande's special education program, so he had decided to hire a tutor and have her take lessons at home.

How much insurance had the late Linda carried? asked McLean. David said that at one time she had almost a million dollars in coverage—but that he had dropped this policy some time ago. A few weeks before her death she had taken out a small policy. He couldn't remember how much it was, he said, but it wasn't much—a few thousand bucks. McLean did not press David on the insurance issue, but made a mental note to check on the policies.

McLean would later learn that David never hired a tutor. Patti Bailey spent nearly all day, every day, at home with David and Linda. Since she didn't know how to drive, on the rare occasions when she left the house, Patti was inevitably with either David or Linda. She was almost never alone outside their house. And after talking to the Bailey clan, McLean learned that everyone in her family agreed that Patti had long had a giant crush on her sister's husband.

* * *

Reading McLean's and Sanders's reports, Newell was convinced there was more to the events of the night of March 19, 1985, than anyone in law enforcement knew. He began to think of the case as an enormous mystery. Why would a sweet, naive, young girl murder her stepmother? What was life like in the Brown household? What was Cinnamon's real relationship with Linda and Patti? Why was David Brown so strict with his daughter? What was Patti's relationship with her sister and her sister's husband?

But as much as Newell was determined to ferret out the whole story, Cinnamon remained the only person he could make a case against. Despite the many questions he had about Patti and David and their actions on the night of the murder, and despite the tantalizing hints that the Browns and Baileys were families with much to hide, in the end there was only Cinnamon's confession. She had pulled the trigger, she told McLean, and she alone would take the blame.

David Brown hired one of Orange County's leading criminal defense attorneys, Al Forgette, to defend Cinnamon. Forgette did not come cheap, but he was a thorough, able advocate, well regarded by peers and prosecutors. He went by Garden Grove Medical Center to see his new client, but she was still unconscious. Forgette gave his business card to the nurse in charge and asked her to call when Cinnamon could have visitors.

One of Cinnamon's first callers was Dr. Seawright Anderson, a psychiatrist hired by Forgette to explore the possibility of an insanity defense. Anderson would later testify that he found Cinnamon alert, reasonably responsive, and entirely clear about what had happened on the night of March 19. But when she told Dr. Anderson about the shooting of her stepmother, she could not differentiate between what she had done and her feelings about it. And, most oddly, she insisted that she never wanted to kill Linda. "Do you think you need to be in a mental hospital?" asked the doctor. "No, no," said Cinnamon, shaking her head.

Anderson observed that although Cinnamon by now

clearly understood that she faced prison, this seemed relatively unimportant to her. Her biggest fear seemed to be about keeping her father's love. She was very worried that he wouldn't love her anymore because she had shot Linda.

Anderson left Cinnamon with a tentative if somewhat imaginative diagnosis: Cinnamon suffered from "major clinical depression" and could not have known the difference between right and wrong when she shot Linda. If a judge bought that, she might go free after only brief hospitalization.

And then a strange thing happened to Cinnamon's memory after her conversation with Dr. Anderson and another with her father. She could no longer remember anything that happened on the night Linda was shot or how she had felt about her stepmother before that evening. It was as though a dark curtain had fallen across her mind, blocking out the horrible events. And no matter how many doctors and investigators questioned her, Cinnamon could only say that she just didn't remember anything about the shooting or how she felt about Linda on the night she died.

Four months after her arrest, Cinnamon turned fifteen and preparations for her trial entered their final phase. Living in Juvenile Hall, visited occasionally by her father, she was completely unaware of the changes that had occurred in the Brown household since the night of Linda's murder.

David, Patti, and Krystal, Linda's baby, had moved into a new house in the nearby city of Orange. Patti now raised Krystal alone, though with constant advice from Manuela, David's mother. Patti prepared the meals and served them to the family from Linda's chair. She now wore Linda's clothes and jewelry. As her late sister had done, Patti accompanied David on business errands. And within weeks of Linda's death, Patti removed all pictures of Linda from their frames, substituting photos of herself.

Over the six months following Linda's death, David Brown systematically deposited the double-indemnity death-benefit checks that trickled in from four insurance companies. Together they totaled $843,626.

\* \* \*

The state's case against Cinnamon had almost derailed a few weeks after her arrest, during a preliminary hearing in Juvenile Court. Just before the hearing, Jay Newell was surprised to learn that the murder weapon did not have Cinnamon's fingerprints on it. Curiously, the gunshot residue test on Cinnamon also came back negative. Perhaps that was because she had lain in her own vomit and urine for several hours, thought Newell. That might have washed away the antimony that this assay sought to find. But the test in itself was not crucial to the state's case, which rested on Cinnamon's confession to Fred McLean at the Garden Grove jail.

But when Al Forgette stood before Judge Robert Fitzgerald in superior court, he argued that since Cinnamon had been under the influence of a massive dosage of painkillers and on the verge of losing consciousness, when she spoke to police, she couldn't think clearly and had no idea of her situation. Although she had been read her Miranda rights, argued Forgette, his client was in no condition to understand them. Therefore her confession ought to be thrown out.

Judge Fitzgerald agreed. Cinnamon's confession to McLean was no longer evidence. Now there was no physical evidence against Cinnamon, and no confession.

Newell began backtracking, looking for evidence that might have been overlooked. If the DA took the case into court now, Cinnamon would surely be acquitted.

One of the documents Newell examined was Cinnamon's medical records from Garden Grove Medical Center. There, buried between many pages of clinical jargon scrawled by doctors, was the clear hand of Kimberly Hicks, who had taken down every detail volunteered by Cinnamon while she lay in her bed, everything about how she had come to be in the hospital—including the girl's confession to killing Linda.

This document survived Forgette's legal challenge, the judge ruling that Kim Hicks had not been serving as an agent of the police when she took this information from Cinnamon. Now Cinnamon faced a possible life sentence, but as a juvenile she had no right to a jury trial. Judge Fitzgerald alone would decide her fate.

The first witness against her was her "aunt," Patti Bailey. She identified the writing on the note McLean had peeled from the girl in the doghouse as Cinnamon's. Questioned by Deputy DA Mike McGuire, who had replaced Fredrickson on the case, Patti told of Cinnamon's escalating arguments with Linda over household duties. Then, noticeably trembling, she described "a silhouette" that had suddenly appeared in her room, fired a shot, and left. In very much the same manner she had adopted while telling her story to police on the night of the murder, Patti said she heard two more shots from the direction of Linda's room. Her testimony of what happened when David returned home was in some minor ways different from what she had told police.

Under Forgette's cross-examination, Patti said that for weeks before the shooting, Cinnamon had seemed depressed and moody.

Patti made a curious witness. She didn't understand many of the words used by both prosecutor and defense counsel. Her manner of speech was flat and monotonal. She had difficulty describing her own emotions and her expression was curiously blank. She was the opposite of animated, and this, despite her natural beauty, made her seem peculiarly plain.

Cinnamon did not understand much of what was going on. She had been told by David, many times, that because of her age the law would go easy on her. But she was living in Juvenile Hall and appearing in court when she wanted to be home with her family. And she did not truly comprehend that if found guilty of murder, she could be sentenced to life in prison.

Next, Kim Hicks testified about the notes she took from Cinnamon in the custodial ward. The medical student was able to shed a little more light on what had happened. Hicks's notes showed that after shooting Linda the first time, Cinnamon said she heard Linda cry out for help. She returned to Linda's room to shoot her again. Then, Cinnamon said, she waited about half an hour before going to the doghouse. She remembered losing control and urinating on herself. She remembered the sirens of police cars and ambulances as she lay in the doghouse.

Finally, Hicks testified that Cinnamon said she shot her stepmother because Linda had told her that she could no longer live with her father. And that when David heard the arguments, he left the house, saying that he couldn't take it anymore.

David, who had continually reassured his daughter of his love for her, did not testify. On the day he was scheduled, he sent word that he was too ill to come to court. His statements to police and district attorney's investigators were offered by stipulation—that is, the deputy DA read into the record David's previous statements, prefacing this with the explanation that if David had been called as a witness, he would have so testified.

Cinnamon understood little of this. Or that the effect of his stipulation was that her father agreed that his daughter was guilty of murdering Linda. But Brown, who had always used his "poor health" as a manipulative tool, had no intention of testifying against his daughter in open court. Had he done so, he would have risked losing his powerful control of Cinnamon's emotions—emotions that had already proved so useful.

Judge Fitzgerald found Cinnamon Brown guilty of murder in the first degree, murder with "premeditation and deliberation, with malice aforethought." He sentenced her to life in prison. In practice, this meant that she would remain in California Youth Authority (CYA) custody until she was twenty-five, at which time, if her case followed the usual pattern for juvenile murderers, she would be paroled. Case closed.

David Brown had replaced his twenty-three-year-old wife with a younger, compliant clone with a voluptuous, youthfully perfect body free from the effects of motherhood. He had removed from his household the only person who suspected that he and Patti had been secret lovers. And thanks to life insurance, he was much richer. David Brown had pulled off the perfect crime.

Almost.

One person was sure that even if Cinnamon had killed

Linda, she had not acted alone. One person whose gut told him that David was a liar and a fraud. One person not willing to forget Cinnamon in prison and Linda in her grave. One who would not—*could* not—let go of this case.

Jay Newell.

Newell had plenty to keep him busy. But whenever he had ten minutes, half an hour, or a morning, he continued to work on the baffling Brown case. Newell began by interviewing virtually everyone—wives, ex-wives, relatives, family friends—who knew David. He went to the archives where public records are kept and searched for references to David Brown.

In time, Newell learned that just three weeks after Cinnamon went off to prison, David bought a new house in Anaheim Hills, one of the area's most exclusive residential communities. The spacious, pseudo-Tudor sat on a grassy ridge, offering a magnificent view of Santiago Canyon. With its swimming pool, it cost David $330,000.

David had paid cash.

Newell dialed up the department of motor vehicles in Sacramento and asked for a computer printout on vehicles registered to David Brown. Between August 1985, when Cinnamon went behind bars, and the spring of 1988, David Brown bought a $60,000 motor home, a $70,000 Mercedes 560 convertible, a $30,000 Mercedes 190, two Ford Broncos, three Nissan Sentras, a Dodge pickup with a camper shell, Ford and Chevrolet station wagons—all together, fourteen expensive cars and trucks.

Newell, who had never met David face-to-face, began spending spare moments tailing him, maintaining detailed notebook records of everything David did and every place he went.

Research into David's credit history revealed a pattern. David had had his share of money troubles, including a lien for unpaid federal taxes. In 1983, however, two years before Linda's death, things improved. David made over $124,000 from his principal client, Randomex. In 1984, his income rose to over $170,000. If David had divorced Linda, under California's community property laws, she would have come away with half of a booming business.

Newell decided he wanted to meet David, to take his measure. But he proved a slippery target who zealously guarded his privacy. David never answered a door or a phone—his family always did this. And they always said David was unavailable—ill, away, or indisposed.

Newell kept up his watch, still stealing time from his other work. Beyond David's new affluence, one thing piqued Newell's curiosity: why did Patti continue to live with David? She was no longer related to him. Yet she always seemed to go with him when he left the house.

As Newell would eventually learn, control was the central issue in David's life. He controlled his family through money and with the threat that if he wasn't obeyed he'd leave. He manipulated them with hints that if he didn't get his way, his ulcers or his colitis or his "dormant" cancer would kick up—that he would leave through death. David reigned as sovereign in his household, a small but disciplined kingdom, the tight little Kingdom of Brown.

Patti Bailey, seventeen at the time she replaced Linda in David's household, was under David's tightest control. She did not go to school. She had no regular contact with people outside the Brown household. She rarely left the house alone or with anyone except David. He insisted that she wear a paging device at all times and "beeped" her constantly, often from the next room, to check on her whereabouts and activities. If she did leave the house to go to a store, David beeped her every few minutes, requiring her to phone immediately to report her location. At home, Patti used the phone only on a speaker or as David listened on an extension. She could speak to no one without his consent.

Patti was a prisoner. David's living love doll.

And even though she loved—and feared—David, the absence of freedom began to be a burden. By 1988 she would be looking in desperation to find out who she was, to get on with her life. And she would fail.

Visiting days at the California Youth Authority's Ventura School were alternate Saturdays. At first, David came as often as allowed, but as Cinnamon's imprisonment lengthened into years, his visits decreased. He kept his daughter's commissary account supplied with funds and allowed her to charge mail-order items to his credit card. But Cinnamon had no way to contact David directly. She could only write to his office or call his answering service. Eventually, her father would reply.

When they were together, however briefly, David seemed the loving father, laughing and joking and boasting and teasing, never mentioning Patti and promising, always, that he was "working" on getting Cinnamon out. He complained about his poor health and the constant demands on him from his family. To Cinnamon, it often seemed as if he had one foot in the grave.

That kind of talk terrified her. She worshipped her dad. If anything happened to him, what would become of her? How would she ever get out of jail?

In her isolation, Cinnamon did not know that her father had bought a magnificent new house and a fleet of pricey cars, that he was speculating in real estate. She did not know just how completely Patti had taken over Linda's role.

Cinnamon didn't even know that her father married Patti Bailey in Las Vegas on July 1, 1986. Or that just before that, Patti had signed the most draconian of prenuptial agreements. If they were to divorce, David would get everything except Patti's 1955 MG and the "future proceeds" of two personal-injury lawsuits stemming from dubious auto accidents she'd had while riding with David.

Even Newell didn't know that David had married Patti. Nor did any of the other Baileys. David had taken pains to falsify their marriage license application, thinking that he could, if necessary, deny that they had ever been legally married. No rings were exchanged. There was no announcement, no honeymoon. But it made Patti happy to know she was David's sixth wife, that he was, finally, all hers.

Cinnamon seemed to adjust very well to prison life. She went to school. The State of California had contracted with several airlines to staff a reservation center within the prison. Cinnamon worked there part-time as a reservations clerk and made a little money. She stayed well clear of the prison's gangs and factions. But she refused psychotherapy and group counseling. At periodic appearances before the parole board, she maintained that she could remember nothing of the events on the night of Linda's death.

But some things she told the parole board about her feelings seemed to contradict what she had told authorities earlier. So the parole board, through channels, asked Jay Newell to try to resolve these inconsistencies by interviewing Arthur Brown, Cinnamon's paternal grandfather.

After moving out of the rented Garden Grove house where Linda had died, David had taken his parents, Manuela and Arthur, into his new home.

Near the end of January 1987, Newell drove up to the Anaheim Hills house to see Arthur. As cover, he carried with him a business card identifying himself as a realtor. He suspected that the old man knew more about Linda's death than he'd ever said—and that he genuinely cared about Cinnamon. Even so, Arthur was very reluctant to talk with Newell. He refused to sit in the investigator's car. But finally, after an antsy game of cat and mouse, he told Newell that he was sure he knew who had planned Linda's death: Patti.

Patti had told David and Cinnamon, in Arthur's presence, that she had overheard Linda plotting David's death on the phone with her twin brother. They wanted him dead, said Patti, so Linda and Allen could steal his business. And Arthur heard Patti say *she* would get rid of Linda to save David.

Before Arthur could expand on this fascinating revelation, David appeared. With a look at Arthur, Newell offered David his "realtor" card. The old man didn't give him away.

So at last Newell talked to David Brown. It was brief and ostensibly about real estate. But even in this low-key encounter, Newell felt there was something very odd about David, something he had a hard time articulating. He just knew, somehow, that David Brown was evil.

That evening, Arthur told his son that the "real estate man" was actually an Orange County DA's investigator.

David cursed his father for a fool. He ordered Patti to burn their marriage certificate and prenuptial agreement in an outdoor barbecue. He tightened security. Now Patti was not allowed any contact with her family. She was not allowed to leave the house at any time.

Patti began to wonder if the magic had somehow left her marriage. So, the next month, she managed to get herself pregnant.

David was predictably furious. He liked Patti's body just as it was, girlishly firm and unblemished. He ordered her to get an abortion. For the first time in her life, she refused something David ordered. She would have the baby. It would be hers forever.

Patti's pregnancy posed a problem to David: Who was the father? David invented "Doug," a boy who drove a Camaro or maybe it was a TransAm and was of Greek ancestry. Doug had made Patti pregnant. Even when David had a florist send flowers with a card signed Doug, the Browns and the Baileys—when David told them—knew it was nonsense. David would never allow any boy to get near Patti. But such was his strange power over everyone in his kingdom that no one questioned aloud his latest absurdity. If he said Doug was the father of Patti's baby, then it was so.

By then, David Brown had complete control of his family. He had become the source of all good things for the Browns and Baileys. The last thing any of them wanted was David angry at them.

Patti bore David's third daughter, Heather, on September 29, 1987. David was so angry that he made Patti pay her own hospital bills with money she got from settling one of her lawsuits. By making herself into her dead sister's clone, Patti had unwittingly cut her strongest tie to David, who lusted only after Lolitas. When Patti, not yet twenty, acquired stretch marks, David began looking for her replacement. He also tried—unsuccessfully—to find an insurance company that would write a policy for several hundred thousand dollars on the infant's life.

Desperately unhappy after David continued to deny his

paternity, Patti made an ineffectual suicide attempt by slashing her wrists. She received minor scars and no sympathy.

With Data Recovery's reportable income topping the quarter-million mark, David decided that another change of scene was in order. He bought a larger property not far from the Anaheim Hills house. He moved his parents into its guesthouse so he had more privacy yet could maintain control.

Cinnamon was seventeen when Heather was born. Except for evading psychiatric examination and refusing group therapy, she was a model prisoner. But in denying any memory of Linda's death, she avoided accepting responsibility for her crime. Since such acknowledgment was required before parole, the California Youth Authority began to press her. In conversations with a psychiatrist, Cinnamon hinted that she was not responsible for the shooting, that she now was angry about being locked up, that she hated whoever was responsible for Linda's death.

It was a tantalizing clue. The doctor suspected that Cinnamon's amnesia was a sham and that she may actually have had little to do with the murder. Of all the Browns and Baileys, she had the least to gain from Linda's death, yet she had been the only one to suffer from it.

Reading Cinnamon's probation reports, Newell was frustrated. He wanted to talk to her but was legally prohibited from initiating contact until she turned eighteen. Until then, he needed a parent's permission.

Newell had begun to appreciate the control David exercised over his subjects. If, as Arthur Brown had whispered, Patti was responsible for Linda's murder, then David must also know. What sort of relationship did Patti and David have? It was the supreme question.

To prod Cinnamon, Newell took pictures of David Brown's princely new estate and of the "old" one in Anaheim Hills. He took prints to the Ventura School and gave them to Cinnamon's parole officer, explaining about the Browns' big houses, their expensive cars, their Las Vegas vacations. Cinnamon should be told about her family's new opulence, said Newell, and about her new half sister.

Newell went to see Brenda Sands, Cinnamon's mother.

She chased him away, convinced by David's propaganda that he was an enemy. But Newell returned, again and again, until Brenda told him something he didn't know: on the day of the murder, David had ordered Brenda to say that Cinnamon had been moody and difficult and threatened suicide.

Two weeks after turning eighteen, Cinnamon called Newell. She had something to say, she told him—but only if she could be sure of protection.

"Protection from what?" Newell asked.

"From my father," sobbed Cinnamon.

Newell convinced Cinnamon that her father would not be told about their conversation.

"He was in the wrong for what he did," said Cinnamon. "And I was too young to realize it. I know now that it's time for him to take the responsibility for the crime that's taken place. . . . I knew what was going to happen, but I didn't actually do the murder."

She explained that Patti and David had told her that Linda was planning to kill David for his insurance—or for his business—and that Linda's twin was in on it. And so, said Cinnamon, when David learned this, he told Patti and Cinnamon that *they* would have to get rid of Linda. Otherwise, he, David, would have to run for his life, abandon the family, abandon Cinnamon.

Cinnamon also reported that weeks before Linda's murder she saw David and Patti kissing. Not kissing like sister-in-law and brother-in-law, but kissing passionately.

Cinnamon recounted hearing endless discussions about how to kill Linda: forcing her out the door of the van while on the freeway, dropping an electrical appliance in her bath, poisoning her. David and Patti had talked about doing away with Linda for more than a year. But always the clear implication was that *Patti and Cinnamon* would have to do the actual killing. David just couldn't stand violence, couldn't stand the sight of blood.

Cinnamon said she had listened and worried. She loved Linda. She loved her father.

"What about the gun that killed Linda?" asked Newell.

"It was Linda's gun. Patti wiped it off with a towel after the shooting," said Cinnamon.

"Do you know Patti had a baby?" Cinnamon asked. "And that baby is my father's?"

Newell now realized that, to Cinnamon, that baby had been the ultimate betrayal. She could no longer deny the feelings she had suppressed for years. She loved her father, but she feared him. He had manipulated her, used and discarded her.

She had suffered enough for him. She hated him.

Newell and Dick Fredrickson, the deputy DA, discussed the phone call. Neither was convinced that Cinnamon had told everything. Both agreed it would be hard to reopen the case. Juries rarely convict on the basis of testimony from a convicted murderer. Just getting a judge to reopen the case would be difficult. The legal system does not like to tamper with matters it considers long settled. There had to be more evidence against David. Newell would have to find a sympathetic deputy DA who was willing to open this can of worms.

He found Jeoff Robinson, a dapper man of thirty-five who at the moment was responsible for prosecuting all homicides in Garden Grove, where Linda had died. Robinson was all but a living legend in the DA's office, a quick-thinking, hard-charging, but humorous man who knew how to win a jury's collective heart. The younger son of a wealthy, well-connected civil lawyer, he was totally committed to the ideal of justice. He loved fighting for the underdog. He worked carefully and seldom lost.

Newell had invested far too many years keeping this investigation alive to stop now. He had little difficulty selling Robinson on the idea of reopening the Brown case. But, said Robinson, he would do so only if Newell could bring him something more than Cinnamon's story. Something a defense attorney couldn't undermine with reasonable doubt. Something no jury—or his own boss—could possibly ignore.

It took three weeks to get the go-ahead. In that time, Newell sweet-talked Fred McLean's supervisor into putting him back on the case.

* * *

Almost three years after the day she was confined to the CYA's Ventura School, Jay Newell and Fred McLean sat down with Cinnamon. The pudgy little fourteen-year-old had become a slender, beautiful young woman who knew how to use clothing and makeup to exquisite effect. The detectives explained that they could not offer her anything in exchange for the truth. It was entirely up to her to decide if she wanted to talk.

It was what she wanted more than anything except her freedom.

Adding considerable detail, Cinnamon told essentially the same story she had told Newell on the telephone. During a seven-month period before the murder, in Cinnamon's presence, Patti and David had frequently discussed ways to kill Linda. This talk about killing had confused and frightened her. At first she thought it was one of her father's practical jokes—until he vehemently set her straight. "Just believe me. I'm your father. I know [Linda] is trying to kill me."

Cinnamon thought of Linda as a second mother. Yet she loved her father even more and was afraid of his temper. She had shuttled back and forth between parents for most of her life, and whenever David complained of poor health or talked about having to leave for good, Cinnamon became fearful that he might abandon her altogether.

She needed someone to talk to about all these things. But she knew if she told her mother, Brenda, it would all get back to her father. So she said nothing.

Then Patti began telling Cinnamon, "I heard them again. They said they were going to kill your father."

Why, Cinnamon asked her father, didn't he just *divorce* Linda?

"She'd still kill me. For the Process. To get my business."

Day after day, week after week, month after month, David and Patti told Cinnamon that killing Linda was the only way out. In time, Cinnamon's fear that her beloved father might actually leave became her dominant feeling. She could face almost anything but losing him. It was the Big Lie, repeated over and over by the most important figure in her life. She had been isolated from everyone outside the household, deprived of any frame of reference except her father's twisted value system, her malleable mind was molded to fit David's paradigm.

After seven months of this, Cinnamon agreed to help. Still, she hoped and wished that her father's problems would just go away. She didn't want to kill Linda.

About a month before the murder, David and Patti took Cinnamon along to a chiropractic appointment. On the way, David said, "We have to get rid of Linda as soon as possible. She's going to kill me soon. We can't delay it anymore."

Cinnamon wasn't sure she could go through with it, so David threw in the clincher. "If you love me, you'll trust me. Just believe what I say. I'm your father. I know what's best."

Neither Newell nor McLean had ever heard of anything so evil, so twisted. They struggled to control their emotions.

David asked Cinnamon to shove Linda out the door of their van while they were on the freeway. He would leave the door loosely latched, but Cinnamon had to be the one to push Linda.

Cinnamon refused, saying she wasn't strong enough.

"Then you *don't* love your father—otherwise you wouldn't have any hesitation. You'd go do it," said Patti.

David's plan to kill Linda inched inexorably forward. The weekend of St. Patrick's Day, he bundled the whole family in their van for a trip to the mountains, where he planned to have Cinnamon shoot Linda. But after hours on the road, darkness approached and Linda insisted that David head home. He had meekly complied.

The next night, Linda died in her own bed.

Finally, Cinnamon told Newell and McLean what had happened on the night of March 19. After dinner and a card game, Linda took a shower. While she was in the bathroom David joined Patti and Cinnamon in the living room. "We have to do it. Any day now, she can kill me. Do you want her to kill me? It has to be done!" he whispered. "Cinnamon, if you *really* love me, you'll do it."

Several days earlier, under David's guidance, Cinnamon

had written several notes. Now David selected one and told her to destroy the others.

When Linda went to bed, David joined her. It left Cinnamon thinking that somehow the miracle had happened and she wouldn't have to kill her stepmother. She went to sleep in a trundle bed that slid out from under Patti's bed. Patti retired, too, and turned out the lights.

About two o'clock, David came into their room and awakened them. "Come with me," he told Cinnamon. He took her to the kitchen and told her to get a glass of water. Then he took out three bottles of pills.

"Take these," he said.

"Why?"

"I want it to look like you tried to kill yourself, in case it doesn't go through tonight."

Cinnamon didn't want the pills, but when David insisted, she dutifully swallowed the capsules from all three vials. They were more than enough to kill her.

On her father's orders, Cinnamon went to the larger of the two doghouses. Dizzy and nauseated, she curled up on the floor. Later she heard David leave in his car. Still later, she heard the shots. More time passed. Then David appeared at the doghouse and said, "Remember what I told you before, you're not going to get in trouble. If they ask, *you* did it."

When Cinnamon was in the hospital recovering from her overdose, David told her that her lawyer said "it's not a good idea to remember" the night of the shooting. And so she developed amnesia, and until this interview had never spoken about the killing again.

The detectives doubted that Al Forgette would ever have suggested amnesia. That wasn't his style; he was an ethical attorney who never bent the rules. But David bent rules whenever it suited him.

Newell asked Cinnamon why she'd decided to talk. Her answer was that her father had lied to her—about fathering Patti's baby, about being too sick to visit her, about sending Patti away after Cinnamon went to jail. And as she had slowly unraveled these lies, noting her thoughts in a journal, Cinnamon began to realize that her father had lied to her about *everything*.

Later, when Newell and McLean had a chance to discuss Cinnamon's shocking story, they wondered if she had told them everything. And if it was the truth. There was a way to find out.

Two days later, Cinnamon—sounding panicked—summoned her father to the Ventura School. The parole board said she would have to stay in prison at least four and possibly seven more years unless she gave them details of Linda's murder.

Sitting with her on the lawn beneath shady trees, David played the tired old record that always worked: things were terrible at home, his health was failing, he was in terrible pain, he was working hard on getting her out. He couldn't believe she'd have to spend so many years in custody for her crime.

Cinnamon, a wireless transmitter concealed beneath the voluminous folds of her oversized sweatshirt, kept trying to get David to tell her exactly *why* Linda had had to die. Once again David spun a web of lies. Linda and her twin had tried to kill him because the Mafia wanted his business. They wanted it because he alone knew the Process, essential to recovering the government's most important secrets. The space shuttle. Secret Pentagon projects. The Stealth bomber. The Mafia wanted the Process so bad they'd kill him for it. Unless she wanted to be responsible for her father's death, said David, Cinnamon was to keep her mouth shut and never talk about the night Linda died.

Cinnamon didn't seem to buy the Mafia angle. So David changed the reason. The *real* reason was that Linda had wanted to kick Cinnamon out. That's why she was moved to the trailer. And her mother, Brenda, had refused to allow her to come back. And of course, Linda wanted Patti gone, too.

No, said Cinnamon. Her mom was glad to have her. She'd gone to the trailer because Patti would no longer share a room.

Okay, said David. If Cinnamon absolutely had to get out

of prison, Patti would confess to the crime and take her place.

"But why can't you just tell the truth," Cinnamon begged.

"Oh no," said David. "Tell the truth and go to jail."

There it was. If David told the truth, David was in jail.

As Newell and McLean, concealed behind a window a few yards away, recorded the conversation, David spoke about how bad Patti felt about Linda's death. He renewed his offer to have Patti take her place.

Cinnamon obliquely suggested that perhaps he could take her place.

"I wouldn't stay here a week," said David. "I'd find some way to kill myself."

David now said that Patti had moved out of his house. A lie—and Cinnamon knew it. He said that if Cinnamon hadn't killed Linda, then his father, Arthur, would have.

Cinnamon wanted to talk about Heather, Patti's daughter. David squirmed. Cinnamon asked who the baby's father was. Patti "wasn't sure," said David, but he thought it was some guy named Doug.

When Cinnamon asked flat out if he was Heather's father, David indignantly denied it.

Then she asked her father about Linda's insurance. David went into a meandering, complicated explanation, the gist of which was that when Linda died, the insurance company canceled all her policies.

Cinnamon knew better.

Before their long, painfully convoluted conversation was over, David was insisting that he had begged Cinnamon *not* to kill Linda. And since he now understood that Cinnamon hadn't actually killed her, it had to have been Patti. So now he was terrified that Patti might kill *him*.

It was an incredible performance by a man who told his biggest lies immediately after saying "honest," or "honest to God"—and he used those phrases constantly. By the time David left, Cinnamon knew for the first time just how casually and completely her father had sold her down the river. And the detectives were, for the first time, convinced that he had used mind control as an instrument of murder.

Two week later, Cinnamon sat with Patti and David beneath the same trees, on the same lawn, with the same wireless microphone taped between her breasts. Cinnamon tried several times to get Patti to name Heather's father. Patti or David changed the subject every time until Patti refused to discuss it. They did, however, discuss various stories for Cinnamon to try on the parole board.

To the detectives listening in, it was a virtuoso performance by a master manipulator. David could get Patti to agree to anything he said. He constantly reinvented history, creating fictitious scenarios calculated to confuse Cinnamon, trying to get her so mixed up that she would no longer know the truth.

Failing, David again trotted out his carload of illnesses, his liver problems, his fading memory, playing on his daughter's sympathy.

Cinnamon *knew* Heather was her father's child. Boldly asserting this, she gave Patti the chance to contradict it. Patti didn't do so. In a momentary lapse, she acknowledged that she loved David and still lived with him.

That wouldn't do. David slowly maneuvered Patti into changing that story. She loved David, as a daughter might. She had moved to Oregon and was raising Heather on her own. She was just visiting for a few days.

Cinnamon again asked about Linda's insurance. This time David said there had been a payout—$175,000—but it had gone to Krystal, Linda's daughter. Data Recovery was doing so well that he didn't even need the insurance money.

Before the afternoon was over, David had said that Linda tried to poison him. That he really wasn't sure now *who* actually killed Linda. Maybe it was her brother Allen. Or her brother Larry. Or his father, Arthur. When Patti moved out of earshot, David said she might well have been the one.

Back in their Orange County office, Newell and Jeoff Robinson listened to the incredible tapes, over and over.

There seemed no doubt that Heather was David's. Now they had a motive for Linda's murder: lust. With Linda out of the way, Patti could have the man she'd always desired. With Linda gone, David could have a new, unspoiled body. And a second motive: money. It didn't take McLean long to turn up four life-insurance policies on Linda, each indicating that it was the only such policy.

With two motives, Cinnamon's confession, the taped conversations, and the fruits of two investigator's work, DA Robinson felt there was enough evidence to get a judge to reopen the case.

Arrest warrants for David and Patti were issued on September 21, 1988. There were two charges: murder and conspiracy to commit murder. At twenty minutes before seven the next morning, Newell, McLean, and two uniformed Anaheim officers arrested David and Patti.

Patti denied ever having had a sexual relationship with David and couldn't remember even kissing him. She said she didn't remember much about the night Linda died and knew nothing about a plot to kill David. To refresh her memory, Newell played excerpts from the tape where David said that Patti had killed Linda and might kill him next. Another excerpt revealed David's offer to have Patti take Cinnamon's place behind bars. When Newell accused her of trying to kill Cinnamon with pills the night of the murder, Patti refused to answer further questions without her lawyer present.

David, however, was sure he could explain away anything. As the video camera rolled he paraded his "recollections" to Newell and McLean. He began by bragging about his sex life with Linda, offering titillating tidbits in the most graphic terms.

Arthur Brown was questioned but not arrested. He said he was sure Patti had killed Linda, and that his son could never be capable of something like that.

Late in October, Newell and McLean decided to go back to Ventura to interview Cinnamon again. Before doing so, Newell telephoned to explain that since her testimony would be the key to convicting David and Patti, if she lied about *anything* on the witness stand, the defense would use that to undermine all her testimony. And so he wanted to know if she had told him everything, and if it was all the truth.

"I was ashamed," said Cinnamon. "I couldn't tell you the

whole truth. I just couldn't say it. . . . I was the one who actually pulled the trigger."

Under California law anyone who aids, abets, instigates, or encourages murder bears equal guilt with the one who pulled the trigger. So, as Newell explained to Cinnamon two days later in Ventura, if David had orchestrated Linda's murder, he was as guilty as anyone else. What he needed now was the whole chronology, with as many details as Cinnamon could remember. She went back through the story, changing or adding a few things. After David had selected one of the suicide notes, he and Patti had spoken together so softly that she could not hear. In the kitchen, after she had swallowed all the pills, David had insisted that upon shooting Linda, Cinnamon was to shoot *herself* in the head. But just a nick. Enough to look like she'd tried to kill herself.

Terrified, she'd refused to shoot herself. Finally, David relented. The medication she'd already taken would have to do for the suicide "attempt."

David said he was going to leave the house, and when he came back he expected Linda to be dead. Just before leaving, he gave Cinnamon a pillow and told her to put it over the gun when she fired. To muffle the noise, he explained.

David had another whispered conference with Patti, then left. A few minutes later, when Cinnamon wandered back to her bedroom, Patti was wiping a .38 revolver with a towel. She handed Cinnamon the gun and showed her where to put the pillow when she fired.

One of them cocked the hammer back—Cinnamon couldn't remember whether she did it or if Patti had.

"Daddy said to go in. Just go in and do it," said Patti. "Fire the gun."

Huge, hot tears slid down Cinnamon's cheeks as she told Newell about accepting the revolver from Patti.

She couldn't remember how she got from her room to Linda's. She remembered only standing in front of the bed, holding the gun out, pulling the trigger. A deafening noise had filled the room. Blinding flame exploded from the gun.

Somehow, the pillow got stuck in the gun's action. Cin-

namon rushed back to Patti's room. The baby, awakened by
the shot, was howling in Patti's arms. With the infant between them, the teenagers struggled with the gun, trying to
pull the pillow free.

It went off a second time, the bullet missing the baby by
inches, lodging in the wall above Patti's bed. Then Patti and
Cinnamon heard a low sound coming from Linda's room. It
was frightening, inhuman, animalistic. *Linda.*

Cinnamon, cradling the baby, watched Patti cock the
hammer back on the pistol. Then Patti took the baby and
gave Cinnamon the gun. Patti told her to go back and shoot
Linda again.

The room was dark and silent when she entered for the
last time, recalled Cinnamon. She pointed and fired the .38
for a third time.

Finally it was clear to Newell. David's plan for the perfect crime was for his beloved daughter to shoot his beloved wife, then take her own life out of remorse. But
Cinnamon had refused to put a gun to her own head. She
had vomited up many of the pills and got medical attention
just in time. She had escaped David's mind control. When
he stopped visiting his daughter regularly, when he could
no longer command her emotions, she had regained domin-
ion of her own will. Now she would testify against her father for his repulsive acts.

While he was being held in the Orange County jail,
David Brown launched a relentless letter campaign to keep
Patti from testifying against him. He sent more than fifty
letters, writing as often as three times a day, each missive
a manipulative masterpiece, designed to punch all Patti's
buttons. The letters were reconstruction work, frantic repairs to the skein of smooth lies that David had woven
around Patti since she was a very young child. And all
were designed to keep her quiet.

David also wrote Patti letters from Doug, the mythical
father of her child. It was his worst mistake. By continuing
to deny that Heather was his child, David exposed all his
promises as hollow, his claims of undying love as lies.

Denying that he was Heather's father was, to Patti, the

ultimate betrayal. It was proof that she and David had no future together.

Eight days after Cinnamon told Newell the truth, Patti, represented by her own lawyer, Don Rubright, sat down in Newell's office. She was under no compulsion from the state to talk. At that moment, the only testimony against her came from a convicted murderess. Few juries would have convicted her on that alone. But Patti was ready to talk.

She told Newell of dozens of conversations she and David had about killing Linda, many of them years before Cinnamon was involved. She said David had tried to get her to kill Linda. He had invented the mythical threat from Linda and the Mafia. When she was eleven, Patti said, David had bought her from her mother for $10,000, the amount Ethel Bailey might have made had Patti been forced to work as a prostitute. Life in the Brown family had been much like life in a bizarre cult—David decided what everyone thought and said and did. David had decided that as long as Linda lived, she was a threat to the family's happiness, Patti stated.

She told Newell that David had started kissing her when she was four or five years old. At eleven, she was performing fellatio. It happened in every family, David had explained, and it was both necessary and completely normal. Unless Patti regularly swallowed his sperm, he insisted, she would never begin menstruating or grow breasts like her older sisters. When, true to his predictions, her menses flowed and her breasts budded, Patti knew that David was the only man she'd ever want. When she was fifteen, he had insisted on sex.

Finally, Patti confirmed for Newell virtually every detail of Cinnamon's account of the events of the night of March 19, 1985.

On December 19, 1988, David was brought to court for a preliminary hearing. Cinnamon testified, laying out the whole story she had told to Newell and McLean. Then Patti testified, confirming what Cinnamon had said.

On Christmas Day, David decided that the carrot would no longer work on Patti. That left only the stick. And he decided that he could no longer tolerate the trouble and in-conveniences brought upon him by Jay Newell and Jeoff Robinson. So he hired a hit on all three.

The intended instrument of their destruction was an un-likely fellow. Richard Steinhart was thirty-five when he met David Brown. He was in jail as a material witness in a case involving murder, counterfeiting, and a motorcycle gang. Steinhart was six feet tall, with massive arms and shoul-ders, tattoos everywhere, and a carefully tended mustache and goatee. He was a martial-arts master, a professional bodyguard and bouncer, a smuggler, a dope dealer. He cheerfully admitted to a thousand-dollar-a-day cocaine habit, snorting $500,000 worth of coke in twelve years.

Money talks, even in jail. David let it be known that he was rich and that he would pay. Since Steinhart was a man of great physical presence—everything David could never be—David admired him as much as he could anyone but himself. He hired Steinhart to arrange for Patti's jailhouse murder and to personally kill Newell and Robinson. Finally, Steinhart would engineer David's escape during a visit to the prison dentist.

Through his brother and attorney, David converted some of his assets to cash, which were passed to the hired killer. After Steinhart took David's money, they spent hours dis-cussing intricate plans for the three murders. When Steinhart was released from jail, the conspiracy continued during dozens of phone conversations. David discussed each murder in detail on a pay phone surrounded by jail guards.

About a week after his release, Steinhart called David to report that he'd put bullets in the heads of both Newell and Robinson. David was ecstatic. Now only Patti's life stood in the way of his own freedom.

But the killings never happened. It was all an elaborate sting. Despite his fearsome appearance and appreciation of physical confrontation, despite the fact that he was one of the toughest men in the Orange County jail, Steinhart was no killer. Learning that a jailhouse snitch had overheard Da-vid talking about the murders, Steinhart went to the author-ities, who set him up with everything he needed to make

David think the murder plot was proceeding as scheduled. In reality, all Steinhart's dealings with David were observed and recorded by Newell and other police officers.

Steinhart got little for his testimony and cooperation except salve for his conscience. He had been placed in protective custody only as a material witness in an unrelated case, but after discovering that he was HIV-positive and probably hadn't long to live, he'd decided to help authorities because it was the right thing to do.

In addition to the murder and conspiracy charges he faced, David Brown was charged with three counts of attempted murder, and with conspiracy to commit murder.

After many delays, David's trial began on April 30, 1990. Patti testified. Steinhart testified. But only after Cinnamon testified about the pills David had forced her to swallow did she realize the whole story: as badly as he had wanted his wife dead, David Brown had also meant to kill his daughter.

Finally, Cinnamon knew the truth.

Patti Bailey Brown pleaded guilty to murder and conspiracy and was sentenced to life in prison. She joined Cinnamon at the CYA's Ventura School. If Patti is handled like most juvenile offenders, she can expect to remain incarcerated until her twenty-fifth birthday. Her daughter, Heather, is being raised by Patti's brother and sister-in-law, Rick and Mary Bailey.

David Brown was convicted on all counts. Because prosecutors had not sought the death penalty, he was sentenced to life in prison without possibility of parole. In handing down his sentence, Judge Donald McCartin expressed concerns for his own safety. "You're a scary person . . . you don't *look* like Charlie Manson . . . but . . . even Manson didn't use *family*. You're a master manipulator. I believe the circumstances of this case are unbelievable . . . if Cinnamon had gone under, you would have walked away. Mr. Brown, you make Charlie Manson look like a piker."

After more than a year of letters, reports, and phone calls to the parole board from Newell and Robinson, Cinnamon Brown, age twenty-one, was paroled in February 1992. "The real story is the courage of this ... fourteen-year-old kid who was completely brainwashed for ... years by her father, who herself has been the victim of terrible crimes, and has now paid her debt to society, maybe even more of a debt than she should have," said Robinson on the day of her release. "Yet her battle will be a very, very tough one, because [she is] a girl who has been marked as a killer for ... life."

And what of the Process, the fabled fluid that David Brown convinced his family was a national treasure? Data Recovery is still in business, still using the Process, and a steady stream of income still flows to David Brown in his prison cell. And by the way, the Process is nothing more than Liquid Ivory Soap.

David Brown concocted a scheme frightening in its diabolical duplicity. He was willing to sacrifice anyone for his own gratification, and he had perfected the black art of mind control to insulate himself from blame.

Brown failed to commit a perfect crime because of two things he couldn't predict or control: Jay Newell's blood-hound instincts and Cinnamon's lucky escape from the pills intended to silence her forever.

# Copycat Killer
# (1986)

**S**UPPOSE THAT A KILLER, IDENTITY UNKNOWN, IS ON THE *loose, his or her exploits chronicled in sensational newspaper headlines and lurid television soundbites.*

*Now suppose that you wish someone dead. If you can mimic the well-publicized techniques of the mystery killer, you stand a good chance that authorities will consider your crime another in a series by the same at-large killer. So even if the murderer is caught, even if he denies your crime while admitting his, you stand a good chance of getting away with murder.*

*This is, of course, always harder in real life than in fiction. Always sensitive to the possibility of false confessions—to say nothing of copycats—police in most sensational cases withhold a few crucial details of most crimes. If demented publicity seekers come forward to confess, they must be able to tell police all the telltale signs that mark each crime. And when similar crimes occur but lack these unpublicized details, police usually have a good idea that there is more than one suspect on the loose.*

*Of course, there's always a chance that the crime is simple in execution, with few peculiarities. In that case, police may not suspect when a copycat prowls the community. . . .*

Crammed into skintight dresses, wearing lots of makeup, and heavy into hair care, Stella Nickell barhopped around

Seattle's many saloons and watering holes. By 1986, she was past forty—and a grandmother. Her husband had quit drinking and spent most of his time moping around the house or watching TV. Stella was bored, bored to death, and she could foresee an old age where money would be scarce and men hard to come by.

Stella had always been poor—but she had rarely lacked a man's company. She was born into poverty in a small town near Portland, Oregon, in 1943. In high school, if she wasn't precisely the town tramp, Stella had little trouble making friends with the opposite sex. By sixteen, she was married and a mom.

With her husband and daughter, Stella moved to Southern California and reinvented herself. After bearing a second daughter, she shed her husband, a few pounds, and many of her remaining inhibitions. In 1969, she was convicted of felonious assault on her nine-year-old daughter, Cynthia. By 1971, she had been convicted twice for forgery.

Stella later moved to Washington State, and in 1976, she married Bruce Nickell. He was a hard-drinking, free-spending man who, when he worked, earned a modest blue-collar paycheck for operating heavy equipment.

A few years after their marriage, Bruce went on the wagon. By 1981, he was employed by the State of Washington, not making a lot of money, often working only a few days a week for the highway maintenance department.

Just about then, Cynthia, now a stunning redhead of twenty-two years, divorced her husband and with her young child moved into a cramped mobile home with her mother, sister, and stepfather. Stella's elderly mother lived next door and required daily attention.

As money became tighter than ever, Stella began to dream about life without Bruce. The only trouble with this, she realized, was that his paychecks would stop, too. Life without her husband would be so much easier, Stella decided, if some serious money could come her way. Enough money, she dreamed, to buy the land under their mobile home and start a business. She'd always dreamed of opening a pet store specializing in exotic tropical fish. But it would never happen if she had to depend on what Bruce brought home in his paychecks.

Stella hadn't had much formal education, but she could read well enough and knew where to find the kind of information that might help resolve her dilemma. For five years, she systematically browsed through public libraries in and around Auburn, her suburban Seattle home. She learned about naturally occurring poisons in the foxglove plant, hemlock, and deadly nightshade.

Stella began cultivating foxglove. When the pretty purple flowers had withered to seed pods, she harvested the deadly kernels and put them in Bruce's food.

She must have miscalculated, however, because the seeds did little but put Bruce to sleep soon after he had ingested them. He awoke the next morning feeling refreshed and hungry.

Stella returned to the library.

Attending alcohol-abuse recovery therapy with Bruce, Stella learned that recovering alcoholics often turn to even more addictive substances when they fall off the wagon. And so she began an informal study of literature describing the toxic effects of cocaine, heroin, and methamphetamines, looking for what might be a lethal dose. She considered the odds that police would suppose that Bruce had simply taken an overdose.

Bruce's life was insured for $31,000 by the State of Washington. If he died accidentally, the payout would increase by an additional $105,000. Considering the risks of murder, this was not quite enough to suit Stella. In the autumn of 1985, she took out two $20,000 life insurance policies on Bruce that listed her as sole beneficiary.

In the spring of 1986, national news attention was briefly riveted on the Chicago area, where the families of seven people who had died of poisoning in 1982 settled suits with McNeil Consumer Products, Inc., a division of giant Johnson & Johnson. All the victims had ingested Tylenol tablets that had been laced with cyanide. The deaths were part of a frightening, widely publicized product-tampering incident. While the tamperers were never convicted, it was known that they had purchased boxes of Tylenol, an over-the-counter painkiller, carefully opening them to remove individual capsules. Cyanide was substituted for granules of painkiller, and the boxes returned to the shelves.

Who may have benefited from these murders, or how, may never be known. Some in law enforcement have speculated that the poisonings were part of a far-reaching scheme to make money in the stock market. After authorities traced the poisonings to Tylenol, the price of Johnson & Johnson stock declined in anticipation of reduced sales and of the heavy expense associated with settlement of damage claims.

A lengthy investigation failed to produce anyone who substantially profited from selling Johnson & Johnson stock short just before the poisonings. Simultaneous investigations turned up no credible suspects who might have had a grudge against the manufacturer of Tylenol. Nor did authorities find anyone who appeared to have significant motives for killing any of the Tylenol victims.

It was a perfect crime.

Publicity surrounding the settlement of lawsuits brought by survivors gave Stella her grand idea: Why not poison Bruce with a cyanide-laced Tylenol tablet? That way, she could not only collect his insurance but also attempt a lawsuit and, perhaps, come away with even more money.

Her first problem was that Bruce didn't use Tylenol; he preferred Excedrin, a competing product. A second problem was that since the Tylenol poisonings, most over-the-counter analgesic manufacturers had taken steps to ensure that their products were far less vulnerable to tampering.

Nevertheless, Stella believed she had a workable plan. She purchased rat poison, which contained lethal quantities of cyanide, and put some of it into Excedrin capsules in a bottle Bruce kept in a kitchen cabinet.

And then she waited.

On June 5, 1986, Bruce Nickell came home from work complaining of a headache. He headed for the kitchen and his appointment with death. He took four tablets—twice the recommended dose of this painkiller, and several times a lethal dose of cyanide—and swallowed them with a little water. A short time later, in obvious discomfort, he went outside. Stella was in the kitchen when Bruce called from their patio.

"Babe?"

"What do you want?" said Stella.

"I feel like I'm going to pass out," said Bruce.

Then he went down.

Stella called paramedics. Bruce was put on a helicopter and whisked to Harborview Medical Center in Seattle.

Claiming that she was "too upset," Stella stayed well away from Harborview for several hours, until Bruce died without regaining consciousness.

When Bruce collapsed, Stella's daughter, Cynthia, immediately suspected her mother of murder. After all, Stella had been discussing Bruce's demise for almost five years. But when Cynthia gave her mother a searching look, Stella shook her head. "I know what you're thinking," she said. "And the answer is no."

Neither the doctors at Harborview nor the coroner detected the presence of cyanide in Bruce's body. The King County Medical Examiner's official report stated that the cause of death was "pulmonary emphysema."

Stella had rid herself of her husband and was about to become $71,000 richer. No one—except, maybe, Cynthia—suspected a thing. She had committed the perfect crime.

Stella didn't see things quite that way.

From her point of view, she was not on the verge of being $71,000 richer. Instead, she was rendered $105,000 *poorer* because the coroner had called Bruce's death "natural." The insurance company wouldn't make the additional "accidental death" payout.

Stella wanted that extra money. She believed she was actually entitled to it—after all, it was absolutely true that Bruce had died, not from natural causes, but from accidentally selecting some of the poisoned capsules that were in his bottle of extra-strength Excedrin. But she couldn't very well tell the insurance company that she had planted the poison.

The more Stella thought about it, the more obvious it became that police would have to believe there was a murderer stalking Seattle's drugstore shelves. Someone else had to die from a cyanide-laced painkiller. So, tempting fate, she set into motion phase two of her plan. Stella made the rounds of supermarkets and drugstores to bring home several boxed bottles of extra-strength Excedrin and Anacin-3.

The result of Stella's tampering was a collection of containers with broken or missing seals. Even the outer boxes were crudely glued and repaired. However, she got the cyanide into the capsules and the reboxed painkillers back on the shelves of three stores without being caught.

One of these was purchased by Susan Snow, who lived about a dozen miles from the Nickells. She bought a bottle of extra-strength Excedrin and put it in her bathroom medicine cabinet.

The poisoned capsules were there very early on the morning of June 11, 1986, when Susan's husband, Paul Webking, forty-five, got ready to go to work. Webking, suffering from arthritis, had the habit of taking two extra-strength Excedrin every day.

He was lucky. The two capsules he swallowed were the real thing—pure painkiller.

Susan, who customarily rose shortly before six each morning, had the same routine; she also took two Excedrin. She took the over-the-counter medicine because it contained caffeine; she liked the little jolt it gave her.

Susan Snow was forty years old, a high school dropout who had quit an early marriage and turned her life around. Through many years of hard work, Snow had risen to the position of assistant vice-president of the Puget Sound National Bank.

Like Stella Nickell, Susan was the mother of two, a grown daughter from her first marriage and a teenager. Unlike Stella, Susan had kept her girl-next-door good looks, her cheerleader's figure, and a blithe optimism about her future.

Her daughter, Hayley, fifteen, found Susan, unconscious, on the bathroom floor. She was still alive when paramedics wheeled her into a hospital emergency room. But Susan was brain-dead; six hours after taking the capsules, her husband tearfully agreed to take her off a respirator. She died almost immediately.

Exactly as Stella had hoped, the King County Medical Examiner's staff found the cyanide in the two Excedrin capsules Susan took. The coroner's report received wide attention in Seattle media.

Stella still could have gotten away with murder—in fact, *two* murders. But blinded by greed, she was far past a rational examination of her situation. Several days after Susan's death, she contacted the coroner's office. She wasn't sure it meant anything, she said, but she now recalled that her late husband had taken extra-strength Excedrin just before he had died.

Since the death had been classified as a result of natural causes, the medical examiner had not retained tissue samples from Bruce Nickell. His body, buried only weeks earlier, was exhumed and tested for cyanide. The results, of course, were positive.

Investigators pawed through Nickell's mobile home and came away with two bottles of poisoned Excedrin, one unopened.

Now there were two victims of product tampering. Fanned by rapt media attention, panic swept King County. Thousands of frightened people ransacked their homes and threw out every sort of painkiller on the chance that someone might have tampered with them. Public-safety officials asked retailers to remove all over-the-counter painkillers from their shelves. As storekeepers hurriedly complied, two more bottles with cyanide-filled capsules were found in supermarkets.

That encouraged Susan Snow's widower, Paul Webking, to file a wrongful-death suit against Bristol-Meyers, manufacturer of Excedrin.

Not long after this, Stella Nickell found a lawyer who supposed that she, too, might have a good case against Bristol-Meyers. Like Webking's, her suit asserted that Bristol-Meyers was negligent in its packaging and had continued to market a product they knew was "easily tampered with, opened, or otherwise contaminated." Stella sought unspecified damages for the company's role in Bruce's death.

Product tampering is among the most difficult of crimes to solve. In most cases, the victim is unknown to the perpetrator. Unless there is some attempt at extortion, the poisoner's motives are unclear. And up to the time Susan Snow was murdered, no one had ever been convicted of this crime. Nevertheless, the police began their careful, labor-intensive investigation.

FBI Director William Webster worried about a nationwide panic. He also told an associate that he worried about copycat poisoners springing up in other parts of the country.

Copycat crimes have been around for ages. Experts on Victorian-era crime give serious consideration, for example, to the notion that some of the murders imputed to Jack the Ripper were actually committed by others who had read complete descriptions of the first murder in London newspapers.

Since the advent of mass media, copycat crimes have become even more common. When the crime is especially sensational, even people in distant countries will read about, see, or hear the most lurid details. Almost inevitably, copycat criminals emerge and adopt the widely disseminated modus operandi as their own. Sometimes the attention focused on the mystery perpetrator brings forth people who confess in order to bask in the glow of publicity.

Mindful of all this, FBI Chief Webster dispatched twenty-five special agents to the Seattle area. Eventually, the joint FBI, Seattle, and Auburn police task force numbered eighty-five.

Authorities soon determined that the chemical "fingerprints" of poison molecules found in both victims' bodies were identical. Further laboratory work confirmed that they also matched poison found in all five recovered containers. Police and FBI agreed that all the poison came from a single source.

In any murder investigation, among the first questions police seek to answer is "Who benefits from these deaths?"

Officials of the U.S. Securities and Exchange Commission pored over the records of millions of transactions, but could find no one who had profited from the sharp, temporary dip in Bristol-Meyers's stock prices.

Paul Webking, a truck driver, had been married to Susan Snow only a short time. He stood to gain from her insurance, and possibly from a settlement from Bristol-Meyers. Webking was asked to submit to a polygraph examination. He agreed, and the results were conclusive: he had no idea who had put the cyanide in her Excedrin, or why.

Despite repeated police requests, Stella steadfastly refused to take a polygraph exam. That lack of cooperativeness interested Auburn Police Chief Jake Evans. He also found it fascinating that of only five known tampered painkiller bottles, *two* had turned up in Stella's house.

It did not take much police work to discover the two insurance policies that Stella had taken out on her husband just a few months before his death.

Suddenly suspicion focused on Stella Nickell.

Stella held firm, but on the advice of her lawyer, she agreed to take the polygraph test. The examiner's conclusion was that her answers were "deceptive." And yet there was no hard evidence against Stella. There was nothing but suspicious circumstances.

The police/FBI investigation ground on. Bristol-Meyers, clearly worried about its image and about the possibility of an endless stream of wrongful-death suits, joined with other over-the-counter painkiller manufacturers and put up a reward. They promised $300,000 to anyone providing information that led to the arrest and conviction of the "Excedrin Poisoner."

Three hundred thousand dollars proved to be exactly the amount of money required to jiggle Cynthia's memory. Or perhaps it was her conscience. Or maybe it wasn't the money at all. Maybe Cynthia really did wish, as she would tell police and the press, "to do the right thing."

In January 1987, some nineteen years after her mother beat her unmercifully, Cynthia went to the FBI. She regaled them with a long, convoluted tale about Stella's oft-expressed wish for Bruce's death. And she told them about her mother's fruitless attempts to poison Bruce with foxglove.

Stella was indicted by a federal grand jury, the first person brought to trial under a 1983 product-tampering statute. Her trial began in 1988, with Cynthia as the key witness.

"I knew she was capable of it," said Cynthia, wiping

away tears. "But when it's your own mother, you don't want to believe she could."

Stella was convicted of causing death by product tampering, the first person ever so adjudged. "These were crimes of exceptional callousness and cruelty," said Judge William Dwyer.

He ignored her lawyer's pleas for "a sentence that would allow some hope," and gave her ninety years. Stella Nickell will be eligible for parole in 2018.

Stella never collected a cent of her husband's insurance. And yet she had committed a perfect crime. Had this killer's intelligence not been overmatched by her greed, she might very well have collected $71,000—enough to start a business and a new life.

All seven 1982 Chicago victims of cyanide-spiked Tylenol died during an eighteen-hour span. While their killer's motive remains a mystery, one long-standing police theory supposes that six were killed to obscure the reason for the seventh's murder. Since the murderer has never been brought to justice, one question has long haunted law enforcement. What sort of person would casually murder innocent strangers?

Thanks to Stella Nickell, we now have some idea.

# The Butler Did It?
## (1987)

*S*INCE *EDGAR ALLAN POE'S "THE PURLOINED LETTER,"* *the notion of hiding a stolen object in plain sight has been a staple of mystery writers. Another favorite fictional device is the fake substituted for a genuine article. And in both fiction and the real life of con artists, the desired end of every con game is to leave "marks" unaware that they are victims until it's too late to do anything about it. In this case, a clever—and lucky—perpetrator combined these three notions to execute what might well have been a perfect crime.*

Rune "Roy" Donell had big problems. A well-muscled six-footer with thinning dark hair just starting to go gray, Donell had finished a hitch in the Swedish navy before emigrating to the United States in 1976. While he held a green card—the document proving he had the right to work in America—he maintained his Swedish citizenship.

Donell's big problem was money. While he had a secure, well-paying job—for eleven years he had served as butler and chauffeur to a wealthy couple—his salary of $25,000 a year, plus room and board, was barely enough to support his two wives. Worse, at sixty-one, he was plagued by ulcers, a hernia, high blood pressure, and psoriasis. As his health declined, Donell began to imagine a day when he no longer had the strength to fulfill his many responsibilities, especially those associated with running his employers' large household. What would he do then?

On the plus side, Roy had virtually unsupervised access to at least one of his employers' household accounts. But while they certainly knew that the $6,000 to $7,000 a month he often spent on food for the small number of people who regularly dined at the estate—plus some occasional dinner guests—was too much, his employers were otherwise so satisfied with Roy's services that not until years later would they voice any suspicion that their butler may have embezzled as much as $20,000 to $30,000 yearly.

Donell's first wife, Christina, was six years his senior. A cook, she worked for seven years in the same household with her husband. But as her age approached the biblical three score and ten, Donell must have worried about the inevitable day when Christina, already frail, could no longer work. Where would they find the money to take proper care of her then, when he was having such a hard time now?

Donell had different worries about his younger wife, the dark, slim, passionately lovely Esther Ariza. Sixteen years younger than Donell, a lively Colombian immigrant with tastes for exotic travel and expensive clothes, she demanded much of his attention and time. She also had a twenty-year-old son, Andy, who needed to complete his education. After their virtually secret marriage in Nevada—Esther thought that Donell had divorced Christina, but wouldn't abandon her—he began paying the rent on her Santa Monica Boulevard apartment in west Los Angeles. He also rented another unit nearby, a place for him and Christina to spend their days off. Between the burden of two wives, two apartments, college tuition, and his growing health problems, Donell sometimes despaired.

Roy Donell worked high above Beverly Hills in Bel Air's posh Stone Canyon. The home at 10659 Bellagio Road was an 11,000-square-foot stone copy of a seventeenth-century French château, a $42 million estate called La Lanterne, after a royal pavilion in a Versailles park. Its owners and occupants were among the world's wealthiest couples. Howard B. Keck, Sr., seventy-one, had made his money the old-fashioned way: He inherited it. Keck was principal beneficiary of a private trust worth over $640 million, a fortune accumulated by his late father, whose acuity in trading drilling services for promising petroleum leases earned him legendary status in the oil patch during California's rough-and-ready twenties.

La Lanterne's owners were not merely wealthy. They were cultured. The Kecks were noted for philanthropy; Big Howard, as the father was called to differentiate him from his son, was a frequent donor to museums, schools, churches, and leading community cultural and educational institutions. Among his most noteworthy acts was a $70 million contribution to the California Institute of Technology in 1985 to build an astronomical observatory. The facility, sited atop Mauna Kea, the dormant volcano on Hawaii's Big Island, boasted an optical telescope with a four-hundred-inch mirror—the world's largest.

Elizabeth "Libby" Avery Keck, Big Howard's wife, was a very attractive woman who looked far younger than her sixty-five years. She wore her light brown hair short, and chose attire that displayed her petite, athletic figure to its best advantage. Libby Keck was widely admired for her artistic tastes as well as her husband's good money. For many years she served simultaneously as a director of the Los Angeles County Museum of Art, the Museum of Contemporary Art, the Huntington Museum, and the Los Angeles Music Center—the apex of achievement for Southern California society culture. She was also an avid patron of the sport of kings: her horse Ferdinand, with Willie Shoemaker aboard, took the roses in the 1986 Kentucky Derby.

But mostly Libby's world was art. She was well regarded as an amateur painter herself, and the word around the gallery and museum Establishment was that Libby knew fine art. She was a relentless, eclectic, world-class collector. Displayed in La Lanterne were the fruits of decades of thoughtful accumulation: priceless paintings, tapestries, sculptures, furniture once owned by Napoleon, Marie Antoinette, and Louis XIV, as well as other, less spectacular objets d'art, chiefly French in origin. Thanks to Libby's acquisitions, La Lanterne attracted a steady trickle of museum curators and art scholars from around the world.

In 1986, the Kecks' marriage began to unravel. Their troubles began when "Little Howard" Keck, their oldest son, filed what he called a "friendly" lawsuit intended to "clarify" his future rights of inheritance. Especially his rights to the enormous wealth of the Keck family trust—and of La Lanterne and its treasures.

Little Howard's suit was answered with countersuits from other members of the family. After thirty-seven years of marriage, Big Howard and Libby wound up on opposite ends of the central issue: would Little Howard get most of the money after his parents passed away?

The money issue stemmed from the way Big Howard's late father had divided his vast wealth among his heirs. William M. Keck Sr. had parlayed his California oil leases into a company, Superior Oil, with billions in assets from producing wells in Oklahoma, Texas, Pennsylvania, and California. When he died in 1964, his estate went primarily to his three children, William Jr., Howard, and Willametta. When the estate emerged from probate fourteen years later, family trusts were set up. In 1983, sometime after his brother's death, Big Howard tried to get his sister, Willametta, to surrender sole control of the trusts to him. She refused and started a nasty proxy battle, during which she referred to him as a "dumb son of a bitch" to a *Wall Street Journal* reporter. In 1984, after Willametta's death, the struggle for control triggered the sale of Superior Oil to Mobil Oil for $5.7 billion. Just before that sale, Little Howard filed his friendly lawsuit.

The Keck trusts provided that their income was to be distributed to the patriarch's grandchildren until the death of his last surviving child, Big Howard. Then the trusts would be dissolved and all remaining descendants of William Keck Sr. would share equally in the distribution.

After Little Howard filed his lawsuit, however, Big Howard suddenly questioned his son's paternity. Was he really his own, or had he been conceived outside of wedlock? Then Big Howard threatened to "go out and have more children" so he could dilute his offsprings' inheritances, especially that of Little Howard. He publicly toyed with the notion of "adopting the entire Marlboro School for Girls."

That was too much for Libby to bear, and she filed for divorce. While that action ground its way through the courts, both continued to live separately in La Lanterne, which was so huge that they rarely saw each other, much less spoke.

The impending breakup of the Keck marriage imperiled Roy Donell's comfortable job. Where would he find another couple so rich that they wouldn't miss thousands of dollars a month?

Despite the demands on his finances from supporting two wives, Donell had managed to squirrel away a little money. But he knew it would never be enough to maintain his double life if he was forced to find another job in a less wealthy household. So he began looking for a way to establish a retirement fund. An imaginative fellow surrounded by great wealth, in due course Donell discovered that way.

After so many years in the Keck household, Donell knew very well that Big Howard cared little for art. Aside from recognizing the huge, priceless Gainsborough that served as the focal point of La Lanterne's enormous living room, Big Howard knew almost nothing about the dozens of other paintings hanging from the walls. But after many conversations with Mrs. Keck, Donell had acquired a certain comfort level with art—and he knew that there were far more paintings in the house than space to display them. The Kecks maintained a storage area for the extras.

In September 1986, Donell took one of the stored paintings, *Fête Gallante,* a miniature by the Frenchman LeClerk des Gobelins that depicted a people-filled urban park. He stashed it in his apartment, and after a few weeks, when no alarm was raised, he took it along on his vacation to Stockholm. Passing through Swedish Customs, he declared the stolen painting and was asked to pay several hundred dollars in duty. A few days later, Donell presented himself at Beijars, Auktioner, one of Sweden's largest art dealers, and inquired about selling the des Gobelins.

He learned from the company's director, Karl-Gustav Petersen, that Beijars did not buy art outright. Rather, they auctioned it. Beijars's resident expert, Louise Lieberg, submitted the miniature to technical scrutiny and confirmed that it was genuine—but no one asked Donell how or where he had obtained it. A few days later, it was sold; after paying the auctioneer's commission, Donell was about $6,000 richer. The money was sent two weeks later to his Beverly Hills post office box. Thus Donell had learned how to sell a stolen painting and became familiar with the necessary procedures to continue his thefts.

Donell did not intend to make a career out of pilfering the Kecks' collection. La Lanterne contained several world-renowned pieces, including the Gainsborough, but taking any of those was out of the question. Not only would Libby be certain to miss such a work, it would be difficult to sell anything so famous, even in Sweden.

Donell instead fastened his gaze on what was, to him, the most salable piece in Mrs. Keck's collection, an 1888 work by Sweden's most distinguished Impressionist, Anders Leonhard Zorn. Libby had acquired it in London in 1982 for a mere $88,506. The painting, oil on canvas, was about three feet wide and two feet high and depicted a nude, middle-aged mother dressing her young son near a sun-dappled country pond. It was titled *I Fria Luften* (In Free Air) but was known, less formally, as *Kvinna Klaer Sitt Barn* (Woman Dressing Her Child).

Before leaving Stockholm, Donell had asked Beijars director Petersen about *I Fria Luften,* and had been assured that resurgent interest in Zorn's works would guarantee a good price in Sweden. So interested was Petersen in selling this work that he gave Donell his home telephone number. A few months later, in February 1987, Donell gave notice to the Kecks: in view of their advancing age and declining health, he said he and his wife Christina had decided to retire, return to Sweden, and spend their golden years in the land of their birth.

By the second week in March they were gone. Had the Kecks checked, they might have found it curious that while Donell indeed flew to Sweden, he left Christina behind in their tiny Manning Avenue apartment. Traveling with Donell was, instead, the lovely Esther—and a large cardboard tube that he kept with him on the airplane. Donell and Esther relaxed in Stockholm until her son, Andy, arrived a week later. Then they toured Europe, staying at good hotels and enjoying themselves.

Donell, Esther, and Andy returned to Los Angeles in April. Four months later, on August 24, 1987, walking through the conservatory, Libby flicked her learned gaze across a painting near the window.

She stopped dead in her tracks.

Summoning her bodyguard and chauffeur, Roger Paine, she howled, "Look at that!" while pointing to *I Fria Luften* on the wall.

"Yes, ma'am," said Paine, scanning the Impressionist masterpiece uncomprehendingly. He looked at the picture in the gilt frame, but Paine didn't know precisely what his boss wished him to see, so he remained silent. After a long moment, an impatient Libby took Paine's hand and led him to the picture. She placed his fingers on the surface. It was perfectly smooth. That's queer, thought Paine. He knew this was supposed to be an oil painting, and oil paintings have textured surfaces. "Well, hell!" said the chauffeur, comprehension dawning. "Somebody has stolen this painting!"

"I know it, I know it," shrieked Libby. Her hands trembled. "It's gone!"

Since it was after four P.M., Libby's security chief suggested that she wait until the next morning before calling police. Otherwise, he speculated, she might wind up talking to "some cop on the beat" who "wouldn't know anything about it." So the very next morning, Libby had Paine report the theft. A uniformed LAPD officer went to La Lanterne to inspect the crime scene, but not until nearly a week later, on August 31, could detectives find an opening in Libby's always hectic schedule that would allow them to speak to her at length. Detective Mike Kummerman did an interview by telephone.

As he did on all such occasions, Kummerman attempted to follow departmental procedures by eliciting some basic personal data from the person reporting a crime. But Libby, long accustomed to the imperatives of great wealth, made the detective work hard for his information. Asked to state her age, she balked. "I don't have to give you all that," she said. "You don't need that. That I'm not going to give you."

Since Kummerman had other ways of ascertaining this date—Libby's driver's license data at the department of motor vehicles was a phone call away, for example—he decided not to make an issue of it. Libby said she didn't know her Social Security number, but if the detective would call her office, someone there could look it up. Asked about a previous address, Libby said she didn't know the number, but she and her husband had lived in the Beverly Hills Hotel for ten years before moving into their estate eight years earlier.

When it came to her occupation, Libby said she really didn't have one, but reported that her husband was "retired." In response to the detective's question, she said she had four children, and while she knew their names, she couldn't vouch for exact ages because she had forgotten their birthdays.

Libby was far more willing to discuss the circumstances surrounding the theft of her painting. "I sit here very often and play cards," she said. "I usually face the window. My back is to the corner where the painting was hanging. And for the last two and a half to three months, I've noticed sort of subliminally that something was wrong with it. But I didn't really go up and check it out. I certainly should have. But—I think it was Wednesday of last week—I went outdoors for something, and when I came back I got a full view of the Zorn. Suddenly I realized the color was completely wrong. So I went up and touched it and it was just a photograph, the exact size of the painting."

Libby went on to say that soon after acquiring the Zorn, she had discussed the purchase with the visiting head of a museum who disclosed that his institution had recently bought another Zorn—but had paid about twice what she had. "I felt like I got a bargain," Libby added.

Libby noted that her estate had twenty-four-hour armed guard service. "They clock everybody in and out, exactly what time you come in . . . I mean, it's like the Gestapo, they keep records and everything," she said.

When Kummerman referred to an earlier telephone conversation that he'd had with Mrs. Keck in which she intimated that she had an idea who might have stolen the painting, Libby emphatically denied that notion. "No. I don't have any, I don't have any suspects. I really don't," she said.

But later, Kummerman returned to this theme. "Do you suspect anybody?" he asked.

"No," said Libby.

"No?"

"Not specifically."

"Have you had any repairmen or servicemen in the house recently who would have any ability to walk off with it?" asked the detective.

"No. This is more complicated than it appears." Libby then described what she thought had happened. To make a copy like the one on her wall, the painting would have to be removed from its frame. "I'm a painter, I've done this a thousand times," she said. "You take the nails and bend them over the holes. Probably they took the whole thing out and rolled up the canvas—it would have been the easiest way. And somebody would have to photograph it very carefully. They would have had to take it down to a place where they could photograph it—you see them all along Santa Monica Boulevard," said Libby. "But they had to have it blown up to the exact size and that's where, probably, the color went wrong. It wasn't too expert a job. If the color had been better, I might not have noticed it for a year."

"Could you think of anybody that would have the time or the ability to do that in your home?" asked the detective.

"Yes. But I don't want to go on record saying that, per se. I don't want to point the finger at anybody."

"I understand," said Kummerman. "But if you would mention the name, it may help in the investigation. It does not imply that you are calling them a suspect."

"I think you're not asking the right questions," snapped Libby. "I think the question you should be asking is 'Who has worked here?' "

"Okay . . . do you have servants in the house that have access to this room?"

"Yes . . . Well, only three who live here. And I've gotten them within the last couple of months. So they're not suspects. . . . I have a Korean cleaning crew that I've had for three years and a cleaning man I've had for two years. . . . Incidentally, about three months ago I let a couple go that I had, and then about a month and a half ago, I had a maid go."

"There were several people then that you had terminated?"

Libby answered in the affirmative, indicating that the former employees included a cook, her husband—a butler/chauffeur—and a maid. All three had left of their own volition.

"Do you believe possibly that the butler . . .?" asked the detective.

"No. I don't believe that. I cannot, I do not say that," Libby replied.

"Okay. Do you think that they would have more knowledge about paintings than the housekeeper would?"

"She wasn't a housekeeper, she was a *maid*."

"The maid?"

"I don't think that they were knowledgeable about paintings one way or the other . . . the only thing I can say is that I had often discussed this painting with the butler and he liked it," said Libby.

"That's interesting," said Kummerman. "What was his name?"

"Roy Donell."

For the last several years in Los Angeles, major felonies involving art have become the business of LAPD Detective William F. Martin, whose recovery rate on stolen paintings far exceeds the national law-enforcement average. After Detective Kummerman's telephone interview with Libby Keck, the case quickly found its way to Martin's desk.

La Lanterne, with its enormously valuable art collection, was protected by an elaborate and sophisticated alarm system. The Kecks' security guards worked for a company owned and operated by a highly regarded man who had recently served as the Beverly Hills police chief. Investigation revealed nothing to cast suspicion on any of the Kecks' guards, and a very careful search of the house and grounds turned up no sign of forced entry.

Despite Libby's repeated protests that she couldn't imagine that her former butler had anything to do with the theft of her painting, she did suddenly recall that Donell had mentioned the painting would fetch a high price in Sweden. With few other suspects, Martin turned his attention to Donell. He soon learned that just before retiring—shortly after the time the painting was thought to have been taken—Donell had vacationed in Sweden.

On a hunch, Martin sent a Teletype message to Interpol, requesting help from Swedish authorities. Did Donell have a criminal record in his native Sweden? Did they have any clues about the stolen painting's whereabouts?

On September 8, 1987, just two weeks after Libby Keck reported the theft, Swedish Interpol sent a long cable to Detective Martin.

THE SWEDISH NATIONALS RUNE GUNNAR DONELL AND HIS WIFE CHRISTINA DONELL HAVE NO CRIMINAL RECORD IN THIS COUNTRY AND ARE NOT WANTED IN SWEDEN.

ON 15SEP86 THE FIRM "BEIJARS AUKTIONER" WAS VISITED BY A PERSON CLAIMING TO BE ROY DONELL, P.O. BOX 532, BEVERLY HILLS, CALIFORNIA. HE BROUGHT A PAINTING BY THE FRENCH PAINTER LECLERK DES GOBELINS CALLED *FETE GALLANTE*. AT THE INSTRUCTIONS OF ROY DONELL THIS PAINTING WAS PUT UP FOR AUCTION AND WAS SOLD ON 19NOV86 FOR AN UNKNOWN AMOUNT OF MONEY.

ROY DONELL SAID THAT IF THEY WERE INTERESTED HE COULD COME BACK WITH A PAINTING CALLED *KVINNA KLAER SITT BARN* (WOMAN DRESSING HER CHILD). THE AUCTIONEERS SAID THEY WERE INTERESTED AND ON 12MAR87 ROY DONELL RETURNED TO SWEDEN TOGETHER WITH A WOMAN OF LATIN APPEARANCE. THE COUPLE WAS MET AT THE AIRPORT BY ONE OF THE DIRECTORS OF THE SWEDISH AUCTIONEER'S OFFICE.

ROY DONELL BROUGHT THE ZORN PAINTING CALLED *KVINNA KLAER SITT BARN*. THE PAINTING WAS DULY ENTERED THROUGH THE CUSTOMS . . . THEN SOLD AT AN AUCTION IN APRIL.

THE CASE HAS BEEN REFERRED TO THE STOCKHOLM CID FOR INVESTIGATION AND WILL BE TURNED OVER TO THE PUBLIC PROSECUTOR'S OFFICE SHORTLY.

PLEASE LET US KNOW ALL RELEVANT INFORMATION YOU POSSESS
ABOUT SUBJECT.

PLEASE NOTE THAT - IF IT IS ESTABLISHED THAT NO CRIMINAL
OFFENSE WAS COMMITTED IN THIS COUNTRY - YOU MUST MAKE
A REQUEST THROUGH DIPLOMATIC CHANNELS IN ORDER THAT WE
MAY SEIZE THE PAINTING ON YOUR BEHALF.

The Donells lived in west Los Angeles, a middle-class
neighborhood, filled with young, apartment-dwelling professionals and older folks living their golden years in modest,
low-slung stucco houses. Martin took Roy Donell into custody as he left his apartment. On the sidewalk, Martin read
Donell his Miranda rights, then asked permission to search
the apartment. Both Roy and Christina each scribbled ap-
proval of this search on a sheet from a lined pad.

As Martin and his colleagues combed through the
Donells' apartment, they turned up a used Scandinavian air-
service ticket and a travel agent's itinerary from Donell's trip
to Stockholm in September 1986. They also found a brochure from Beijars Auktioner. Elsewhere in the apartment
police found money transfer receipts from Beijars Auktioner
to the Security Pacific Bank in Los Angeles. One, dated
March 18, 1987, was for $633. Seven others, dated March
17, 1987, were for $5,000 each. Altogether, the receipts from
Beijars totaled $85,633.

Police also found a brochure and price list from Rossi Pho-
tography Custom Lab. And they found two 35mm cameras,
a zoom lens, strips of color negatives, and a handwritten paper identifying Roy Donell as a freelance photographer.

Donell was booked for grand theft at the Los Angeles
County Jail. At his arraignment, bail was set at half a million dollars. Insisting that he was unable to raise the 10 percent fee required by bondsmen, Donell began what would
be a long stay behind bars.

So far, the case looked like a slam dunk to Detective
Martin. Intent on building an airtight case for the prosecutors, he paid a visit to Rossi Lab, on Santa Monica Boulevard in what the Los Angeles art community calls the
"Photo District." Tom Rossi, the owner, told Martin's part-

ner, Detective Donald Hrycyk, that early in 1987 a man answering Donell's description brought in a 35mm color slide and ordered a print. While photo enlargements are usually made to standard sizes, such as eight by ten or sixteen by twenty, the man, who spoke with a thick Swedish accent, explained that he needed an odd size because it had to fit exactly into a particular frame.

When he returned a few days later to pick up his print, the man was not happy with the results. The colors did not match the original, he said, and the size was not exact. Rossi then explained that while it was possible to match a print to the slide, it was difficult to duplicate the original unless it was available for comparison. He also pointed out that blowing up even the sharpest 35mm slide to more than twenty times its original size introduced a lot of fuzziness and grain. Rossi suggested that the Swedish man bring the painting in to be photographed with a larger-format camera, which would yield a far more pleasing print.

The Swede agreed. A few weeks later, said Rossi, he returned with the painting, minus its frame, and watched while it was photographed with a view camera and a special "flat-field" copying lens. "He stayed with the painting continuously while I photographed it," recalled Rossi.

Rossi sent the four-by-five-inch negative to be enlarged and had the print dry-mounted on poster board. But when the Swede returned to pick up the photo, he found that the print was about a half inch too small for the frame. Rossi sent it back out for a remake. Finally, almost two months after his first visit to Rossi's establishment, the Swede left with an enlargement that was exactly the right size.

Roy Donell had left an indelible impression on Rossi. When it came time for the photo-studio proprietor to testify, the fact that he had no paperwork would make little difference.

While he had established that Donell received over $85,000 from the sale of the painting, Martin now sought to recover the rest of the money. A Swedish industrial firm had bought the painting for 3.1 million kronur, approximately $550,000, and Beijars had retained 20 percent of that. That left over $350,000 missing. Detectives found only an insignificant amount of cash in the Donell apartment, and a laborious check of California banks turned up no other accounts. While searching Donell's apartment, Martin and Hyrcyk had also found a receipt for a safe-deposit box in a Beverly Hills bank, and another from a storage company where Donell kept his twenty-five-foot motor home. Armed with a search warrant, detectives opened the motor home, where they found the two rejected photographic blowups of *I Fria Luften*. They also found the copy negative.

*Gotcha!* thought Martin and Hrycyk. They now had motive (money), opportunity (for eleven years, Donell was the Kecks' most trusted servant)—all neatly documented by a paper trail and credible witnesses linking Donell every step of the way from theft to sale of the painting.

The only thing missing was the money, but Martin was confident that it would turn up. And even if he couldn't track it down, thought Martin, most crooks would eventually decide that a few hundred thousand dollars was too much to hide when it might mean several extra years behind bars. When Donell realized that he was going away for theft, Martin was fairly sure he would talk in exchange for a reduced sentence. But until then, maybe the mysterious "woman of Latin appearance" Interpol mentioned might lead him to the loot.

With all Donell's financial records at their disposal, Esther wasn't hard to find. But she said that while Donell had mentioned that their stop in Stockholm was "to sell an asset, something that was already in Sweden," he never mentioned a painting during their trip or after. Yes, a man named Petersen had driven them from the Stockholm airport to a suite he'd reserved at the Royal Viking Hotel. But, Esther stated, she had no idea he was the head of an art auction firm. She recalled Donell had mentioned he was meeting with a gentleman about selling the "asset" and that the transaction looked "favorable." However, she said, he had never intimated it had anything to do with a painting. Esther was less than fully cooperative, but Martin could find no evidence that she was Donell's accomplice.

Even when confronted with what prosecutors felt was overwhelming evidence, Roy Donell refused to cop a plea.

That meant a jury trial, open to the press and public. And the testimony given at this trial blew the lid off one of the juiciest divorce cases Southern California had seen in decades.

The divorce proceedings, which would enrich the Kecks' attorneys by some $15 million before all issues were resolved, began in December 1986. A judge soon clamped a gag order on all participants and their lawyers. But as Donell's trial for the theft unfolded, quirky details of the Keck family's greed, jealousy, betrayal, and alleged illegitimacy leaped from the pages of Los Angeles newspapers.

When Donell took the witness stand, he freely admitted that he had copied the painting, replaced the real article with the copy, taken the original to Sweden, and sold it. But he was innocent, said Donell, because everything he did had been on Libby's orders. That was the reason, he claimed, that most of the money from the sale of both "stolen" paintings had never been found. Donell testified that he had kept only a 20 percent commission and had handed the rest over to Libby.

"The story that he told on the witness stand was unbelievable," said Detective Martin. "He said that while traveling around Europe, he sent several increments of $20,000—cash, American currency—by ordinary mail to Mrs. Keck. Absolutely absurd! Knowing what the post office is like, how many of them would get through?

"But there was so much money," continued Martin, "that even in $20,000 chunks, he said he couldn't get it all back while he was traveling. So, he said, after he returned to California, when he brought Mrs. Keck her breakfast tray every morning, he put a stack of money under a linen napkin next to her coffee cup. I'm sure that anybody who heard that must have thought, 'This is stupid, why didn't he just give her the money in one lump?'"

Donell also testified that it was none of his business that the Kecks had accepted $500,000 from their insurance company to compensate them for the loss of the painting. Under cross-examination from Deputy DA Michael Montagna, Donell insisted that Libby got most of the money from the sale of the Zorn, and that she needed it to help pay her divorce lawyers.

An accomplished prosecutor, Montagna headed the district attorney's Career Criminal Unit. Aided by Martin's investigation, he did a very thorough job of preparation and was by all accounts effective in presenting the government's case—until he called Libby to the stand to refute Donell's allegations.

Dressed to the nines, Libby was a commanding presence. She haughtily told the jury, "The suggestion that I would conspire with my butler to sell these paintings for a sum of money which is but a small fraction of one month's income of myself and my husband is ludicrous."

Indeed, documents filed with the court showed that pending the dissolution of her marriage, Libby got a $5,000 monthly grocery allowance, plus $1,200 a month for lunches, $3,300 for dinners, $10,000 for dinner parties, and $25,000 for clothing. In addition, Libby Keck had $11 million of her own money in accounts she controlled. She said she didn't need the $354,000 that Donell claimed he had given her from the sale of the Zorn painting. "I could have written a check for the whole amount," she testified.

Donell testified that Libby had given him *I Fria Luften* in the parking lot of the Bel Air Hotel. But on the witness stand Libby said, "I've never been to that hotel in my life."

On cross-examination, however, Donell's attorney, Don Randolph, reminded Libby that before marrying Big Howard, she had been married to the man who then owned the Bel Air Hotel. Libby, however, stubbornly refused to change her statement. The jury's reaction was unseen—but at that moment many in the courtroom felt something moving beneath the surface of the state's case against Donell.

"I knew we were in deep trouble the moment she testified," said prosecutor Montagna. "The jury did not seem to like her. It was her attitude, the way she carried herself."

In any criminal case, a courtroom is full of lawyers—the prosecution team and defense attorneys. But sitting in the courtroom audience for this trial, each seeking some tiny fact that they might use in defense of their client's interests during the divorce settlement, were still more lawyers working for Big Howard, Libby, and their children.

"When a defense attorney asked Mrs. Keck a question

about her finances, a lawyer in the audience got to his feet and shouted, 'We object!' " said Martin. "The judge told him that he had no standing in this case and to sit down and be quiet."

The prosecution called Big Howard, who testified that as legal owner of the stolen paintings, he had indeed received the insurance money. But Big Howard, concerned about saying anything that might cost him millions in a divorce settlement, was choosing his words carefully. So when defense counsel Jackson asked him if his wife lied or was dishonest, he replied, "I don't think she is a truthful person."

The jury wasted little time finding Roy Donell not guilty. Afterward foreman Joel Nenzell hastened to tell reporters that while the jurors did not "necessarily believe Donell was innocent," his story had seemed more believable to the jury than Libby Keck's.

"I think they found reasonable doubt only because of Mrs. Keck's wealth," said Martin. "While she was always gracious to me, the jurors took a dislike to her because she acted like she had so much money that this was a drop in the bucket to her. But those jurors also admitted afterward that they didn't believe Donell."

Montagna, the prosecutor, was left with the strong impression that there was more to the incident than either Donell or Keck had told. "Maybe she suggested to Donell that he should steal the paintings and share the money with her—and then he double-crossed her. But I guess we'll never know," he said with a sigh.

Martin nevertheless remains certain that Libby played no role in the theft. "It makes absolutely no sense," he said. "Number one, she didn't get the insurance money, her husband got it. And if Mrs. Keck wasn't getting the insurance money, why would she bother reporting it at all?

"Number two, half a million dollars is a lot of money to most people, but it was not significant to her. With her own money and with what her husband was giving her to run the house, she was scraping by on about $200,000 a month. And she was obviously going to get a major settlement when they divorced.

"Not only that, but if Mrs. Keck was in on it, why steal

the first painting, the French miniature, which brought only $6,000? The only purpose of that theft was so Donell could see how the Swedish art gallery ran, see if he could get away with it, see how he would get his money, and to establish himself as somebody who sold art. If Donell was working with Mrs. Keck, he'd never have had to do this test.

"And since Mr. Keck admitted that he knew nothing about art, there would have been no reason to replace the Zorn with a photograph, because if Mrs. Keck was in on it, she didn't need to dummy up a photo. Her husband would never have noticed if she sold the Zorn and put another picture on the wall," added Martin.

Days after Donell was released from jail—he had served ten months before and during his trial—Libby's attorneys filed a civil suit against him asking $31 million for alleged theft, slander, invasion of privacy, and infliction of emotional distress. Her attorneys were from Trope & Trope, among the most prestigious litigators in a city all but overrun with lawyers. "I want the truth out. I don't want to live with the lies that have been cast upon me by the bludgeonings of fate," said Libby, explaining why she filed suit.

Donell, who claimed to be surviving on only his small Social Security payments, said that he could not afford to hire an attorney. He wrote to Big Howard, asserting that since the alleged theft had taken place while Donell was an employee of La Lanterne, his legal expenses should rightfully be covered by the Kecks' homeowner's insurance.

Big Howard didn't see things that way, so Donell instead somehow found the money to pay a lawyer to help him prepare court filings. Otherwise, he served as his own attorney, representing himself in all proceedings. He also filed a cross-complaint against Libby, alleging malicious prosecution, abuse of process, false imprisonment, and intentional infliction of emotional distress.

In June 1989, Donell responded to a deposition subpoena by Libby's lawyers. He visited their offices but refused to answer any substantive questions. Donell said he wouldn't answer because he didn't have an attorney present. Trope & Trope rescheduled the deposition for the following month, but Donell again refused to answer questions. This time he claimed the protection of the Fifth Amendment, citing the allegation that Deputy DA Montagna, following Donell's jury acquittal, had threatened to send the case to the U.S. attorney's office so that prosecutors there could seek an indictment on federal charges.

Libby's attorneys then filed a motion to prevent Donell from testifying at the civil trial because he hadn't allowed himself to be deposed. In August, a judge ruled that Donell could not claim Fifth Amendment protection because he had waived these rights by testifying in his criminal trial. He ordered Donell to pay Libby's lawyers, five hundred dollars for their trouble and to make himself available for a deposition.

Instead Donell responded by filing a motion with the court. While he still claimed to be representing himself, that motion appeared to have been written by Donell's former attorney, Don Randolph. Asserting again his claim for Fifth Amendment protection, Donell cited the federal statute of limitations on interstate or foreign transportation of stolen goods—five years—and indicated that he would be willing to testify only after August 1992, when that threat had expired. The judge agreed.

In May 1992, the court dismissed Libby's case for "lack of prosecution" by the plaintiff. Her attorney at Trope & Trope, vague about why Libby had failed to follow through, suggested that the suit was "not economical to pursue" because Donell had no money.

Somewhere, probably abroad, remains $350,000 of the money paid Donell from the sale of the Zorn. And if that money still exists, Rune "Roy" Donell, once the trusted servant of the fabulously rich and cultured Kecks, has been free to spend it since late 1992.

# Secret Lives
# (1989)

**T**HERE CAN BE NO PERFECT CRIME WHEN THE PERPETRATOR
*depends upon others to accomplish his or her
purposes—even when the principal plotters have good reason to believe they exercise complete control over their un-
derlings. This case illustrates the folly of involving others in
a murder plot.*

Daytona Beach lies along Florida's mid-Atlantic coast,
basking in the year-round sunshine. The city everyone
knows is a spring-break playground for college kids, a
mecca for motorcycle clubs, the beach where expensive,
juiced-up cars roar full-tilt down hard-packed alabaster
sand, a carefree town of hard-rocking nightclubs, skimpy
bikinis, free-flowing beer, all-night parties, and tolerant
cops.

Daytona is not always what it seems.

After dark, much of the city is a sleazy jungle of drifters
and desperadoes selling drugs, snatching purses, stealing
cars, burglarizing hotel rooms, and dealing in the sex trade.
Attracted by warm weather, relaxed law enforcement, and
year-round crowds of free-spending tourists, Daytona's
"boardwalk"—a collection of fast-food stands, arcades, gift
shops, souvenir shacks, saloons, and restaurants dotting a
broad ribbon of concrete paralleling a few miles of
beachfront—is home to a population of transients. Some are

young runaways from northeastern cities. Most are alienated from society and mistrustful or contemptuous of the law. Nearly all use alcohol, crack, pot, coke, LSD, hallucinogenic mushrooms, PCP, heroin, or the designer drug of the moment. Daytona's lost generation own little but a few clothes and an assortment of raging addictions. They will do anything to stay high—anything to avoid a harsh descent to reality and the unbearable pain of narcotics withdrawal. Anything at all.

In the summer of 1989, a beautiful, petite, but bosomy woman of twenty turned up on the Daytona Beach boardwalk. Deidre Hunt, who also answered to Dee or Cherie, had an angelic face, thick brunette hair falling straight below her shoulders, huge, smoldering eyes that radiated an aura of sexuality, and the bubbly laugh of a teenage waif. Few could fall into her orbit without feeling intense, primal attraction. Deidre was a superb actress, confident in many roles: hungry urchin, imperious queen, happy hooker, haughty debutante, even nymph next door. She was a ninth-grade dropout with a mind like a silicon chip, able to add, subtract, multiply, or divide boxcar-length figures in her head with unfailing accuracy and blinding speed. And yet she understood pathetically little of the ways of the real world. Her hopes and dreams were often those of a child: improbable wishes and fantasies that could never be realized, yearnings for magical solutions to life's real problems.

Parading herself around the boardwalk in the barest of bikinis, within weeks Deidre became the undisputed queen of Daytona's demimonde. She was trailed around town by a scuzzy entourage of thugs and hookers who did her bidding—and often shared her bed.

Deidre had been born in South Weymouth, Massachusetts, and grew up in Manchester, New Hampshire. Her mother was an alcoholic and mental patient who treated her as a slave, beating, neglecting, and finally abandoning her. At age eleven, Deidre was raped by an adult neighbor. Her mother refused to report the incident. Deidre's father denied his paternity, rebuffing her every attempt to make contact. Seeking escape from her hellish childhood, at age seven Deidre was regularly abusing street drugs and stealing her mother's booze. Soon she was seducing schoolyard bullies she couldn't dominate with her fists. She began her sex life at age ten. By twelve, Deidre was fiercely independent, dating grown men, selling her body, sampling coke, smack, 'ludes, Ecstasy—anything and everything available from drug pushers.

Ever desperate for attention, in her early teens Deidre made herself the brightest star among dozens of outrageous characters in the Combat Zone, Manchester's tough red-light district. She worked as a barmaid. She danced topless in saloons. She sold herself to anyone with money—but she seemed to prefer especially abusive men. She also had a succession of lesbian affairs, usually with tall, slim, blond hookers. Men or women—Deidre had no strong preference, as long as she could define the relationship on her own terms. The word on the street was that sexually speaking, Deidre was willing to try anything at least once. She shared company with con men, burglars, drug dealers, robbers, killers. In July 1987, after a night of partying on LSD, Deidre put four .25-caliber bullets into a total stranger, a woman sitting in her own car. Miraculously, the victim survived. In a plea bargain that brought her a short period of probation, Deidre agreed to testify against a girlfriend who was with her at the shooting. At trial, the victim identified Deidre as the shooter, and the jury acquitted the friend.

Deidre thought she'd discovered a way to beat the system. She could be sweet, supportive, childlike, incredibly charming. She could erupt into murderous rage at the slightest provocation—and suffer few consequences.

If Deidre Michelle Hunt was seldom what she first seemed, she was exactly what Kosta Fotopoulos was looking for. The man christened Konstantinos X. Fotopoulos was born in Greece in 1959 and grew up in a prosperous Athens suburb. His father was an engineer for Olympic Airways, the Greek national airline. Four uncles emigrated to America via Australia and built small but successful businesses in the Chicago area. In his senior year, Kosta went to Aurora, Illinois, to live with an uncle while finishing high school and earning a bachelor's degree from Lewis University. Kosta loved flying and enrolled in a master's program at Daytona's Embry-Riddle Aeronautical School. He waited tables in a barbecue joint to earn spending money.

Kosta was over six feet tall, fit and well toned from regular exercise. Very much the old-world-style charmer, he exuded a dark, brooding sex appeal that made it easy for women to surrender themselves. Many did; by his late teens, Kosta had learned that most females found him nearly irresistible. Always appearing extremely sure of himself and seeming to fear no one, his macho qualities magnetic to both genders, Kosta slipped easily into the role of best buddy. He was a raconteur, given to spinning long tales of adventure and valor, spiced with colorful tidbits from his own mysterious past.

He spoke English with a thick Greek accent and made it his business to meet many of Daytona's large, thriving Greek community. He was unfailingly polite to his elders. By and by, in the manner of the old country, he was introduced to a suitable young woman.

In 1985, Lisa Paspalakis was twenty-six, the same age as Kosta, and the daughter of one of Daytona's leading businessmen. She had earned a degree in accounting from the University of South Florida, in Tampa.

Lisa's life revolved around her family and their business interests, principally a boardwalk amusement center called Joyland. When speculators began pushing to condemn the crumbling patchwork of beachfront properties along the boardwalk and replace them with luxury hotels, Lisa— young, poised, and telegenic—emerged as an effective spokesperson for the boardwalk's business association. She helped draft and sell to local government a master redevelopment plan that allowed for a few hotels *behind* the boardwalk along with a cleanup and complete makeover for the small, family-owned businesses like Joyland. The threat to the boardwalk receded, and around Daytona, Lisa Paspalakis became a minor celebrity.

Lisa was widely admired for her brains, character, beauty, and warmth. And her wealth: Though her father had been a penniless immigrant, the business he had built was worth millions. Lisa and her younger brother, Dino, would one day inherit it.

Lisa was exactly what she seemed.

She wasn't much interested in marriage, she told her father, Augustine—everyone called him Steno—before he finally persuaded her to meet Kosta in the late spring of 1985. Three weeks later, following a whirlwind courtship, the couple announced their engagement. In October 1985, no longer able to restrain their conjugal urges, Lisa and Kosta were married in a discreet civil ceremony. The formal wedding in the Greek Orthodox church took place January 4, 1986, followed by a lavish reception at the Daytona Hilton. Steno Paspalakis spent $50,000 to share with friends and relatives the happiness of his only daughter's marriage.

Afterward, Lisa was a busy woman. She had Joyland to run, and she had to keep house for her husband. Kosta quickly made himself part of Lisa's extended family, attending clan gatherings and ingratiating himself with the older generation. They saw him as a young man with much promise, a good match for Lisa.

With Lisa's younger friends, however, Kosta was polite but distant. When several couples got together, Kosta usually fell asleep on the couch or retired early. On evenings when there were no social activities, he found frequent occasion to go off on his own. Lisa was no clinging vine, and she gave Kosta the space she thought he needed.

Kosta drew three hundred dollars a week from Joyland while finishing his master's degree at Embry-Riddle. But he lived like a rich man in a condo Lisa had bought. He drove a spiffy black BMW, purchased with a loan cosigned by his wife. After graduation, he did not seek an appropriate position with an airline or aircraft manufacturer. Instead, he did little except hang around Joyland, doing menial tasks, dreaming of his own business, his own success. He became very good at dreaming.

Unlike his uncles, Kosta wasn't willing to start small and work hard. He asked his father-in-law to bankroll him in a succession of "can't miss" enterprises—but each time that Lisa and Steno, ever the practical business minds, ran the numbers, it was clear that Kosta had chosen poorly. Soon it was apparent that he had no head for business.

Eventually Kosta talked Steno into a $10,000 "loan," which he was to use to start his own enterprise. In June 1987, Kosta took Steno's money and another $10,000 he'd somehow scraped together and flew to Milan, Italy. There he bought a box of counterfeit hundred-dollar bills.

Back in Daytona, Kosta told his best pal, Peter Kouracos, about the funny money. Kouracos was the scion of a wealthy, well-connected Daytona family and very active in local business, Jay Cees, and Young Republican affairs. Kouracos was alarmed, but Kosta was his best friend. Kouracos said nothing about the bogus bills.

The relationship between Kosta and Kouracos was odd. Kouracos had known Lisa her entire life and it was natural that he would get to know Kosta. They were, on some level, soul mates, sharing an almost obsessive fascination with firearms. Kouracos had a federal gun license, allowing him to buy and sell weapons. Often accompanied by Kosta, he attended weekend gun shows and swap meets all over Florida. They spent a lot of time together, frequently with Lisa.

Kosta and Kouracos considered themselves "survivalists." They lived as though in expectation of some apocalypse, a disaster followed by the breakdown of civilization. Each owned an arsenal: handguns, shotguns, assault rifles, knives, ammunition in vast quantities. Kosta covertly acquired a small stock of plastic explosives and several hand grenades. He secretly modified semiautomatic assault weapons to fire on full automatic—a felony. And he manufactured and sold silencers for handguns—even though mere possession of a silencer is a felony.

As a self-proclaimed survivalist, Kosta studied the martial arts and learned to tolerate pain. He liked to demonstrate his steely willpower to casual acquaintances by applying a lighted cigarette to the skin of his arm for as long as five minutes without flinching or showing pain.

Kosta carried an automatic pistol in a shoulder holster at all times, reveling in the power it made him feel. He liked to see strangers react when he opened his coat so they caught a glimpse of the gun. He kept another automatic in his car, two revolvers at Joyland, an automatic under his bed, and several assault rifles close at hand in the bedroom. He told friends and acquaintances that he'd been trained by the Greek army and the Mossad in counterterrorist tactics and that he had worked as a contract killer for the CIA.

The Mossad doesn't answer inquiries regarding its personnel—but both the CIA and the FBI acknowledge having rejected his employment applications.

Kosta had two college degrees, but after graduation from Embry-Riddle, most of his reading was action-adventure comic books, survivalist publications, and *Soldier of Fortune* magazine. He spent many evenings prowling the swamps and wild palmetto scrub around Daytona, burying and digging up mysterious metal boxes and plastic bags.

Lisa knew about Kosta's fascination with guns and survivalism. She was a very bright young woman, but she had little experience with men except her father and her sweet and gentle younger brother. To Lisa, the guns and knives, the camouflage uniforms, and nocturnal trips to the woods, often with Peter Kouracos, were "a guy thing," a male-bonding ritual that she could never hope to understand. She tolerated Kosta's eccentricities—but didn't know about the darker side of his fascination with weaponry. He was her husband and she loved him very much.

Kosta used Vasilios "Bill" Markantonakis and his wife, Barbara, to pass tens of thousands of dollars in counterfeit. The Markantonakises, Greek by birth, were new Joyland employees. Barbara was one of Lisa's best workers; Bill, hired to do repairs and construction, had proven less reliable, and after several months, Lisa let him go. He continued to hang around the arcade, however, often accompanying Kosta to gun shows.

In the fall of 1987, the Markantonakises made an auto tour of the southern states, passing bogus bills in small-town stores. They kept half the cash they got in change, and gave the rest to Kosta.

In the third week of November 1987, while the Markantonakises were on the road, Kosta became a U.S. citizen. The same day, Lisa's father collapsed and died. He had a history of heart problems and attending physicians attributed Steno's death to a coronary embolism. Probably. At least one doctor wasn't sure, because there had been some strange symptoms. He asked permission to do an autopsy, but Lisa and her mother, Mary, refused, citing religious grounds.

Oddly, Kosta's whereabouts at the time Steno collapsed are a mystery, though Lisa, thinking back to the event years later, found reason to believe that he might have been with Steno. Steno's symptoms on the day he died—confused thinking, balance problems, abdominal pain, and shortness of breath—were consistent with mercury poisoning. But no one in the family recalled that Kosta had a bottle of mercury, which, he told Lisa, he used in reloading cartridges "to make the bullets go faster."

Her father's death left Lisa in charge of the family business. To help ease her mother's transition into widowhood, she and Kosta rented out their condo and joined Mary and Dino in the Paspalakis home, a huge, luxurious house backing on a broad river in the best part of Daytona.

Joyland and other family businesses were in a trust, jointly controlled by Lisa, Dino, and Mary. The trust provided that should any of the principals die, the survivors would jointly hold the business. This was a subtlety that Kosta never quite grasped. He became convinced that if Lisa was to die, *he* would inherit her share of the family holdings.

Lisa also had a hefty life-insurance policy: $350,000, with a double-indemnity provision covering sudden death. The proceeds were to be divided equally between her husband and brother. Kosta, however, believed that *he* would get everything upon his wife's death, that Dino could inherit only if he, Kosta, was also dead. There was a vast difference between what Kosta fancied and what he actually stood to inherit. But as many times as Lisa and Dino tried to explain it to him, Kosta either couldn't or wouldn't grasp the reality. He was convinced that he would become very rich if Lisa were to die.

On March 18, 1988, Barbara Markantonakis was arrested for passing a phony bill in a Georgia supermarket. Bill was arrested soon afterward. They were indicted on federal counterfeiting charges. Before they came to trial, Kosta gave the couple nearly $5,000 in cash and told them to go to Greece, where it was very unlikely they would be extradited. To make sure Bill understood the situation, Kosta explained things to him: if he ever mentioned Kosta's name in connection with the counterfeit, he was a dead man. And if he or Barbara ever set foot in the United States again, they were both dead. Kosta would personally kill them. He would also kill their son, and Barbara's parents, who remained in Daytona, as he had killed Steno Paspalakis, Kosta told Bill.

The Markantonakises hurriedly departed for Greece.

Early in 1989, Kosta found a spot for a business of his own, at the north end of the boardwalk, far from Joyland. Remodeling what had once been a recording studio, Kosta and two partners opened a bar and pool hall, calling it Top Shots.

Lisa was angry. A pool hall would attract precisely the element that brings speculators and redevelopers out of the woodwork. A boardwalk beer-and-pool joint was exactly the opposite of the image that Lisa and her business association colleagues wanted.

But Kosta was adamant. Top Shots was his business, not Lisa's. And it was a surefire moneymaker. Nothing Lisa could say would stop him.

Lisa well knew that Kosta did not like to be challenged. He was the sort of man who would never admit to being wrong about anything. Early in their marriage, she had learned that for Kosta it was a matter of macho pride. To keep the peace, she bit back her objections.

Top Shots was everything Lisa feared. The clientele was mostly young drifters, sleazy bikers, hookers, petty thieves, and assorted lowlifes. But Top Shots was exactly the kind of place Kosta wanted. He knew little about business, less about record keeping, and most of the people he hired to tend bar and serve up sandwiches were typical boardwalk miscreants. Since Top Shots was a cash business, the help pocketed money at every turn. Kosta didn't care. The real purpose of the establishment was not to sell beer or rake in quarters from the pool tables.

Kosta was now thirty-one, a decade older than most of his clientele. He was tall, handsome and athletic, and dressed very well. He drove a gleaming BMW, wore a gun, flashed huge rolls of cash, and convinced nearly everyone around the bar that *he* owned Joyland and other businesses and that Lisa took orders from him.

He also convinced many of the boardwalk bunch that he was rich and powerful because he killed people for a living.

Top Shots was never intended to be more than a front for Kosta's secret life. He quickly made himself the board-walk's godfather, with Top Shots the heart of a rapidly ex-panding criminal empire. It was a convenient place to recruit hookers for his outcall prostitution ring and to hire thugs to steal and torch expensive cars for insurance scams. It was a location frequented by second-story men whom Kosta dispatched to burgle specific hotel rooms. The bar was conveniently situated for Kosta's cocaine-dealing activ-ities, wholesale and retail. There was no shortage of penni-less transients willing to borrow two hundred dollars (often in counterfeit) from Kosta and, by buying and reselling street drugs, pay him four hundred in real money only hours later. And there were plenty of kids available to pass a phony hundred or two in a local supermarket.

So Kosta didn't care how much the help stole—even when they got caught. That is exactly what happened to Mark Ramsey, a petty thief, pimp, male prostitute, and purse snatcher of eighteen whom Kosta hired to tend bar. Kosta's partner, Tony Calderone, caught Mark red-handed, skimming money from the till behind the bar. Kosta laughed it off.

But several weeks later, Ramsey told Kosta that he knew about the counterfeiting ring. He wanted a few thousand dollars for his silence. Otherwise, said Ramsey, he'd tell the police.

Kosta knew how to deal with blackmail. He told Ramsey he'd kill him if he ever came into Top Shots again.

Calderone was thirty-nine, a dark, burly man who sold cars and owned two restaurants. He was a successful businessman who knew a line of bull when he heard it, but he found Kosta amusing and charismatic. In a lapse of judgment, he invested $6,000 to help start Top Shots. But when Calderone saw how Kosta ran things, he demanded his money back. Kosta agreed. But he was too busy to manage the pool hall, so he hired Calderone to run the place in exchange for a small salary, a cut of the profits, and a large dose of excitement. Much later, Calderone would wonder why on earth he had ever allowed himself to associate with Kosta.

Soon after returning to Top Shots, in September 1989, Calderone hired a waitress who called herself Cherie. Her real name was Deidre Hunt.

Calderone was at once drawn to her sensuality. Although he was married, he soon set her up in a nearby hotel room, visiting her daily to enjoy her special brand of steamy, no-holds-barred sex.

But not for long. When Kosta met Deidre, it was magic. Each recognized in the other a kindred soul. Instantly they became lovers. Kosta told Calderone that he was to stay away from Deidre. On pain of death.

Probably, no one will ever know who manipulated whom. Probably each used the other, often simultaneously. But whatever the nuances of their relationship, both craved the same things: sex, power, and money. Almost from the moment they met, Kosta and Deidre became intimately involved in each other's lives, embarking on a bizarre and savage pilgrimage to the gods of death and deception.

As streetwise, wild, and willful as she was, Deidre had never met anyone like Kosta. While those in Lisa's sophisticated circles would smirk at Kosta's self-aggrandizing tales, Deidre believed that Kosta earned big money as an assassin. She saw his car and the opulent, grandly furnished house where he lived with Lisa and her family. He even sneaked Deidre in for a room-by-room tour. She had never seen anything like it. She wanted to believe that Kosta was everything he claimed to be. And she wanted everything he could give her.

Kosta moved Deidre from one hotel to another, then to a small house he rented for her. At each, she insisted on bringing Lori Henderson, her eighteen-year-old, six-foot-tall lesbian lover. Kosta tolerated Deidre's lesbian affairs, but made it clear she was not to have sex with other men.

Nevertheless, Deidre had sex with whomever she pleased—and she pleased dozens of men. She just made sure none was around when Kosta arrived at 7:30 each weekday morning.

Through Kosta, Deidre began to enjoy material things that had eluded her throughout her brief and impoverished life. Besides paying her rent and utilities, Kosta gave her cash. He let her steal as much from Top Shots as she liked. He bought her clothes, jewelry, lots of drugs.

One day he told Deidre about the "Hunter-Killer Club," an organization of assassins who earned top dollar for murdering selected individuals. Although the "club" existed only in his imagination, Kosta spun tales in great detail, throwing in his own exploits. He was such a great assassin, boasted Kosta, that he was now the *head* of the Hunter-Killers. And he told her that she, too, could become a Hunter-Killer. All she had to do was murder someone, record the event on videotape, and give it to another member of Hunter-Killers. The video would be held by some unknown third member, he explained. That way, no one would ever rat out another; if he did, the betrayer's own video would go to authorities.

Deidre liked guns and liked the idea of killing. She wanted the money that would come to her if she became a Hunter-Killer. Another young woman might have challenged Kosta's fanciful tale of a CIA-sanctioned ring of killers-for-hire, but Deidre was driven by money and power. Another woman might have worried about the consequences of murder, but she had committed hundreds of crimes and had never served a day in prison. She had no fear of the law. Deidre told Kosta she wanted to become a Hunter-Killer.

Kosta explained that she would first have to prove her ability as a killer. He selected her first victim: Mark Ramsey. Before Kosta had appeared on the scene, Ramsey had briefly lived with Deidre. He worshipped her. He trusted her.

He was marked for death because he had tried to blackmail Kosta. And whatever slight affection Deidre might once have felt toward him was unimportant beside the opportunity she saw in Kosta's club of killers.

Once she was "blooded," Kosta continued, Deidre would be ready for her first assignment: engineering the death of Lisa. With his wife dead, Kosta explained, he would collect $700,000 in life insurance, plus Lisa's share of the Paspalakis business. And with Lisa out of the way, he said, he'd be free to marry Deidre. Deidre could have it all—the big house on the river, the jewelry, the cars, the carefree lifestyle funded by Joyland and several other businesses.

It sounded good to Deidre. Very good. She shared her plans and dreams with her other lover, Lori.

On the afternoon of October 3, 1989, Deidre told Ramsey that Kosta wanted to see him that evening.

Ramsey wasn't so sure he wanted to see Kosta. The last time they'd spoken, Kosta had promised to kill him if he ever went back to Top Shots. But Deidre assured him that Kosta was no longer angry. He had a little job for Ramsey, one that paid well, and he was willing to forgive and forget.

Ramsey wasn't completely at ease, but he knew Deidre. She had given him money and drugs. They had shared hash and coke and speed and had spent many a passionate afternoon exploring the highs and lows of kinky sex.

Later that night, they met on the boardwalk, near where Kosta waited in his BMW. Kosta said he wasn't angry anymore; he had a job to do, a job that involved braving "enemy fire." To prove that Ramsey was man enough for the job, Kosta would fire an assault rifle into the ground near Ramsey's feet. The whole thing would be videotaped and Kosta would send the tape to his "employer" to prove that Ramsey didn't flinch at gunfire.

It was three in the morning and Ramsey, sitting in the backseat, wasn't so sure about all this. According to later courtroom testimony, as the black BMW sped out of Daytona toward a thickly forested area, Ramsey kept saying how hungry he was. He begged to stop for some fast food.

Deidre, as reported in subsequent testimony, thought that if they let Ramsey out of the car, he'd run away.

"You can eat later," she said. "This won't take long."

The car turned off the main highway and bounced over a dirt road. Deep in the woods, Kosta braked to a halt and they all got out. Kosta told Ramsey to take a look around to make sure they had privacy.

When he returned, Kosta and Deidre were ready. To keep him from accidentally moving into a ricochet, said Kosta, he'd have to immobilize Ramsey. Still complaining of hunger, Ramsey allowed Kosta and Deidre to tie him to a tree trunk. Again Kosta assured Ramsey there was absolutely no danger, that he would fire his AK-47 Soviet-style assault rifle at his feet.

The only light on the scene came from Kosta's Mag flashlight. He slung the AK-47 over his shoulder and hefted the video camera in his right hand and the flashlight in his left. When Kosta briefly shone the light at Deidre, she complained angrily. "Don't shine that shit in my eyes," she said. The camera was rolling. The remark was recorded on tape.

Kosta kept the camera on Ramsey as Deidre approached the tree. She took a .22 semiautomatic pistol from the waistband of her jeans and pointed it at Ramsey.

Ramsey screamed when the first bullet hit his chest. He raised his left leg, struggling against the ropes. As the second and third bullets tore into his chest, he screamed again and again. Then he slumped back against the tree, quiet but still breathing.

Needing no instruction, Deidre walked up to the tree, grabbed Ramsey's hair, and jerked his head up. She put the pistol to his left temple and squeezed the trigger.

Deidre turned from her work flashing a prideful grin.

Ramsey was dead, or very nearly, but Kosta was not satisfied. The body still twitched. He leveled the AK-47 and fired a last shot into Ramsey's head. Deidre caught the expended cartridge with her jacket before it hit the ground.

They put their weapons and gear into the BMW's trunk and drove off.

\* \* \*

Beyond her singular beauty and her voracious sexual appetites, Kosta saw in Deidre one of few people in the world who could both insulate him from responsibility and efficiently carry out his myriad criminal schemes. Deidre was the queen of the boardwalk, and many of the common low-lifes haunting Daytona's waterfront jumped at her slightest suggestion. With Deidre as his sidekick, relaying orders, supervising the details, and dealing out discipline in his name, Kosta became the commandant of a ragtag legion of thieves and thugs. It was an arrangement that suited both.

Calderone, Top Shot's manager, was still fascinated by Deidre. But although she flirted outrageously with him, he feared Kosta too much to tempt fate. As Kosta's affair with Deidre became common knowledge on the Top Shot end of the boardwalk, he became increasingly bold about where he went with her. When Calderone mentioned this to him, he was told to mind his own business. Later, conversing with his wife, Calderone remarked on how Kosta was courting disaster by flaunting his affair.

Several weeks before the murder, Calderone's wife had phoned Lisa to tell her about Kosta's relationship with Deidre, begging her never to reveal where she had gotten her information.

When Lisa confronted her husband, he denied that he had anything but a business relationship with Deidre. He agreed to fire her from Top Shots—but so vociferously did he deny an affair that Lisa chose to believe him.

At least, she *wanted* to believe him. Desperately. But Lisa went so far as to tell Kosta flat out that if she ever found proof of his infidelity, she would divorce him immediately, leaving him with nothing. While Lisa knew that Kosta had great difficulty expressing emotion of any kind, she had no idea that her husband was a violent, unfeeling sociopath who had married her only for the opportunity to enrich himself.

Having received notice that Lisa would not tolerate his affairs, Kosta began planning her death, still convinced that he would inherit at least half the business and $700,000 in life insurance.

The day after Ramsey's murder, Kosta called Deidre. He

used a simple code, a string of numbers that told her what time to be at a specific pay phone for his call. All this rigamarole was required because Kosta now feared that Lisa had hired a private detective who had tapped his mistress's telephone.

When they finally connected, Kosta told Deidre to find someone to kill Lisa. He would offer the killer $10,000, but the assassin would never collect this fee. As soon as Lisa was dead, Kosta would leap from his hiding place and shoot her killer. In that way, he explained, not only would he take full control of Joyland, he would also appear as a big hero for coming to his wife's assistance. And of course the dead assassin would be unable to implicate him.

It would be a perfect crime.

So, Kosta went on, Deidre was to select someone "expendable" for the job. Surely there was someone among her dozens of followers who would not be missed, who would not be mourned.

Deidre was wildly excited about the plan. It was all she could think about. She had to tell everything to Lori.

Lori listened and said she thought the whole thing was "pretty weird." Shocked when Deidre told her how she and Kosta had killed Ramsey, she became even more afraid of Kosta. Later, when Deidre asked to spend the night, Lori said no. Instead she found Teja Mzimmia James, late of Brooklyn, a tall, good-looking, light-skinned black of nineteen. He was a Top Shots regular, a sometime Kosta gofer, a young man somewhat better educated than most of the boardwalk riffraff, but not above breaking a law or two for fun and profit. Lori told him all about the plan to hire an assassin to kill Lisa—and about the plan to kill the assassin.

Meanwhile, Deidre selected Matthew Chumbley, better known on the boardwalk as Mike Cox. He was a homeless, unemployed drifter with no local relatives, few friends, and a modest record of criminal offenses. She gave him a long, convoluted story about Kosta's Hunter-Killer Club. He could make ten grand a week, she said, doing political assassinations. There was very little risk, because Kosta had connections to the CIA. And all Chumbley had to do to get started was to go to a certain business on the boardwalk,

walk into the office, and kill the woman he would find there.

After he'd shot her, said Deidre, a man would come out of the rest room and hand him $10,000 in cash.

Chumbley wanted that money, but he was no fool. He figured out that the victim would be Lisa Paspalakis and that the man with the cash would be Kosta.

He agreed to kill. However, before meeting Kosta to pick up a gun, Chumbley broke into a house and was nabbed by police.

Kosta was furious and ordered Deidre to find another killer. He suggested Teja James, whom he knew as a tough and capable young man.

Deidre said that she thought Teja would do a good job killing Lisa, but that if *he* was used for the job, the plan would have to be changed. Teja was Lori's friend and he knew all about the original plan. Kosta agreed. Teja would make the hit, get his $10,000, and leave town for several months.

Deidre and Kosta went to Teja and made their pitch. Teja was reluctant, but Kosta made it very clear that he had no choice. He could kill Lisa and collect the money—or he could refuse, and be killed.

Teja finally agreed to kill Lisa. Following Kosta's plan, he would go to Joyland in the morning, when Lisa was alone in her office. He would force his way into the office and stab Lisa with a butcher knife Deidre had bought at a Pick 'N Save discount store.

At eleven on a late October morning, Teja sat with Deidre in a rented car outside Joyland, waiting for Lisa's brother, Dino, to leave on his regular daily trip to the bank.

For reasons never explained, Dino skipped the daily deposit that day.

Deidre went back to Kosta and told him what had happened. He was almost beside himself with anger. He couldn't believe that Lisa could be so lucky—or maybe that Deidre was an incompetent killer.

Lisa's murder was rescheduled for the following day: Halloween. Kosta and Lisa would attend a costume party at Razzles, a popular nightclub. Teja was to wait until Lisa went to the ladies' room, follow her into a stall, and stab her to death by jamming a long, razor-edged butcher knife between her third and fourth vertebrae, puncturing her diaphragm so she couldn't scream, then stabbing her again, slightly higher, in the heart.

Teja turned up at the party, the knife concealed in a rag. As the only attendee without a costume and a mask, he was oddly suspicious. Feeling naked and vulnerable, Teja followed Lisa around for hours, waiting for his chance. In the end he could never get up the nerve to stab her.

Kosta's anger was an awesome sight.

The next day, Teja was back in the parking lot with a .22 automatic, a gun Deidre had found in a pawnshop. Teja had test-fired it, but the gun jammed after each shot.

Deidre had told Kosta about the malfunctioning pistol, but he ignored this information. Teja was to shoot Lisa in the back of the head. One bullet would be enough.

When Dino left, on schedule, Teja waited a few minutes, then knocked on an outer door. Before leaving her office and opening the locked door, Lisa pulled open a desk drawer to get the gun she usually kept there. It was gone.

Leaving her office, she opened the door a crack and saw Teja. He looked vaguely familiar, but she couldn't place him.

"Is Kosta here?" he asked.

"No," said Lisa, putting her foot against the door.

Mumbling something about a promise of a job, Teja asked Lisa when she thought he might return.

Suddenly she noticed the pistol stuck in his waistband. Lisa flinched backward as Teja pulled out the .22 and ordered her back into the office.

Lisa knew there was no escape from the room. She didn't want to be in there, alone, with an armed man. She released the door and tumbled backward to the ground.

"Get up, bitch! You're going to die," shouted Teja.

Lisa scrambled to her feet as Teja cocked the pistol.

"Get back in the office!" he ordered.

"*You* get back in the office," said Lisa, whirling to run through the arcade.

Teja pointed the gun at Lisa as she scampered away. But

he had only one shot and no illusions about his ability to hit a rapidly moving target. As Lisa made it to the safety of a restaurant in the adjacent Marriott Hotel, Teja pulled the gun back in his jacket and fled.

Kosta was predictably angry when he learned of yet another failure. But he was a brilliant actor, rushing to Joyland to comfort his wife, who found him warm and supportive. Even as he held Lisa in his arms, murmuring endearments, Deidre was recruiting yet another killer.

Bryan Chase was just eighteen, a big, good-natured Ohio farm boy who lived with his parents in Daytona and held down a full-time job in a beachfront hotel. He was painfully shy around women and probably never met anyone remotely like Deidre.

Deidre seduced Chase—possibly for her private amusement—then turned him into a wannabe bad guy who hung around with the boardwalk lowlifes. He bragged about seducing Deidre while desperately hoping he'd get another opportunity to be with her. Chase was hooked. He would do anything she asked.

Deidre was ordered to crank up Bryan Chase for yet another attempt on Lisa's life. She gave Chase the same gun Teja had used and promised him $5,000 for killing Lisa. All he had to do was follow Lisa's car with his own pickup truck, slam lightly into her car at an intersection, and when she got out to exchange license and registration information, shoot her in the head.

Kosta would be in his BMW a few cars ahead. When Chase shot Lisa, he'd jump out, run back, and shoot him to death. Of course, Deidre neglected to mention this last detail to Chase.

At Joyland, Kosta suggested to Lisa that they rent a video and spend a quiet evening at home. It sounded like heaven to Lisa.

She followed her husband to the video store, thinking it odd that he took dark, narrow side streets when their usual route was along a well-lighted major thoroughfare. Glancing in her mirror, she had the distinct impression that someone in a pickup truck was following her. But she made it to the video store and then home without incident.

Bryan Chase told Deidre that he just couldn't find an opportunity to bang his truck into Lisa's car. It just wouldn't work.

Later that night, after talking to Kosta by phone, Deidre found Chase on the boardwalk. She told him that since his first attempt failed, he'd have to do it the hard way. He'd have to break into the Paspalakis house, find the upstairs bedroom where Lisa and Kosta would be sleeping, and shoot Lisa in the head several times. Then, to make it look like robbery, he could take a few valuable items and escape. Kosta would pay him $5,000 and he'd be in the Hunter-Killers.

Deidre also promised a little party, just the two of them. Driven by the thought of all that money and more sex, Chase agreed.

Wandering around the boardwalk before his appointment to end Lisa's life, Chase ran into another of Deidre's lovers, J. R. Taylor, a nineteen-year-old burglar who had been her first boyfriend when she came to Daytona.

Kosta didn't like J.R. because Deidre still had feelings for him. He'd once caught him in Deidre's room and fired a shot at him. But that had not stopped Kosta, in the months afterward, from making broad hints about hiring J.R. to kill Lisa. When J.R. checked with Deidre, however, he'd learned that it was a setup, that whoever Kosta hired to kill Lisa would never live to spend the money.

J.R. told Bryan Chase all about this as they sat on the boardwalk, smoking cigarettes.

Chase was in a fearsome double bind. No doubt Kosta would kill him whether he shot Lisa or not.

Nevertheless, urged on by Deidre, he turned up at three in the morning in the backyard of the Paspalakis house. Chase was to break a small basement window, one that was not protected by the house's elaborate alarm system. If he couldn't fit through the broken window, Kosta would be waiting to turn off the alarm, let Chase in the back door, then reactivate the security system.

When Chase tried to break the window, nothing happened. The glass was too thick. He returned to the boardwalk and found Deidre. More than a little upset, she sent

Chase back to the house and told him he had to break in, no matter what. She made it plain that if he didn't murder Lisa that night, Kosta would surely kill him. But Chase just couldn't break in. When a neighbor's dogs began to bark, he fled.

The next day, Kosta told Deidre to give Chase an X-Acto knife, which he could use to remove the putty holding the glass. Then he could remove the whole pane. That night, after three, Chase returned yet again to the Paspalakis house. The X-Acto knife was of no use. Once again Chase returned to the boardwalk.

Deidre flew into one of her monumental rages. She almost took the gun and shot Chase on the spot. What worried her now was that after so many failures, Kosta would insist that Deidre herself kill Lisa. So she sent Chase back for a fourth attempt at breaking into the house. And once again he failed.

But driven by fear, sex, and money, he agreed to try yet again the next night. The new plan was for Kosta to leave a light burning in the basement stairwell. When Lisa was sleeping soundly, he would get up and turn the light off, a signal to Chase.

Under cover of darkness, Chase returned. After several minutes, he eased into the street in front of the house and found Deidre, waiting in a parked car. It was no use, he said. He just couldn't get in.

"Go back and try again," Deidre ordered.

Soon after he arrived in the backyard, the stairwell light went out.

But it was not Kosta who turned the switch; it was Dino, Lisa's brother, who was suffering from a cold and had woken up with a sore throat. He went to the kitchen for water and turned off what he thought was a useless light. Dino washed down some aspirin with milk and went back to sleep.

Moments after Dino went upstairs, Kosta came down. He smashed the window with a hammer, then let Chase into the house and led him to the bedroom where Lisa lay sleeping.

Kosta lay down on his side of the bed as Chase approached Lisa, gun in hand.

By the dim glow of a tropical-fish aquarium, Chase put the .22 to Lisa's temple and pulled the trigger. A bullet penetrated Lisa's skull near her ear.

When Chase tried to fire again the gun jammed. He didn't know what to do.

"Fuck it," he said, heading for the door.

Kosta leaped from bed, his gun blazing. He put seven shots into Chase's chest. Then he stood over the body and carefully put one more in his head.

Downstairs, Dino heard what sounded like firecrackers. He rushed to the bedroom, as did Lisa's mother, Mary.

On the bed, Lisa opened her eyes. "I'm all right," she said, struggling to remain conscious.

The bullet had penetrated the thickest part of her skull, losing most of its kinetic energy as it did so. For this reason it did minimal damage to her brain.

The first to suspect that Kosta was involved was Dino. While ignorant of the details, he told police he was very suspicious of his brother-in-law. Soon after Dino voiced his fears, J. R. Taylor, worried that Kosta might come after him, telephoned police detectives to say that he'd heard that Kosta was behind the plot to kill Lisa, that Chase had been marked to die before he broke into the house.

But beyond the musings of a boardwalk transient, what most interested Corporal Greg Smith, the detective assigned to investigate the shooting, was that if Chase had entered the bedroom intent on robbery, and if he had intended to shoot someone, then surely he would have shot *Kosta* first. Even if he'd had no idea who the sleeping couple were, Kosta was larger and would have posed more of a threat. Instead, Chase shot Lisa first.

Nor could Smith understand how Kosta, just awakened from deep sleep, had been able to shoot Chase eight times within seconds of opening his eyes. Smith shared his feelings with his boss, Lieutenant William Evans of the Daytona Beach Police. It didn't add up for Evans, either.

For several days following the shooting, Daytona's media portrayed Kosta as a hero who had saved his wife's life.

Reveling in the attention, Kosta speculated to police and reporters that those who wanted to tear down the boardwalk's family-owned businesses and make millions through redevelopment were behind the plot to kill Lisa.

At the same time, Kosta went right on plotting her death. He told Deidre to have Teja make a bomb out of laundry detergent and gasoline and smuggle it into Lisa's hospital room, which was under round-the-clock police guard.

On the evening of Tuesday, November 7, Mike Chumbley, out on bail, tried to score enough money to buy drugs. He snatched a heavy medallion from a man's neck and ran into the night. Unfortunately, Chumbley's victim was a police decoy who chased him down. Once in custody, Chumbley bargained what he knew about Kosta's plan to kill his wife against the hope of a reduced charge. Now there were two people who had told police they knew who wanted Lisa dead.

Lori was brought in for questioning and she volunteered that Teja had built a bomb to finish off Lisa—and anyone else who might be in her room.

When police arrested Teja James, he said, truthfully, he'd never even built the bomb. Then he told them what he knew about the plot to kill Lisa, including his own abortive efforts at Joyland.

That was enough. Deidre and Kosta were arrested.

Lisa, at first, refused to believe that her husband was behind the whole sordid plot. She would later—very painfully—come to accept that she had married a sociopathic killer.

During several long and convoluted interrogations, Deidre told police that Kosta had controlled her every action with fear, that she had acted to save her own life. She claimed to have gone along with Kosta's plot to kill Lisa because he had threatened to send police the videotape of Mark Ramsey's murder. Deidre told police she shot Ramsey only after Kosta had applied lighted cigarettes to her breast and threatened her. Even then, she said, she shot him only because Kosta had an assault rifle trained on her.

Deidre was a bright young woman who had succeeded at manipulating many at society's fringes through her formidable sexuality and her willingness to enter into almost any depraved bargain. But she had never had to deal in earnest with honest citizens. She knew society had its rules, but felt that she was special and so not bound by these rules. Attempting to manipulate the legal system, she used the amoral techniques that had served her on the streets. They did not work for her. She fought constantly with her court-appointed attorney. She switched her plea from guilty to not guilty and back again to guilty, several times. In her calculating way, Deidre granted interviews to newspaper reporters, replete with lurid details intended to make her seem more victim than perpetrator. And she strove to create an elaborate myth to conceal the true nature of her involvement with Kosta.

The videotape of Ramsey's murder, seized from its hiding place at the Paspalakis home, was shown to juries at both Deidre's sentencing hearing and Kosta's trial. It was a devastating blow to Deidre's claim that Kosta had held her at gunpoint when she shot Mark Ramsey. The tape convinced jurors that Kosta had held a video camera in one hand, a flashlight in the other. Deidre, armed with a pistol, had plenty of opportunity to shoot Kosta instead of Ramsey.

Worse, the tape clearly conveyed the obvious relish with which Deidre had killed Ramsey. It was the most damning evidence possible.

Deidre pleaded guilty to Ramsey's murder. She agreed to testify against Kosta and the judge postponed her sentencing until he was tried. But when she testified, she lied, evaded, and dodged questions. She wore down the patience of a long-suffering judge, in the process convincing prosecutors that she could never be trusted to tell the truth.

Kosta testified in his own defense, denying any involvement in the deaths of Ramsey and Chase, and the attempts on Lisa's life. He maintained that the voice on the Ramsey murder video was not his, despite overwhelming scientific evidence to the contrary. Kosta claimed that his prosecution was politically motivated, that he was framed by wealthy businessmen who had hoped to kill Lisa as part of a plan to reap millions of dollars by redeveloping the boardwalk.

A jury found Kosta guilty of murder in the first degree.

He was also convicted on a raft of lesser charges, including counterfeiting. Kosta and Deidre were sentenced to die in Florida's electric chair.

Teja James was convicted of conspiracy and sentenced to four years in prison. Lori Henderson, who helped Deidre plot Lisa's murder, was similarly convicted and sentenced.

An autopsy was performed on the remains of Steno Paspalakis. The results were inconclusive. Officially, the cause of his death remains natural causes.

Lisa was incredibly lucky. Had Bryan Chase followed Deidre's instructions and shot Lisa in the *back* of the head, she probably would have died instantly. Instead, she made a nearly complete recovery. The bullet, however, remains lodged in her brain; doctors decided it would be less risky to leave it than to open her skull and probe for it.

Lisa and Kosta were divorced after Kosta's convictions.

Kosta Fotopoulos and Deidre Hunt believed they had planned the perfect crime. They failed because the people they selected as their instruments of murder were flawed, unreliable, and inept. Kosta's scheme started out clever and daring, but soon became almost a parody of itself.

# No Body
# (1955)

AN ONE BE CONVICTED OF MURDER IF AUTHORITIES CAN-
not prove that a supposed victim is actually dead?
And if police cannot produce a dead body, or enough of it
to identify the victim beyond a reasonable doubt, can any
court convict an accused killer? If there is no body and no
witness who can testify to seeing the accused kill, or even
that they heard him acknowledge the victim's death, can the
state prove a murder has occurred?

In 1955, no California court had ever convicted without
at least a body, or a witness, or a confession. So, reasoned
L. Ewing Scott, a shrewd and very poised man, if he could
kill his wife with no witnesses, dispose of her body without
a trace, and keep his mouth shut about what he had done,
it would be impossible for prosecutors to get a conviction.
He would have committed the perfect crime.

Robert Leonard Ewing Scott was tall, broad-shouldered,
and movie-star handsome, always well groomed and impec-
cably attired. He was a smooth, nearly unflappable man
who projected a polished, cosmopolitan image. Many
women, especially those of a certain age still looking for
romance, found him an irresistible package.

Scott was born in St. Louis in 1896. He was raised as an
only child, though he had a half brother and half sister from
his father's prior marriage. Scott's father was a hard-

238

drinking, womanizing, wildcat oilman whose finances and fortunes swung wildly between poor and worse. Scott spent several childhood years living with grandparents and aunts; at nineteen he moved to Chicago and struck out on his own as a clerk.

As a young man, Scott worked in a stockbrokerage, where he observed the outward signs of success displayed by investment counselors. He had a singular talent for mimicry, and over time, imitating the dress and mannerisms of men in whose shadow he toiled, Scott developed an impressive facade. To casual acquaintances he came off as intelligent, well heeled, politically conservative, worldly wise, and knowledgeable. But Scott had little formal education; most of what he knew was culled from self-improvement articles found in the men's magazines he devoured. He was a bright fellow, affable and convivial, but nowhere near as smart as he believed. Beneath his carefully constructed surface, Scott was cold, cruel, calculating, self-centered—and totally ruthless.

Nearing forty, no longer young enough for entry-level jobs, and weary of failed business attempts, Scott finally discovered his calling. He became a con artist and gigolo, presenting himself to likely candidates as a successful "financier." For his con games, he used several aliases; for pursuing moneyed women, he restyled his real name, dropping "Robert" and reducing "Leonard" to an initial.

As cool, unruffled L. Ewing Scott, he affected an urbane knowledgeability about real estate developing, investing, and finance, a complex world far beyond his real experience and understanding.

In 1934, after his last failure at starting a stockbrokerage, Scott moved to Los Angeles, a town where almost everyone reinvents himself at least once. There he met, wooed, and married Alva Brewer, the no-longer-young heir to a Canadian mining fortune.

Scott and Alva divided their time between a San Fernando Valley squire's "ranch" and luxury cruise ships circling the world. Scott's pretensions and shallowness did not survive the intimate daily commerce of marriage. Alva came to know the real L. Ewing Scott as a calculating misogynist and fortune-hunting heel. After enduring five years of his abuse, she sued for divorce. Scott came away with a generous financial settlement and membership in the exclusive Jonathan Club, whose members were and are a who's who of Southern California's elite.

During World War II, Scott parlayed a childhood friendship into a low-level job in the Office of Price Administration in Washington, D.C., thus neatly sidestepping the draft. But although his duties were no more than those of a glorified clerk, after a few months of picking quarrels with fellow workers, failing to show up for normal working hours, and displaying general incompetence, he was fired. Scott would nevertheless thereafter describe his brief government service as a major contribution to the war effort. Pressed for details, he would airily explain that it was all "hush-hush"—important, classified matters that remained secret.

Unwilling to work for a living, dependent on what he could con from rich women or the unwary, Scott became a world-class tightwad. While dining—usually on funds provided by others—in luxurious restaurants or traveling around the world in extravagant style, he rarely condescended to tip waiters or porters; indeed, on several occasions he was seen pocketing tips left by others. When he bought something with his own money, a rare event, he haggled with the élan of a bazaar merchant.

Between 1945 and 1948, Scott was married to a wealthy Italian woman. When they divorced, it cost her family $200,000 to rid her of him. Embarrassed by having fallen for such an obvious fortune hunter, the woman kept her marriage secret for several years.

By 1949, Scott was living in a small room at the Jonathan Club and working intermittently as a salesman for housepainters; his bank account had dwindled to $3,000. He spent much of his time dodging businessmen whom he had conned or swindled.

And then he met Evelyn Throsby.

Evelyn, a Pasadena society matron, had been married four times. While her first two marriages were to abusive alcoholics and ended in divorce, her next two husbands were both chronically ill and rich. Each had the grace to die and leave her a tidy fortune. When she met Scott, Evelyn was worth almost $1 million.

To Scott, Evelyn must have seemed heaven-sent. Although four years his senior, she appeared far younger. She was slender, fastidiously groomed, rich—and despite a life crammed with social engagements, lonely.

He was fifty-three, showing the first hint of fleshiness and aging, and he might have felt that Evelyn was his last chance at a rich woman. Mustering considerable charm, he pursued her. In August, after weeks of chaste dinner and luncheon dates, Scott persuaded Evelyn to accompany him on a long auto trip through Mexico. He was attentive, caring, romantic. They were married, south of the border, on September 3, 1949. Uncertain if the marriage was valid in the United States, Scott insisted on a second ceremony in Carson City, Nevada, two weeks later.

Evelyn had a wide circle of friends, with whom she regularly dined, chatted over the telephone, or visited. Among them were many wealthy and socially prominent people, including the actress and singer Jeanette MacDonald, one of the top film stars of her era and a woman admired for her philanthropy almost as much as her talent. In an act calculated to isolate his wife and make her more dependent on him, Scott persuaded Evelyn to sell her comfortable Pasadena home and move to Bel Air, a newly fashionable foothill section of Los Angeles just north of the Los Angeles campus of the University of California.

Evelyn's household had long included a secretary, a cook, a chauffeur who doubled as handyman, and a maid. Soon after moving into her Pasadena house, in the name of economy, Scott began firing the servants. Not long after moving to Bel Air, he fired his wife's live-in maid.

Evelyn became increasingly isolated, dependent upon Scott for almost everything—everything, that is, except money. Ewing, as he asked his friends to call him, had no income except what he got from Evelyn.

Evelyn was a warmhearted, sensible woman of well-established habits. For many years, she had kept a weekly appointment with her hairdresser. She regularly visited her physician for treatment of a chronic but nonthreatening intestinal condition. She required reading glasses and so kept regular appointments with her optometrist. She wore a partial denture, and to maintain it properly and care for her natural teeth, she regularly saw her dentist. Most of her fortune was conservatively invested in stocks and bonds, and since she was a knowledgeable and interested investor, she spoke frequently with her stockbroker. She also spoke often with her attorney; an incessant traveler, before each departure Evelyn left him an itinerary so he could contact her if something unexpected came up. A woman of solid predictability, she continued her regular routines even after moving to Bel Air.

Shortly after their marriage, Scott laid the groundwork for a grand scheme. Using all his powers of persuasion—and sometimes a few punches, slaps, and other forms of physical intimidation—he pursuaded Evelyn to begin converting her wealth from blue-chip stocks and triple-A bonds into hundred-dollar bills.

Scott's rationale was an incredible three-part fiction. He convinced Evelyn that he was extremely knowledgeable about financial matters; that the stock market was unreasonably high and so must surely decline; and that although this was a time of world peace, a nuclear war was inevitable, likely to begin soon, with Los Angeles a target. So, said Scott, until this danger passed, at least, it made sense to get out of stocks and bonds and stash the cash in safe-deposit boxes in major cities around the country. That way, he explained, if they had to flee Los Angeles, they would have adequate money in banks anywhere they might seek refuge.

It made no sense at all. If a nuclear bomb exploded near Los Angeles, the Scotts would have had far more to worry about then a ready supply of cash. But Scott never let up on his plan, harping on its virtues day and night to Evelyn both alone and in the company of her friends. Such was Scott's hold on his wife's failing self-esteem that in the end, partly just to shut him up and to restore tranquillity to her home, she succumbed. By early 1955, she had liquidated some $600,000 in securities, placing most of the cash in safe-deposit boxes around the country. While Evelyn later confided doubts about the wisdom of her husband's ideas to her friends, she never publicly questioned his honesty.

After liquidating Evelyn's assets, Scott fired her stockbroker, explaining that as he himself was a knowledgeable investor, he would be managing Evelyn's portfolio should she reenter the securities market.

On the afternoon of May 16, 1955, Ulrich Quast, a recent immigrant from Germany and an auto salesman, hoping to sell the Scotts a new Mercedes-Benz 220S, rang the doorbell of the Scott's Bel Air home.

It was Evelyn who had made the appointment and who had expressed the most interest in the car. The couple was contemplating an extended European vacation, she told Quast, perhaps to Spain. They were considering buying a Mercedes in Germany, having it delivered to Spain for their trip, and bringing it back to California when they returned.

After pointing out the advantages and safety features of German engineering, Quast got behind the wheel and took the couple for a test-drive. Grudgingly admitting that the car rode well, Scott complained that $2,600 seemed like far too much money for a mere automobile. Quast left without an order but with Scott's promise that he would consider the purchase carefully and telephone in a few days.

Ulrich Quast was the last person, aside from her husband, to see Evelyn Throsby Scott alive.

May 17, 1955, was a Tuesday, the day of Evelyn's weekly beauty-salon appointment. A few minutes after the shop opened that morning, an unidentified male caller telephoned to cancel Mrs. Scott's 9:30 appointment. Manager Ellen Richmond was surprised. She was even more surprised when the man said that all Mrs. Scott's future appointments were also canceled. Later, much later, she would remember his exact words: "I'm canceling all her appointments, for good."

Two days later, Scott appeared at the Westwood branch of Security First National Bank, where Evelyn kept a safe-deposit box. The box was in Evelyn's name only, but Scott had a plan. He handed a completed bank form naming himself as the box's co-renter to the young female clerk. Looking it over, the clerk noted that it bore the signature of

Evelyn Throsby Scott. But although the clerk was new on her job, she knew that documents like corenters' agreements had to be signed in the presence of a bank officer.

Very politely, she told Scott that he could not have access to the box unless Mrs. Scott signed the agreement in the bank.

Scott threw a fit. He demanded to speak to the clerk's supervisor. Assistant Manager Bill Dawson listened as Scott, purple-faced with fury, demanded an explanation for the clerk's bad manners. What kind of a place was this, he raged, that wouldn't let a man into his own wife's box when he had a perfectly legal document showing he was entitled to enter?

Dawson was apologetic as he compared the signatures on the corenters' agreement with Evelyn's on-file signature card and Scott's driver's license. Satisfied, he told the clerk to give Scott access to the box.

Evelyn received regular monthly income from a Milwaukee apartment complex she owned. Scott's next move was to set up a system to divert this income to his own use. Step one was to open a new account in the nearby Westwood branch of the Bank of Los Angeles. The initial deposit was five hundred dollars in cash, taken from Evelyn's safe-deposit box. Over the next few days he added another six hundred to the account, including three hundred in traveler's checks made out to and apparently countersigned by Evelyn.

Scott opened a new joint account in his and Evelyn's names with the Bank of America. Evelyn already had accounts in the two nearest Bank of America branches, so Scott drove to Van Nuys, forty-five minutes away, and presented a clerk there with a joint-tenancy account form signed by Evelyn, and four hundred-dollar bills.

While in Van Nuys, Scott asked a clerk to make up a rubber stamp of Evelyn's signature. She traveled so much, explained the distinguished-looking man, that it was difficult to make her deposits. The stamp, he added, would simplify the procedure, because while few banks would accept facsimile signatures on withdrawals, most found them acceptable for deposits. With the signature stamp, Scott could deposit checks coming to Evelyn into their joint account. And by writing out other checks from her private account to "Mrs. Evelyn Scott," he could also deposit them in the joint account. He could systematically transfer every cent she had in her Bank of America accounts to the joint account.

In early July, Scott, ever the tightwad, canceled $6,000 insurance coverage on Evelyn's jewelry, including a necklace with a hundred small diamonds, a gift of her last husband. He demanded that the cancellation be backdated to May 17 so he could get a rebate on the premium.

The insurance company dutifully sent him the refund: $3.47.

As weeks passed with no word from Evelyn, her friends became concerned. Scott ignored most of the letters and notes, responding to telephone calls by saying that Evelyn was suffering from an acute mental disorder and was in an East Coast sanitarium. He told some of her close friends that Evelyn had cancer and had gone east for treatment.

As time went on, Scott began to say that Evelyn was an incurable alcoholic; that she had tried to poison him; that she often vanished for days at a time without saying where she went. Scott, barely suppressing the anger in his voice, confided that this was because, in addition to her alcoholism, Evelyn was a lesbian who often enjoyed clandestine assignations with a coterie of female lovers. He wasn't worried about her, he told everyone. She'd often done things like this before.

Then, suddenly, the phone at the Scotts' Bel Air home was disconnected. There would be no more phone calls to disturb L. Ewing Scott's tranquil life. Scott fired his once-a-week cleaning lady and his chauffeur, explaining that he would be closing the house and moving to the East Coast to be closer to Evelyn's hospital.

Not long after that, Gladys Baum and Opal Mumper, two of Evelyn's closest friends, drove from Pasadena to Bel Air to see for themselves what had happened. They rang the doorbell. They knocked on the door. There was no answer. They went into the backyard and knocked on the back door. As they were about to leave, Opal saw Scott staring silently out of the window, motionless except for his singular characteristic gesture, twirling his eyeglasses by holding the frame and rapidly rotating his wrist.

In late July, more than two months after Evelyn was last seen in Bel Air, Scott gave a dinner party at the Jonathan Club. One of his guests brought a very beautiful and very rich widow, Harriet Livermore. Soon Scott was seen squiring Mrs. Livermore about Southern California's most elegant establishments.

Just about that time, two of Evelyn's friends separately contacted the Los Angeles County District Attorney's Office, each to ask for help in finding their mysteriously absent friend. One of these was songstress Jeanette MacDonald, who personally called S. Ernest Roll, the District Attorney. To mollify one of his more famous constituents, Roll ordered an informal investigation. But the DA tiptoed into the case. All he had was a reportedly slightly eccentric woman of considerable means who hadn't been seen for some time by her friends. Her husband, ostensibly a respected financier, was a pillar of the community, a member of the exclusive Jonathan Club, and judging by his failure to file a missing person's report, not at all alarmed at her absence.

L. Ewing Scott was to be treated with kid gloves, said Roll. There was probably a perfectly good reason why his wife had dropped out of sight, and with an election year coming up, the last thing Roll wanted was to anger a prominent member of the local Establishment.

DA investigators conducted a delicate interview with Scott, which netted little information but left them scratching their heads. Affable and unruffled, Scott described his wife as an alcoholic and insisted she had a serious problem with cancer. He seemed so open, so coolly unflappable, that detectives were reluctant to press him, even though they couldn't get him to give a single straight, unequivocal answer. The best they could do was extract a statement that the last time Scott had seen his wife was in May, when she had sent him to a drugstore for a can of Effermin tooth powder. When he returned, said Scott, his wife had vanished. And while Scott's vagueness seemed suspicious, investigators had not a shred of evidence that a crime had occurred.

But since Evelyn had still not surfaced, the investigators decided to poke around and see what they could learn about either one of the Scotts. Evelyn was known to be wealthy, so on a hunch, investigators began checking with stockbrokers. They soon located the E. F. Hutton office where Evelyn's accounts had been kept until February 1955. The check that closed out that account was cashed at the Westwood branch of Security First. Talking to the branch manager, investigators learned about the peculiar but apparently legal manner whereby Scott had gained access to Evelyn's safe-deposit box on May 19. Calls to other banks in the area turned up Evelyn's three other bank accounts. Oddly, no checks had been written against any of them since the first part of May. Several hundred dollars in traveler's checks, however, had been deposited in the joint account Scott had set up in the Van Nuys branch of the Bank of America.

Probing Ewing's background proved unexpectedly mysterious. He was by all accounts a prosperous man—yet Evelyn's tax returns did not include him and he had not filed a return of his own in eight years. DA investigators were unable to discover any business licenses in Scott's name, nor even one former employer. Everything about L. Ewing Scott was a riddle.

Scott meanwhile was living very well, depositing to his account the monthly sums from the Milwaukee firm that managed Evelyn's apartment building. He secreted, somewhere in the large home on Bentley Drive, a very large wad of hundred-dollar bills, more than $57,000.

Some of this doubtless went to entertain the enchanting Mrs. Livermore, of whom Scott was seeing more and more. But Harriet Livermore was no one's fool. She was not reassured by Scott's vague answers to her increasingly probing questions about his past and about his wife's whereabouts. When, in September 1955, he invited her to accompany him to Central America, making plain that he expected her to share his bed, she broke off their still-chaste relationship. She filed away in her formidable memory just what an odd duck was L. Ewing Scott.

It was nearly a year after Evelyn was last seen before investigators had their first hostile interview with Scott. In the meantime, however, Bill Brawner, a friend of Evelyn's fourth husband, had been busy checking East Coast hospitals and sanitariums for any trace of Evelyn. And he tracked down her younger brother—and only relative—Raymond.

In October, Brawner met Raymond and told him that Evelyn had been absent for months. Raymond Throsby made an appointment with District Attorney Roll, who proved unable to tell him much except his men were looking into her disappearance. Raymond joined the search himself, staking out the Bel Air home, noting Scott's comings and goings. Finally he confronted Scott on the sidewalk in front of the house.

All that came of this meeting was that Scott insisted that Evelyn was an alcoholic who frequently wandered off; Raymond accused Scott of killing his sister.

In November, when Scott attempted to gain access to the Security First safe-deposit box, the branch manager refused. Scott argued, threatened, created an ugly scene. The manager, quietly briefed by police, stood his ground. Scott left, empty-handed, in a huff.

Not content with passive measures, on February 13, 1956, Roll sent his detectives to the Jonathan Club to escort Scott back to his Bel Air residence. There, beginning at ten in the evening and lasting until late the following afternoon, they interrogated him at length. He remained a smooth and unflappable subject until the very end of this interrogation.

Before they left, the investigators managed to get Scott to contradict his earlier adamant assertion that he had gone out for tooth powder. Before the long interrogation was over, Scott insisted that the DA's men had it all wrong, that he had always claimed it was *Evelyn* who had gone out for the tooth powder and never returned. A few days later, Scott elaborated, he had found her parked car in nearby Westwood, and had used the spare keys to drive it home.

While being questioned, Scott, under the curious eyes of

detectives, chewed his lower lip over and over. Eventually the lip bled. At the same time, he repeatedly rubbed the area beneath his eyes with a hard knuckle, first one side and then the other. The next day, Scott told newspaper reporters that the DA's men had worked him over, offering as proof his bruised face, blackened eyes, and torn lip. Whether they believed him or not, it made a good story and some editors gave it page-one treatment.

In March 1956, the story of Evelyn's disappearance finally hit the front pages when Raymond Throsby filed for trusteeship of her estate. Scott hired an attorney and challenged Throsby's claims. Alerted by the newspaper stories, Los Angeles Police Chief William Parker bitterly criticized District Attorney Roll for concealing a possible crime, and ordered his own men to enter the case.

There was still no evidence against Scott, still no proof even that Evelyn was not in perfect health. But the Los Angeles newspapers, always eager to share newfound facts about the lives of the wealthy and prominent, were in full cry. If Evelyn Throsby Scott was still alive, why didn't she come forward and say so?

More to the point, having had time to assess Scott's peculiar behavior, both police and district attorney's detectives began to dig deeper into his convoluted story. They quizzed Bel Air neighbors and learned that some of them had smelled smoke from the Scott residence—and something more: an indescribably but awful smell that had emanated from the Scott incinerator shortly after Evelyn disappeared.

As investigators dug further they learned that Scott was dating other women, and that one, the most attractive but penniless Marianne Beaman, had spent several nights in the Scott home, and had twice accompanied him on overnight trips to San Diego and to Las Vegas.

The District Attorney's office was intrigued to learn that Scott in Las Vegas, at a chance meeting with old friends, had introduced Beaman to them as "Mrs. Scott."

On March 10, a small army of investigators descended upon the Scott home. They probed every foot of the grounds with long poles, looking for a body. They turned the house upside down without finding either Evelyn or her money. In the incinerator were the remains of a feathered corset, and a fragment of lamb-chop bone.

They were also curious to find a book that Scott had written, under a pseudonym. Titled *How to Fascinate Men* and ostensibly a handbook for female gold diggers, it reflected the musings and insights of a man whose experience as a high-level gigolo had afforded him rare insights into the art of manipulating women.

On the other side of a wall separating the Scott incinerator from the neighbor's property, investigators found a partial denture, five artificial teeth. Also discovered in dense foliage were the partially decomposed remains of several prescription drugs, and two pairs of women's reading glasses.

Under intense questioning, Scott declared that he never met Evelyn's dentist or her optometrist; thorough police work turned up these two professionals. The optometrist confirmed that he had made the reading glasses for Evelyn. The dentist's artisan who fashioned the partial denture was equally adamant that he had made the device for Evelyn, and that no one else could have worn it. Equally damning were the dentist's and optometrist's clear recollections that they had met L. Ewing Scott several times and had spoken to him at great length.

In looting Evelyn's safe-deposit boxes and bank accounts, Scott had left an extensive paper trail. The district attorney's own "questioned documents" expert, Donn Mire, subjected the signatures to intensive analysis. While they appeared to be Evelyn's, under infrared light, these signatures yielded up their secrets: they had been traced from real signatures, but they had not been written by the hand of Evelyn Scott.

Scott was arrested in April 1956, on the only charges that could be made, theft and forgery. En route to the police station for booking, detectives took a leisurely detour to an isolated, ridgetop fire station. There, unhindered by the Supreme Court's yet-to-be-written Miranda ruling, which years later would require police to stop questioning a suspect when he asked to see an attorney, they attacked Scott's story. He refused to budge an inch.

Finally booked, Scott was released almost immediately on $25,000 bond, a sum he paid, in cash, from a cache mysteriously hidden in his house.

A day or two later, after considerable haggling, Scott bought—for cash—a used green Ford, a powerful car capable of going eighty miles an hour. It also had a large trunk; Scott very carefully measured to make sure it would hold all his luggage before he agreed to buy the car. Since his picture had been in all the newspapers and he had given an interview aired on a local television station, it's not surprising that the car salesman was well aware of his customer's identity.

Within hours of accepting Scott's money and watching him drive off, the salesman called a friend—an LAPD detective—and gave a description of the Ford. He also reported Scott's comments about needing a car that could outrun the highway patrol.

Police doubled surveillance of Scott and his house.

A few days later, Scott gave his typewriter and several personal items to Marianne Beaman, along with several expensive pieces of jewelry belonging to Evelyn.

On April 27, Scott appeared before the Los Angeles County Grand Jury, where he was questioned by a deputy DA about his wife's disappearance. He refused to answer any questions, but late that afternoon the grand jury returned an indictment, charging him with nine counts of forgery, four of grand theft, and thirteen of fraud.

Once again, Scott put up bail money, mostly in cash. Pleading cash-flow problems, he borrowed several thousand dollars from his attorneys.

A few days later, Evelyn's red coupe was found parked on a street not far from Marianne Beaman's apartment. A pair of bullet holes were found in it. Police recovered an expended .45-caliber cartridge from the car's interior.

But L. Ewing Scott had vanished.

When he failed to show for a succession of court appearances, a fugitive warrant was issued. Police turned the Bel Air house upside down, probing the backyard once again. The only thing they found of interest was a professional wiretapping device in the basement.

Scott had actually managed to get a twelve-day head start on his pursuers, but in the process he drove his green Ford off a narrow, twisting Sierra Nevada road above Bishop, a central California town near the Nevada border. After having the car towed, he took a hotel room and spent three days waiting for repairs. He continued on to Ontario, Canada, by a circuitous route, arriving a few days before police noticed he was missing and posted all-points bulletins.

Scott holed up in a succession of comfortable resort hotels around Lake Ontario. He sold his Ford, bought another used car, sold it weeks later and bought still another, sold it and bought a fourth car, then traded that for a fifth. He kept to his various rented rooms, telling innkeepers and hoteliers that he was an accountant desperate to finish some enormous project that required his constant work. He dined alfresco on hot dogs and other cheap street-vendor repasts. He changed his name as often as he changed cars, and he stuck to resort towns along the Great Lakes, where strangers were common the year around.

Time passed. Scott found a modest apartment in Toronto. He might well have gone to earth in Canada, waiting, until the hubbub in Los Angeles faded. He might easily have established a new life under an assumed name. He had enough cash with him when he left Los Angeles to reinvent himself, find an undemanding job, and live the rest of his life in obscurity.

But he was L. Ewing Scott! He liked fine restaurants and good clothes and beautiful women. He was confident and assured. He went through life acting as though he was as smart and successful as he tried to make others believe. It was his big mistake.

Scott decided he wanted a new and documented American identity and hatched a scheme to get it. On the evening of Monday, April 9, 1957, he crossed from Windsor, Ontario, to Detroit. After lengthy shopping for the best price, he bought a new Ford Fairlane 500 from a dealership. Before paying for it, however, he talked the salesman into driving him to Ohio, where he could get a driver's license without having to show a birth certificate. Scott, who had already impressed the salesman as a skinflint, told the salesman that if he could get an out-of-state license he'd avoid paying about $125 in Michigan sales taxes. The salesman drove him to and from Toledo, Ohio, a two-hour trip, then did it again so Scott could pick up his license. The hungry salesman even provided Scott with an out-of-state address.

Driving a new car and armed with a new identity, Scott crossed the Canadian border on April 15. His distinguished-looking appearance caught the eye of a Canadian immigration officer with a good memory for faces. As Scott filled out a lengthy form ostensibly required to import his new car, the officer skimmed "wanted" bulletins. Soon, American FBI agents escorted L. Ewing Scott back to Michigan.

But Scott was far from done. He held an impromptu press conference in a Detroit courthouse hallway, declaring his innocence and increasing the pulses of dozens of comely Michigan matrons who flocked to the courthouse to see the handsome and cultured man accused of murdering his wife.

Scott hired a Michigan lawyer, fought extradition, and succeeded in delaying his departure for the Golden State. After three weeks, Deputy L.A. County DA Art Alarcon, representing California in the extradition proceedings and anxious to return home, told Scott's attorney that if his client didn't stop fooling around and waive extradition immediately, the DA's office would suspend their efforts and just turn Scott over to federal agents.

That would leave him facing federal charges of unlawful flight to evade prosecution—for which he had absolutely no defense. As Alarcon explained it, because federal penalties were so stiff and parole less likely, Scott would probably spend the rest of his life in prison.

If he returned to Los Angeles to face murder charges, however, the state would have an uphill fight to prove its case without benefit of the victim's body or any physical evidence. If Scott was acquitted of murder, the state's fraud case against him would seem considerably weaker; should his highly respected lawyers manage to win a not-guilty verdict or even a hung jury, Los Angeles might back off. Under those circumstances, few federal prosecutors would risk a trial on unlawful-flight charges of a man twice proven innocent.

It was a long shot, but as Alarcon laid it out, by coming back to Los Angeles, Scott had an outside chance of avoiding prison. Continuing his fight to stay in Michigan would only buy him hard time in a federal pen.

Encouraged to accept reason by his attorney, Scott waived extradition, confident that without a body, he would never be convicted of murder, even though the Los Angeles County Grand Jury had indicted him for that crime while he was a fugitive in Canada.

Once back in Los Angeles—in the county jail—Scott was his old self. He hired the best attorneys, he radiated confidence, he declined to make any statement under oath. So confident of victory was Scott's new attorney, P. Basil Lambros, that he agreed to defend him without a retainer. His only fee would be half the sum for the movie rights to Scott's story. Lambros expected a huge sum after Scott's acquittal.

And he was sure there would be an acquittal. Not only did police have no body, they also had no witnesses and no physical evidence of a murder.

There had been very few successful prosecutions of no-body cases and Lambros had read them all. There was, for example, the New Zealander convicted of killing his bride after World War II. He told police that she had died during the war, having sailed on the S.S. *Empress of India*, which had been torpedoed and sunk by a Japanese submarine.

Since there had never been a ship by that name, the jury found the husband guilty of murder and sentenced him to be hanged.

On the other hand, there was the case of the unfortunate John Miles, hanged in nineteenth-century England for the murder of his friend William Ridley. After Miles was executed, Ridley's body was found. Thoroughly drunk, he had accidentally fallen into a very deep hole under an outdoor privy—but that was of small comfort to Miles.

In another British case, an uncle was hanged for the murder of his niece—but the niece had only run away, and returned home to claim her uncle's estate after his execution.

There had been a few no-body convictions in California. One was an 1880 case where José Alviso was convicted of killing John Ruhland. But Alviso, after shooting Ruhland, had merely burned his victim's body beyond recognition. The state had a witness, a man who was with Alviso at the time and testified to the killing and disposal of the body.

There was a 1925 San Diego case, where E. Drew Clark was convicted of murdering George Schick. Schick's body was never found, but a witness testified that Clark had admitted the killing to him. Some of Schick's possessions, including his jewelry, were found in Clark's possession, and that, with the witness, convinced a jury to convict Clark. The verdict was sustained on appeal.

And there was the 1951 conviction of Raymond Cullen for the murder of his wife and her stepfather. Their bodies were never found, but a witness testified that Cullen told him he'd paid a long-haul truck driver to dispose of the bodies. His conviction was also upheld on appeal.

But no one in America had ever been convicted of murder without a body, or a witness to the killing, or without a confession. Lambros was confident that the district attorney had nothing that could convict L. Ewing Scott of murder. Nothing but circumstantial evidence.

But the DA's office *did* have something else. Something—or rather, someone—Lambros had overlooked.

J. Miller Leavy.

At fifty-one, Leavy was the heavyweight champion of the Los Angeles DA's staff. He had won convictions against Barbara Graham, the killer beauty who inspired Susan Hayward's Oscar-winning performance in *I Want to Live*; against rapist and kidnapper Caryl Chessman, the so-called Red Light Bandit, who survived twelve years on death row; and against many other celebrated defendants, as well as dozens of less famous perpetrators.

Leavy was born in Tucson, Arizona, in 1905, the son of a merchant. His parents moved to Los Angeles when Miller was an adolescent, and so after high school he attended UCLA. He received a law degree from Michigan in 1930, passed the California Bar exam in 1931, the base of the Great Depression, and went to work as an unpaid volunteer for the district attorney. Not until 1933 did he begin drawing a salary.

Miller Leavy was everything L. Ewing Scott pretended to be: poised, learned, calmly efficient, principled, and handsome. He was also willing to work long and hard to see justice done. If the state's case against Scott for the murder of his wife lacked a dead body, it had an abundance of circumstantial evidence, including ninety-eight witnesses. At trial, Leavy put forward the testimony of a parade of witnesses. Among them were old friends of the vanished Evelyn, who testified that she was a bright, capable, well-groomed woman of regular habits. Leavy placed in evidence the denture found on Scott's next-door neighbor's property, questioned the dentist and technician who had created it for Evelyn, and showed the jury a giant photo of Evelyn wearing the denture, and then another with her five missing teeth blacked out, to show how she would look without the denture.

The jury quickly got the point: Evelyn without the denture looked like no one a proper Pasadena widow would ever be seen talking to.

Similarly, Leavy introduced as evidence two pairs of reading glasses found with the dentures. Her optometrist testified that Evelyn needed the glasses to read and her friends testified that reading was a daily activity very important to her.

Leavy brought in the west's foremost expert on handwriting to show the jury how Scott had traced Evelyn's signatures. He produced the paper trail that Scott left as he systematically looted Evelyn's estate. He put Marianne Beaman on the stand to testify that Scott had told her, very early in their relationship, that he planned to wait seven years and then have his wife declared legally dead. Harriet Livermore testified that Scott had told her the same thing during the months they had dated.

Evelyn's friends were mature, well dressed, and highly credible witnesses. They testified about Scott's fanciful assertions about his financial expertise and the influence he had exerted on Evelyn to get her to convert her stocks and bonds to cash. Two businessmen he'd defrauded testified about how Scott conned them out of money.

Mildred Schudhardt, frail and elderly, testified from her wheelchair about her long, close friendship with Evelyn. "During the many years that you knew Evelyn," asked Leavy, "and as you were less able to get around, did you and Evelyn always keep in touch with each other in some way?"

"Yes, sir. By telephone, literally every day."

The prosecutor then established that the last time these two best friends had spoken was May 5, 1955, just before Mildred sailed for London in the company of a nurse. When she returned from this trip six weeks later, said Mildred, Scott had called to say that Evelyn had become mentally ill and there were only three places in the entire country where her "neuroses" could be properly treated—all in the east.

Mildred continued her testimony, recounting that she had asked to speak to Evelyn, only to be told by Scott that this was impossible, that his wife was standing naked in the bathroom swilling whiskey straight from the bottle and screaming words that would cause a sailor to blush. Then he hung up.

Finally, Mildred testified that despite her weeks of pleading phone calls to Scott, despite the dozens of times she begged to know where Evelyn had been sent to recover from her "illness," Scott never told her.

Leavy produced a parade of other witnesses who testified about all the different stories Scott had told them to explain his wife's absence. He even brought the jury out to the Scotts' Bel Air home to show them where the dentures and spectacles were found, where the incinerator stood, and the general layout of the house and grounds.

Miller Leavy wanted very much to cross-examine L. Ewing Scott on the witness stand, but despite appeals calculated to appeal to his vanity, Scott would not be lured to testify.

Instead, his attorney argued eloquently that the state had failed to prove even that Evelyn was dead, much less that Scott had killed her. To that end, Lambros even subpoenaed

Leavy and put him on the stand to testify that in fact, authorities were still actively looking for Evelyn. Evelyn was still very much alive, argued Lambros, and might very well appear at any moment. But even if she were dead, even if she'd been murdered, argued Lambros, there was no proof that the murder had taken place within the jurisdiction of the court.

For Scott to win acquittal, jurors needed only to believe that the evidence showed some possibility that Evelyn was alive, that there was a reasonable doubt that she was dead and that Scott had killed her.

They believed there was *no* reasonable doubt. Just before Christmas 1957, L. Ewing Scott became the first man in America to be convicted of murder without a dead body, without a confession, without an eyewitness.

In California capital cases, juries also decide whether the victim will be sentenced to life without parole or executed. Usually, the penalty phase of a trial is delayed at least thirty days after the verdict. While Scott was in jail awaiting sentencing, two men working for him schemed to plant a human arm and hand, taken from the corpse of an elderly woman and injected with blood of Evelyn's type, in a shallow grave at a beach house owned by Evelyn's old friend Bill Brawner. The hand would have been wearing Evelyn's wedding ring, plucked from its hiding place in the Bel Air house. The scheme was foiled when one of the men tried to bribe actor Leo Carillo, best known for his television role as the Cisco Kid's sidekick, Pancho, to say that he'd seen Evelyn alive in Rio de Janeiro after she had disappeared from Los Angeles in May 1955. Carillo, son of an old Santa Monica family that included several prominent lawmen, immediately went to the police.

Still claiming innocence, Scott entered San Quentin Prison. He occupied his days with jailhouse lawyering, peppering state and federal officials, including two U.S. presidents, with letters protesting his incarceration. In 1974 the parole authority set his release date, but Scott angrily refused to accept parole because, he said, it would imply an admission of guilt.

Scott served more than twenty years. In March 1978, his

sentence was commuted to time served and an unrepentant Scott was released to live out his remaining years free, if impoverished. On July 27, 1984, at age eighty-nine, he told an ABC television audience "I did not kill my wife. That's the truth, the whole truth, and nothing but the truth."

But only weeks after that interview, Scott told another story to Diane Wagner, a young, beautiful, brilliant, and most persistent writer. Wagner was writing a book, *Corpus Delicti*, about Scott and the mystery surrounding his wife's disappearance.

After many interviews, most at bedside in the Los Feliz district apartment where Scott lived, a curious friendship developed between the young lady and the old lady-killer.

On the afternoon of August 6, 1984, Scott telephoned to say he had something to tell Wagner—something he knew she'd want to hear. Later, at his apartment, he described how he had used a hard rubber mallet to kill Evelyn with a single blow to her head. A blow with no warning, no preamble, no conversation. Evelyn's last words, said Scott, were, "But I haven't done anything." Scott said he removed her clothes, wrapped her nude body in a gardener's tarpaulin, and loaded it into the trunk of his 1940 Ford.

Scott said he then drove to a spot in the desert near Las Vegas, six miles east of the Sands Hotel, where he spent all night digging a deep grave in the soft sand. Despite his endless protestations to the contrary, he had killed his wife, he said, and he was not sorry about it at all.

"I think he wanted to enjoy his last moments—that he really had been smarter than everybody else and had kept them guessing. His physical health was beginning to fail, [but] he was clear mentally," said Wagner in a 1992 interview.

"The reason Scott murdered his wife was ... self-protection and greed. My feeling was that Evelyn was, probably, considering divorcing him or [she had] realized that she had made him too good a bargain. ... That would present problems for him ... he wanted to protect himself," added Wagner. "I don't think he wanted to start all over, looking for a new meal ticket."

Scott came very close to committing a perfect crime. He

had grasped the larger concept and executed his plan with no major flaws. But little pieces of evidence, piled one atop another, tipped the scales against him. Had he disposed of Evelyn's dentures and reading glasses as completely as he had her body—not a difficult task in the months before authorities began their probe—then it would be hard to imagine most juries agreeing with the same certainty on his guilt.

L. Ewing Scott died in 1986.

Evelyn Scott's body has never been recovered.

# Deadbeats
# (1988)

**T**HE MAIN PROBLEM WITH LIFE INSURANCE IS THAT YOU MUST *die to collect. That necessary detail has inspired generations of grifters to an extraordinary selection of ingenious ruses, faking the deaths of heavily insured relatives and partners.*

*That such schemes rarely succeed is a function of the difficulty of faking a death. Extra dead bodies are rare, so schemers often attempt to create a believable illusion, a strong reason to believe that someone has died, but under circumstances such that their body disappears. Insurance companies being skeptical, this method rarely succeeds.*

*Others, more bold and resourceful, have tried to offer, as proof of an insured's death, a different body, often that of a vagrant. Such schemes usually collapse on issues of identity, or on the cause of death, because those making insurance claims must rely on government authorities to identify the victim and cause of death.*

*But what if the insured's own doctor is part of the scam? What if he kills a stranger resembling the insured and identifies this body as the insured? And what if this doctor kills in such a way that the cause of death seems natural?*

*In such a case, only bad luck—or some unusually suspicious and stubborn authorities—can prevent a perfect crime.*

* * *

Gene Hanson and John Hawkins moved out of their pricey, midtown Lexington Avenue apartment on a frigid Manhattan morning in 1985. They hired professionals to pack and carefully move their genuine Victorian furniture, expensive objets d'art, and first-rate lithographs and original paintings. Protected by padding and covered with tarpaulins, the contents of their home filled a large U-Haul truck. At lunchtime, with only a few more boxes to load, Hanson took the movers around the corner for a hearty lunch while Hawkins ran an urgent errand.

When the movers were out of sight, Hawkins drove the U-Haul a few blocks to where a second, identical truck was parked. He left the first truck, with its precious load, and drove the second back to the apartment. The second truck, rented from a different agency by an unsuspecting friend, was filled with a few hundred dollars' worth of thrift-shop junk. Shrouded beneath similar pads and tarps, it evoked no suspicion in the movers when they returned from lunch.

The first truck, full of valuable antiques and art, was driven to the tony decorator's agency where Hanson and Hawkins had rented the furnishings some months earlier. When the second truck was ready to go, Hawkins drove it to New Jersey, where its cargo of junk disappeared into a landfill.

The empty U-Haul turned up in Harlem the next day after curious passersby called police to report that someone was pounding and shouting from inside an illegally parked truck.

Freed by police, Hanson told of being hijacked at gunpoint by his Latino movers. They had driven him to a warehouse, he said, unloaded the truck, then locked him in back and abandoned it on a street. Hanson's descriptions of the desperadoes—vague, contradictory, and racist—provided few leads for police to follow.

The story sounded a little odd to NYPD detective John Miles. But after decades on the job, Miles had seen many victims, and he thought that if Hanson was a little inconsistent on details, it might well be from shock and stress.

The NYPD took a full report—except that Hanson never revealed that the hijacked goods were rented.

So when Hanson and Hawkins enclosed a copy of the police report with a claim on their homeowner's insurance, it sailed through the Chubb Insurance Company's system with only perfunctory examination.

A few weeks later, Hanson and Hawkins got a check for over $109,000.

Another perfect crime. And up to then, their largest score.

Hawkins, who had spent most of his young life committing one felony or another, was very fond of insurance fraud. Some months earlier he'd bought a badly mistreated, barely running Porsche with a rubber check for $5,000, then torched it on a deserted Lower Manhattan street and told police that he'd been the victim of gay bashing. Submitting to the insurance company a phony bill of sale for $9,000, he covered his check and cleared four grand for an evening's work.

Another time he flew to Los Angeles, got a friend to rent a car, and staged a fake hit-and-run accident. Hawkins, "struck" in a pedestrian crosswalk, claimed major injuries. After his physician, Dr. Richard Boggs, certified that Hawkins's injuries were severe and he would be unable to work for at least three months, an insurance company was glad to settle with the young man for $25,000.

John Hawkins was born in 1963 in St. Louis, Missouri. His parents divorced less than two years later. John's mother, Jackie, was a stunningly beautiful woman. She had no trouble finding work dealing blackjack in a Las Vegas casino.

Little Johnny was a gorgeous child, with deep blue eyes, dark skin, and wonderfully curly dark hair. In childhood, he learned that his beauty captivated many people, especially women. His striking good looks and honeyed, ingratiating manner allowed him to manipulate many. And so, unlike most people, Hawkins never did learn why he had to obey anyone's rules, why he couldn't do exactly as he pleased.

Hawkins dropped out of school in the eleventh grade. By then he was an accomplished seducer who had brought temporary comfort to both teenage girls and many women his mother's age. His mother, by most accounts, was proud of her son's amorous achievements.

Hawkins drifted down to Florida to hook up with his father, a welder, and learn that trade.

But welding is hot, dirty, often painful work. Before Hawkins turned seventeen, he was sure that his destiny did not involve anything quite so pedestrian. He went back to Las Vegas, bought his mother's van, and lit out for the land of milk and honey: Southern California.

In Los Angeles, he tried his hand at stand-up comedy, in hopes of getting into the movies. But the area is filled with good-looking young men, and Hawkins had no patience for the years of study and work required to become successful.

So he turned to the one thing at which he excelled—hustling. John Hawkins hired himself out as a gigolo, escorting moneyed older women—and soon men—through Southern California's glittering nightlife. He turned up at party after party, rubbing elbows with Hollywood's beautiful people, its nouveaux riches—and its enormous corps of pretenders. And in 1981, at a glitzy party, he met Gene Hanson. It was love at first sight—at least on Hanson's part.

Melvin Eugene Snowden Jr. was born in 1941 in Ocala, Florida, a ranching and farming community far closer in geography and temperament to south Georgia's heart-of-Dixie spirit than to Miami's pulsing Latin beat. His parents split up while Melvin was in diapers. When he was five, his mother married Cecil Hanson, and soon Melvin Eugene Snowden Jr. became Gene Hanson. In 1965, ending two years of indifferent scholarship at Florida State, Hanson enlisted in the army. After basic training he enplaned for Europe, where he mostly enjoyed himself until 1968, when his discharge came through. The only lasting residue of Hanson's service was a fondness for things European—and a set of fingerprint cards buried deep in a Pentagon archive.

For a few years after his army service, Hanson kicked around at odd jobs, turning up in Atlanta in the early 1970s. He went to work for Rich's, a regional department store, and through hard work, an innate sense of style, and a mutual attraction with his mentor, the store manager, quickly moved up to become the store's star merchandiser.

It was during this time also that Hanson, following his mentor's lead, came to terms with his own homosexuality. While he kept his private life private and devoted most of his time to hard work, he was out of the closet and, over time, comfortable with his sexual identity.

Moving on to jobs in Richmond, Virginia; Scottsdale, Arizona; and Portland, Oregon, Hanson became both a sophisticated and worldly fashion buyer and a somewhat jaded habitué of the gay underworld.

In 1979, Hanson landed a job as a shoe buyer for Robinson's, a chain of department stores headquartered in Southern California and catering to the more affluent. With a salary of $50,000 a year, he had finally arrived.

When Hanson met Hawkins at a party in the summer of 1981, they both sensed an immediate attraction. Not long after that, they moved to New York, where, with Hanson posing as the younger man's stepfather, they took their first apartment together.

Hanson accepted a job with a $75,000 annual salary from a division of the Abrams company. His principal duty was to build a line of imported shoes for New York's elite department stores, a task requiring extensive European travel.

Hawkins, with introductions from his Hollywood glitterati pals, landed a job as a bartender at Studio 54's exclusive back bar. There he quickly established himself as a comer, the one fellow who *must* be invited to exclusive private parties—often for fees that ran as high as $5,000 for an evening's sexual entertainment. That was because to certain wealthy New Yorkers, Hawkins's immensely magnetic personality, his knockout good looks, and his raging, anything-goes sexuality were easily worth that kind of money.

Hawkins also prospered from his ability to provide a wide assortment of prescription drugs, notably unlimited quantities of Quaaludes. At Studio 54 and private parties, he often took in thousands of dollars during a single evening from the illicit sale of opiates, tranquilizers, and stimulants. The drugs, bottles and bottles of them, came from a down-and-out Glendale, California, physician whom Hanson and Hawkins knew during their Los Angeles years. His name was Richard Boggs.

Richard Peter Boggs was born in the tiny town of Hot Springs, South Dakota, in 1933. It was the depths of the Great Depression, and Richard's father, Pryde, made a precarious living as a supervisor for an oil company. In 1939, Pryde was transferred to California. The family moved to Glendale, a quiet, conservative community near Los Angeles. During World War II, however, Pryde abandoned his family, leaving his wife to eke out a livelihood as a drugstore clerk.

As first son, Richard was expected to contribute to the breadwinning effort. He did not disappoint his mother, Beulah. Dick Boggs delivered newspapers, washed cars, mowed lawns, swept floors, made flower corsages in a mortuary flower shop, even emptied hospital bedpans.

He worked very hard, and early in his life displayed a near obsession with money. But little Dick Boggs was a smart youngster who got good grades and who, long before adolescence, had picked his career: medicine.

After graduating high school in 1951, Boggs did two years at Glendale City College, during which time he was elected vice-president of the student body. He spent his junior and senior years at UCLA, finishing with a B.S. in zoology. Then it was on to medical school at Loma Linda University, an obscure Seventh-Day Adventist institution about sixty miles east of Los Angeles. He met his future wife, Lola Cleveland, while visiting an even smaller Seventh-Day Adventist campus in Lincoln, Nebraska. They married in 1961, just before Dick became a doctor.

Ironically, just about the same time, Dick Boggs was beginning to realize that he was more sexually attracted to men than to women. The Boggses adopted two infants, a boy and a girl, in their first few years of marriage. Later Lola would bear Richard two more children.

Boggs did his internship at County General in Los Angeles, where his skills, both medical and political, won him election as head of the interns and residents' association.

Then it was on to Harvard on a full scholarship. Afterward, Boggs completed a residency in neurology, doing clinical work at Boston City Hospital and part-time work at Presbyterian Intercommunity.

It was during these years in Boston that Boggs performed his first homosexual sex act. He found it wonderfully gratifying—and said nothing to his wife, Lola, about his newly emerging sexual identity.

Returning to Southern California, the Boggs family, Richard's star ascending, settled in Glendale. Within a few years, it looked like Boggs had it all. Although he no longer adhered to the strict tenets of Seventh-Day Adventism, Boggs the physician and leader was widely admired for his indefatigable energy and his searing intelligence. Boggs, the father of four, was a hero to each of his kids. And Boggs the man? He was still in the closet, sexually, but finding more and more opportunities to sample the gay lifestyle.

Still in his midthirties, Boggs was offered the opportunity to head the neurology department of Rancho Los Amigos, an internationally celebrated hospital in nearby Downey. It was the kind of job that few of his medical school peers would ever get a shot at, and so he was quick to accept.

With money pouring in, Boggs bought a spacious hacienda with an expansive view of the Los Angeles basin on a mountain ridge above Glendale.

Within three years, however, still under forty years of age, he had quit. Few at Rancho Los Amigos were sorry to see him go, because Boggs, despite his obvious intelligence, never missed a chance to cut a corner, to find the easy way out. He was long on promise, short on delivery.

He returned to Glendale and seemed, for a time, to work hard to build his practice. He was also affiliated with a group practice. But he was no more the wunderkind. His patients often found him distracted, absent. He was late for appointments, gave only perfunctory attention to details—and sometimes, despite a full schedule of patients, never bothered coming in to his own office.

Richard Boggs was living a double life. At night he haunted Southern California's gay bars and bathhouses, seeking men like himself, seeking the short, sweet satisfaction of an anonymous sexual encounter.

But still he remained in the closet. Society did not yet accept gay physicians, and to maintain his affluent lifestyle meant persevering with the illusion that he was a happily married family man.

In the early 1970s, Boggs thought he saw a shortcut to the kind of income that would allow him to come out of the closet. With several investors, he started one of Southern California's first health maintenance organizations (HMO). There, for a flat monthly fee, most routine medical services were available from a staff of physicians. Through the power of preventive medicine, serious medical services were held to a minimum but still included in the monthly fee.

But Southern California, long on the cutting edge of social change, still wasn't quite ready for HMOs. At least, not the way Dr. Richard Boggs practiced the business of administering medicine. For all his medical brilliance, Boggs had no idea how to run anything so complex. Satellite Health Systems, with offices from San Diego to San Luis Obisbo, never turned a profit. Everything that could have gone wrong did go wrong, from hassles with medical equipment suppliers, failure to win essential contracts with government agencies—and most of all, failure to attract enough paying patients to cover the enormous overhead.

As Satellite fell into bankruptcy, it nearly wiped out Boggs's personal fortune. Depressed and anxious, he came out of the sexual closet. He moved to Laguna Beach, a sparkling jewel of a community, semi-isolated on the beautiful coastline south of burgeoning, business-oriented Newport Beach. Laguna was an artists' colony, and large numbers of gays lived there, many flaunting their sexual preference. After divorcing his wife in 1976, Boggs bought a beachfront condominium and plunged into the sort of life he had furtively experienced for well over a decade.

But Laguna was too small a community to support a neurology practice, and the surrounding area was populated with some of the most politically and socially conservative people in the United States. Boggs soon learned that few would accept a gay physician.

So he bought a condo in West Hollywood, another center of openly gay activity not far from Glendale. For several years, a stream of young men flowed through Boggs's bedroom, many of them his sons' ages. Often they were new arrivals from parts of the country where the openly gay were not welcome.

Now feeling free to experiment with all forms of sexuality, Boggs entered a netherworld of leather, chains, sadomasochism, and all the drugs he could buy.

Although once a superb physician, by the early 1980s, Boggs had lost staff privileges at every hospital that had formerly offered them. As his medical practice dwindled to a handful of patients, he squandered whatever money flowed through his pockets on drugs and sensual gratification. Most of his income came from dealing cocaine and methamphetamines and from supplying prescription drugs to people like Gene Hanson and John Hawkins, men he had met in the tightly knit circle of West Hollywood's gay bars and bathhouses.

By 1988, Richard Boggs, M.D., was reduced to sharing a shabby, barely-furnished Glendale apartment with his lover, Hans Jonasson, a twenty-two-year-old Swedish nurse. Jonasson worked for Boggs, both in the ruins of his neurology practice and in his illicit sideline, dealing drugs. But not for long. Boggs was behind in his rent and the landlord was trying to evict them.

Hanson and Hawkins decided to leave New York in 1985, largely because Hawkins's star standing at Club 54 meant little after scandal—and the panic over AIDS—closed down the glitzy center of Manhattan nightlife. After skipping out with $109,000 in insurance-scam money, Hanson and Hawkins settled in Lexington, Kentucky. They were determined to become rich—and Hanson, a sophisticated merchandiser, had imported from Southern California an idea that had tremendous potential.

With the money from their Manhattan antique-furniture scam, and with sizable chunks from several other investors, in June 1985, Hanson and Hawkins opened Just Sweats. Just Sweats stocked all kinds of sweatshirts, sweatpants, and closely related athletic gear. Staffed by healthy-looking and attractive college-age men and women, it was an immediate success.

Within a few months they moved to Columbus, Ohio, and opened a second store across the street from Ohio State's expansive campus. It, too, was a big success. Hanson and Hawkins, local retailing legends almost from the moment of their grand opening, established relations with local banks and lawyers, hired dozens of young salesclerks, and began opening stores all over Ohio.

Soon the partners had only two problems: how to manage the all-important details of their exploding business, and when to find time to party in a style befitting their sudden celebrity.

Managing a business like Just Sweats through its explosive growth was a challenge even for those well trained in retailing. But Hanson's strength was buying, not selling, or hiring, or controlling costs, or managing inventory, or the thousand details demanded by a busy chain of stores. Hawkins's only real talents were dispensing sexual pleasure and doing drugs.

By 1987, Just Sweats was going through growing pains. These were worse than usual, because almost from the first, Hawkins and Hanson had treated the business like a personal piggy bank, raiding cash registers at closing time for a few hundred dollars in walking-around money, pigeonholing bills, operating in the blind with no accurate sense of inventory, stalling creditors with elaborate concoctions, muddling through planning, begging short-term bank loans—and refusing to hire professionals to create and supervise the financial and other systems needed to manage a large and expanding business. All that work took too much time away from the many beautiful, willing, even eager young men and women around them. Hawkins and Hanson despaired of ever getting to all available sex partners. But they tried.

The partners did find time, however, to sit down with an insurance agent. If one of them died, said Hanson, the other would be hard-pressed to keep the business going. A chunk of insurance money would help make it possible to hire appropriate talent to fill the void, they said. The partners left the agent's office with three policies each. If either died, the other would inherit more than $1.5 million.

And not long after Just Sweats made the first of the monthly insurance payments, Gene Hanson began to complain to his key employees that the stress of running Just Sweats was getting to him. He wasn't yet fifty, but his heart was going, fast. Stress was killing him. His days were numbered.

Later in December 1987, Gene Hanson sat down with his corporate merchandise chief, Melissa Mantz, and laid down the law. The day after Christmas, December 26, was traditionally the busiest retail day of the year. Just Sweats needed cash, and lots of it. So for that day, and that day only, said Hanson, everything in every store was marked down 50 percent. That ought to generate some quick cash.

Mantz thought it was a pretty good idea. So she was stunned when, late on the afternoon of December 26, Hanson told her that the sale would continue for three more weeks.

Mantz was worried about depleting inventories more than accumulating cash, especially because the sale discounted all merchandise, including much-in-demand higher-priced goods. She tried to argue Hanson out of extending the sale, but he would not be moved.

Hanson had his own agenda. For the last several weeks, after taking check-writing duties away from his chief accountant and sending him off to Europe for a two-week, all-expenses paid vacation, Hanson had squirreled away all payout invoices. He stopped paying Just Sweat's bills.

Then he vanished, taking with him $1.8 million—practically all the corporation's cash.

Hawkins, away on vacation, came back to find Mantz frantic with worry. Without that cash, she told Hawkins, the company would go under in a few weeks.

Hawkins seemed very angry. How could his trusted partner do this to him? But he was also cool. Don't worry so much, he told Mantz. Everything will work out.

But when Mantz and the company's attorney said they'd have to go to the police and the FBI, Hawkins got edgy. Not so fast, he said. He thought he might know where to find Hanson. Give him a few days.

Hawkins caught a plane for Los Angeles, returning in triumph a few days later with a duffel bag full of cash and bearer's bonds.

Recounting a long, convoluted story about how he tracked Hanson down, Hawkins concluded by saying that Hanson was very ill. But there was nothing to worry the FBI about. He hadn't really stolen from the company. It was just that he wanted to sell his share of the company, and he'd thought $1.8 million was the right price.

But, said Hawkins, after a long discussion, Hanson had settled for $243,583.06. And Hawkins showed Mantz and the company attorney a notarized statement. Hanson was out, leaving Hawkins in sole control. The rest of the cash and bonds went back into company coffers.

The real reason for Hanson's flight would not surface for many months. Not until after a murder.

Just before leaving for California, Hanson had made an appearance in a Columbus probate court. He had rewritten his will, he told Judge Richard Metcalf, and since he was in poor health, with probably only a few months to live, he was winding up his affairs. He sought a ruling that his new will would survive any challenge that might arise after his death.

It was an extraordinary request, if not quite unprecedented. Probate courts rarely get involved in the affairs of the living. But in this case, the judge told an all-but-empty courtroom, he would make a ruling.

Hanson's will left everything to John Hawkins, who would also serve as executor of his estate. His previous will was void, and after his death, a codicil directed that his body be cremated—and that none of his relatives be notified.

Judge Metcalf questioned Hanson closely, then ruled that the will was legal. When Hanson died, his instructions would be followed to the letter.

* * *

In early April, Barry Pomeroy, a tall, wiry computer operator—and a remarkably passive individual—appeared at the Glendale, California, Police Department and asked to file a complaint. Eventually, he was interviewed by Detective James Peterson.

Several days earlier, on the night of March 26, said Pomeroy, he had allowed a man to pick him up in a West Hollywood gay bar called the Spike. After a coffee-shop meal, the man, who said he was a doctor and called himself Peter Richards, took him for a ride to enjoy viewing Glendale's latest office-building architecture by moonlight. Then he took Pomeroy home. A few days later, on April 1, Richards called and asked him for a date.

Pomeroy accepted, and Richards came to pick him up in his Cadillac. On the way to dinner, Richards said he had to stop at his office and use the phone, so Pomeroy came up to wait in an examination room. Then Richards asked if he'd like to have an EKG test. Anxious to please, Pomeroy agreed.

But when he went into the room with the electrocardiograph, Richards attacked him with an electric stun gun.

In great pain and fearing for his life, Pomeroy fought back. After a long, violent struggle, Richards abruptly stopped, put the stun gun away, and apologized. Something had come over him, he said. He apologized again.

Pomeroy let Richards take him home, still apologizing and offering to seek psychiatric help.

The next day, Pomeroy, with a friend, went back and searched through several office buildings until he found the office. Asking around, he learned that the only doctor in that office was Richard Boggs, and after getting his description, Pomeroy decided that he was the man who had assaulted him. Now he wanted to bring charges.

Detective Peterson was reluctant to press the issue, explaining that he'd known Dr. Boggs for over twenty years, that he was an outstanding citizen, much beloved in the community. Peterson didn't reveal that he was friendly with Boggs's younger brother, William, a Drug Enforcement Agency supervisor and former Glendale PD detective sergeant.

Peterson called Dr. Boggs and asked him to explain what had happened with Pomeroy. Boggs said that while it was true he'd been out with Pomeroy, Pomeroy had picked *him* up. When they got to his office, said Boggs, Pomeroy had groped him—attempted to fondle his genitalia.

That wasn't his style, said Boggs. So he had defended himself with the stun gun.

To Peterson it looked like a "Mexican standoff," one man's word against the other. And Boggs was a physician, with deep community roots.

When Pomeroy tried to get the district attorney's office interested, he ran into a wall of disinterest. No one seemed to want to get involved with what they saw as a lovers' quarrel between aging homosexuals.

What no one in law enforcement realized until weeks later was that the Pomeroy assault was not supposed to end with Pomeroy alive. While Pomeroy waited in his office, Richard Boggs, alias Peter Richards, had telephoned both Hanson and Hawkins. Afterward, he called again. They agreed that Boggs would wait a few days, then try to find another victim.

A few minutes after seven on the Saturday morning of April 16, 1988, Glendale Emergency Services got a call on their 911 telephone system. The caller was Dr. Richard Boggs, who asked for paramedics.

"What's the problem?" asked a fire-department dispatcher.

"Uh . . . I had a patient call me. He's having chest pains. He came in the office and he's collapsed. I'm trying to give him resuscitation."

Paramedics rushed to Suite 201 at 540 North Central Avenue. According to local standard operating procedures, a fire truck with a company of firefighters was also dispatched.

There was some delay getting into the building because the outer doors were locked. Firefighters and paramedics milled around in the parking lot until a testy Dr. Boggs unlocked the front door. At once, he began to berate them for taking too long. A paramedic supervisor, Thomas Brooks, who had arrived after the ambulance but fewer than five minutes from the 911 call, was surprised at this attitude.

But someone might be dying, Thomas thought. This wasn't the time to argue with Boggs.

Paramedics found a bearded man on his back on the linoleum floor of a small examination room. His trousers had been removed and his feet were on a pillow. Paramedic David White put down his oxygen tank and touched the man on the floor. He was dead.

White, very surprised, checked the patient's vital signs again, with no luck. The man was beyond help.

White was confused. If the victim had gone into cardiac arrest in the previous hour, as Dr. Boggs claimed, his body should still have been warm.

The paramedics noted other signs, all indicating that the victim had been dead far longer than the forty-five minutes Boggs claimed. For openers, the body was already showing unmistakable signs of lividity, the purplish skin tone that comes from blood settling, under gravity's effect, into the lowest parts. And rigor mortis, the stiffening characteristic of bodies dead more than a few hours, had already begun to show in the victim's fingers, jaw, and neck.

Attracted by the activity in the parking lot, two Glendale policemen, Tim Spruill and James Lowrey, arrived. When it was apparent that the victim was beyond medical help, these officers looked through the victim's pockets, extracting a brown leather wallet that held credit cards, a photocopied birth certificate, and other documents bearing the name of Melvin Eugene Hanson. None bore a photo of Hanson, however. No one at the scene was particularly bothered by this.

Next, the patrolmen questioned Boggs. He said that he had been home, sleeping, when the phone rang, between 3:00 and 3:30 in the morning. The call came to his bedside via a device known as call forwarding; any call to his office number was automatically switched to his home.

Boggs said he always let the answering machine pick up the call until he could find out who was calling. On the line was his longtime patient Gene Hanson, said Boggs, complaining of severe chest pains. He'd been drinking, was very frightened, and wanted to see Boggs immediately. Boggs picked up the phone, shutting off the answering machine.

Boggs told Hanson to meet him at his office. When he got there, said Boggs, he waited until almost five before a light brown Honda entered the parking lot. From his window, Boggs directed the car to the back door and went down to open it. After Hanson staggered into the building, the Honda departed.

Hanson smelled like a grogshop, said Boggs. He helped him upstairs to his office, where he took his blood pressure, measured his pulse, and gave him an EKG.

Alarmed by the jagged lines of the EKG printout, said Boggs, he suggested that Hanson needed to be hospitalized immediately.

But, said Boggs, Hanson refused. He was afraid of hospitals and afraid of most doctors. Boggs was the only one he trusted.

Hanson lay down on an examination table to rest, and Boggs went into his office to make some notes. A few minutes later he heard a loud thump from the examination room and rushed in to find Hanson on the floor. He wasn't breathing and his heart had stopped.

Bogs said he started CPR, then interrupted himself to call 911. When he got a busy signal, he went back to work on Hanson. He tried 911 again a few minutes later and got another busy signal, and when he tried a third time a loud squeal came from the phone. It took him about forty-five minutes to get through.

Wasn't it odd, asked a paramedic, to see a patient at that hour?

Not at all, said Boggs. He had lived most of his life in Glendale, he treasured his patients, and he would do anything to make things easier for them. Hanson was a busy Ohio retailer who came to Southern California on buying trips for his chain stores. Usually, he was pressed for time. Boggs always tried to accommodate him.

If was unfortunate that Hanson died, said Boggs, hefting the thick file that detailed seven years of office visits, but hardly a surprise. He smoked too much, drank too much, never exercised and had been complaining of heart problems for a long time.

The police were disturbed by what they saw and heard. By an extraordinary coincidence, Lowrey was far more knowledgeable about medicine than most police officers. The son of a Glendale cardiologist, during his childhood he'd often accompanied his father on house calls. He also knew Boggs by reputation, knew that his once-promising career was in ruins.

Lowrey skimmed through Hanson's file. One of the things he noticed was that Hanson had taken an AIDS test some months earlier. The results were negative.

Officer Lowrey was puzzled by other things Boggs told him. He thought it was very odd that a man with chest pains would go to his doctor's office at that hour, when it was probably easier and made more sense to go to a hospital emergency room.

He challenged Boggs on that subject, and Boggs promptly admitted that he had made a mistake. "I probably shouldn't have done that," he said.

Lowrey pressed the point. Didn't Boggs's actions leave him open to malpractice charges?

Boggs mumbled that maybe his insurance company wouldn't be too happy.

And why, asked Officer Lowrey, had Boggs found it necessary to remove Hanson's trousers?

Well, said Boggs, it was partly to make it easier to attach the EKG electrodes. And partly because Hanson said he needed to urinate.

Lowrey picked up the phone and dialed 911. His call went through in a few seconds.

Looking Boggs over critically, Lowrey decided he was too fresh for a man who had performed CPR for forty-five minutes. After lengthy questioning, he was convinced that Boggs wasn't being straight. Something was wrong here, and although he didn't know what it was, Lowrey called the doctor a liar to his face.

But Lowrey was only a patrolman. Detective James Peterson arrived to take charge of the investigation. The office filled with more police and with investigators from the Los Angeles County Coroner's Office.

Peterson, forty-eight, knew that Boggs was gay. Some two decades earlier, he had arrested him in a Glendale city park rest room after the doctor grabbed a police decoy. Boggs had been released in the custody of his brother, Detective William Boggs, and that had been the end of the matter. Peterson was also aware that Boggs had been experiencing financial difficulties. He had been summoned to Boggs's office more than once to calm things down when some of the doctor's creditors created a disturbance with their demands for payment. Peterson asked Lowrey and Spruill to brief him, then dismissed the patrolmen after telling Spruill not to bother filing a supplementary report. It wasn't necessary.

Peterson took it upon himself to inform Hanson's next-of-kin. He found John Hawkins's name in Hanson's file and used the doctor's office phone to call Hawkins in Columbus, Ohio. Hawkins said he already knew about the death. Boggs had phoned him earlier.

Peterson asked Hawkins if he knew Hanson was gay. Yes, said Hawkins, he'd known that for a long time. But when Peterson asked if there was anything between the victim and his doctor, Hawkins set his mind at rest. Each was into very different things, he said. It wasn't likely that they were involved beyond their professional relationship.

Sergeant Terry Jones, who had called Peterson to the scene, took the precaution of following Boggs over to the doctor's apartment, where he listened to the answering-machine tape. As Boggs had said, there was the voice of Gene Hanson, sounding scared and complaining of chest pains. Jones took the tape cassette and later gave it to Peterson as evidence in his investigation.

Coroner's investigator Craig Harvey conducted a careful examination of the corpse as it lay in Boggs's office. He looked for bruises, cuts, scrapes, bumps—anything that might show foul play. He also looked for needle marks, on the chance that the victim had been injected with something. When he learned from Peterson that Boggs was gay, Harvey did a careful check of the victim's body, looking for any sign that he had been sexually molested. There was nothing unusual about the corpse.

Peterson told Harvey that a few days earlier, Boggs had been accused of using a stun gun on a gay man in his office. But his tone of voice made Harvey believe that Peterson didn't take the accusation seriously. Peterson left the scene without once speaking to Boggs.

The only odd thing Harvey found in Boggs's office came after measuring the temperature of the corpse's liver and comparing it with room temperature. Based on standard tables, he estimated the time of death at between two and three in the morning. But Boggs put the time of death at about six.

Harvey's professional observations also confirmed what Officer Lowrey had noticed: rigor mortis had already begun, another indication that the time of death was much earlier than Boggs said.

All this went into Harvey's report, but it was not his job to draw conclusions, only to note facts.

Harvey accompanied the body down to the morgue, where it was photographed, fingerprinted, weighed, and measured. He put an identification tag around the big toe of each foot and wheeled the body into a refrigerated vault kept at forty degrees Fahrenheit.

The autopsy was conducted by Dr. Evancia Sy, a forensic pathologist. She found no evidence of strangulation, no fractures or bruises, nothing to indicate a violent death. Yet nothing indicated that the victim had fallen from an exam table to the floor a few minutes before death, or that CPR had been performed.

She did find an unusually high concentration of alcohol in the victim's blood—.29 percent—about three times California's legal threshold of intoxication. That was consistent with her observation of the victim's fatty liver, which showed many years of alcohol abuse. There was no evidence of a heart attack. Dr. Sy took tissue, blood, and other samples, and sent them off for laboratory analysis.

Dr. Sy was stumped. She could find no reason for the death. However, seeing no reason to do otherwise, she released the body to a mortuary for burial.

A week went by, and then Dr. Sy got a call from Dr. Boggs. What had she learned about the cause of Gene Hanson's death?

Sy said only that no conclusions had been announced. This was partly because of her own cautious nature, but mostly because the coroner's office had a well-defined and long-standing policy about prematurely disclosing information.

Boggs became very chummy. One physician to another, he confided certain details of Hanson's medical history. There were the chest pains, he said. Hanson had complained for almost a year, all the while refusing to consult a cardiologist.

Did Hanson ever suffer from viral infections? asked Dr. Sy.

Yes, said Dr. Boggs. And only a few days before he died.

Dr. Sy took this as a clue. She reexamined slides of the victim's heart tissue. Now she noticed a tiny area around the arteries supplying blood to the heart muscle. It seemed to her, on extended scrutiny, that there had been a recent infection there.

Dr. Sy decided that the man identified as Melvin Eugene Hanson had died of nonspecific focal myocarditis, "inflammation" of the heart muscle. A death certificate was prepared stating that the cause of death was natural.

The corpse identified as Gene Hanson was not buried. John Hawkins, who had arrived in Southern California late on the afternoon of April 16, had made arrangements with a local mortuary for cremation. Two days later, the ashes were scattered at sea.

A few days after this, Hawkins filed copies of Hanson's death certificate with Farmer's New World Life Insurance, a Seattle-area company, and with Golden Rule Insurance of Lawrenceville, Illinois.

Gene Hanson, however, was not dead.

Using the name Wolfgang von Snowden, he paid some $20,000—in fifty-dollar bills—to a Miami plastic surgeon. The surgeon spent over eleven hours in two operations, removing wrinkles from Hanson's face. When the bandages came off, "von Snowden," who spoke with a peculiar, not-quite-German accent, looked like a man in his early thirties.

Wolfgang von Snowden rented a luxury penthouse overlooking Biscayne Bay in Miami and enjoyed as much of the good life as an apparently endless supply of cash could buy.

After a few months, however, Hanson/von Snowden moved to Key West. Now calling himself Ellis Greene, he opened a bank account and rented a cottage. But Hanson felt naked in Key West, which had an active gay community but was also crawling with law-enforcement types, most involved in trying to stem the drug traffic through the area.

So in October, again calling himself von Snowden, he bought a piece of historic old St. Petersburg, putting down $25,000 in cash and signing a note for $33,000 more for a house near the beach of Tampa Bay. But the house was infested with termites and had to be torn down.

While deciding what to do next, "von Snowden" rented a luxury resort hotel room and made short excursions to the Cayman Islands, where banking secrecy laws protect those with piles of cash they don't wish to explain. He also visited Acapulco, where he considered the possibility of opening a saloon or bathhouse.

In Columbus, Ohio, John Hawkins counted the days as he waited for the $1.5 million due him from insurance companies in compensation for Gene Hanson's death. Just Sweats, however, was going through very tough times, very low on inventories as a result of Hanson's "checkout" sale and unable to order more until they paid for earlier shipments. Pressed by creditors, Hawkins finally acceded to the wishes of his lawyers and accountants and hired professionals to run the company. But he expected the company's salvation almost any day from the insurance companies.

That day came on July 8, 1988, when Farmer's New World Insurance Company's check for $1 million arrived at the offices of a Columbus law firm Just Sweats kept on retainer. Jubilant, Hawkins picked up the check and sped down to the bank to deposit it.

The check came to the law offices, instead of to Hawkins's home or office, because the insurance companies, slow to pay Hawkins's claim, were kept under almost daily pressure from Hawkins's lawyers, until, lacking any legal reason to delay any longer, they cut him a check.

Another check, for a little over $450,000, was mailed from the Golden Rule Insurance Company. The clerk who addressed the envelope, however, overlooked the change of address in Hawkins's file, and sent the check, via registered mail, to his old address. Hawkins had moved several weeks earlier, but neglected to turn in a change-of-address form at the post office. Consequently, the check was held at the post office for several days while officials looked for his new address.

It was a lucky break for Golden Rule. Not long after their check went astray, Hawkins vanished.

The first questions about the man who died in Boggs's office were raised by Norman MacRae, a private investigator working for Equifax, which did insurance investigations. Farmer's New World, concerned because Hanson's death had occurred so soon after coverage began, suspected that Hanson had concealed facts about his medical condition on his life-insurance application. If so, then the company might not have to pay, or might be able to negotiate a smaller settlement.

MacRae paid a visit to Boggs and asked to review Hanson's medical records. Pleasant and cooperative, Boggs gave them to an investigator.

About the same time, and for the same reasons, a claims investigator from Golden Rule contacted Hawkins. Hawkins refused to give the investigator any information about Hanson's family, explaining that Hanson had disinherited them shortly before his death. Despite this lack of cooperation, Golden Rule almost immediately sent Hawkins a check for $10,000 to help pay burial expenses.

In June, after Dr. Sy ruled that Hanson's death was of natural causes, Farmer's claims clerk Shelly Navarre sought to close out his case file so the full amount of insurance could be paid. But like every insurance company, Farmer's had its bureaucratic procedures. Navarre asked Glendale PD detective Peterson for a photo of the deceased and a copy of his driver's license.

It took two requests and over five weeks before Peterson got the duplicate license from Sacramento. At first glance, everything seemed in order. The man who died in Boggs's office was five feet, ten inches tall, weighed about 145 pounds, had blue eyes, balding brown hair, and sported both mustache and beard. However, Peterson thought the two photos seemed to be of different men. The victim appeared somewhat younger than Hanson's forty-six years. While police almost always check the fingerprints of those who die under suspicious circumstances to confirm their identity, it is not the usual procedure for a death arising from what are thought to be natural causes. And since "Hanson" had died in his physician's office and had been ID'd by him, there was never a question about his identity. But Peterson was quite surprised at the differences in the two photos of what was thought to be the same man.

So, departing from standard procedure, he compared fingerprints taken by detectives from the corpse with the thumb print on Hanson's driver's license. They didn't match.

To double-check, Peterson requested copies of Hanson's fingerprints on file at the Pentagon.

It took several weeks to retrieve them. But when Peterson compared the two sets of prints, there was no longer any doubt: the man who died in Boggs's office was not Melvin Eugene Hanson. He immediately called Shelly Navarre at Farmer's and was told that with no legal reason to further delay payment, a check had been issued and cashed.

Farmer's hired a Columbus, Ohio, private investigator, Vince Volpi, to get its money back—but Hawkins had already disappeared.

Golden Rule was luckier. Their check—over $450,000, including interest from the day of Hanson's "death"—was still floating around the post office. It was a simple matter to stop payment.

Peterson's startling discovery was whispered about in

law-enforcement circles almost as soon as he told his superiors. Not long after this, a retired LAPD detective called the coroner's office and told the chief of the department's Special Operations Unit that he had heard rumors of a possible insurance scam in Glendale. Checking out this tip—and being discreet while he did so—fell to twenty-nine-year-old Karl Stoutsenberger.

Stoutsenberger knew only that the body identified as Gene Hanson was somebody else—and that the latter person might have been murdered. He got in touch with Officers Spruill and Lowrey and the firefighters and paramedics who had answered Boggs's 911 call. All agreed that Boggs had acted suspiciously. Examining the statements Boggs gave that night, Stoutsenberger saw a glaring inconsistency. Boggs had told the police "Hanson" was driven to his office and dropped in the parking lot. But he told paramedics that he, Boggs, had picked Hanson up at a West Hollywood hotel.

Next, Stoutsenberger talked to medical examiners who had visited the death scene. They commented on Boggs seeming overeagerness to have the body removed to the morgue—and the strange fact that their calculations of the time of death varied sharply from Boggs's account.

Convinced that he had stumbled on, at least, an insurance scam, Stoutsenberger had several mysteries to contend with: If the man who died in Boggs's office wasn't Gene Hanson, who was he? If he didn't die of a heart attack, what killed him? And what was Boggs's role in all this?

He telephoned Glendale PD detective Peterson and was stunned to learn there was no homicide investigation. As Peterson explained, the death was certified as the result of natural causes. So, he asked, how could they be investigating a homicide?

Stoutsenberger contacted Dr. Sy, the forensic pathologist who autopsied the body. He was surprised to find her extremely cooperative; most physicians, in his experience, were defensive when laymen questioned their findings. But Dr. Sy had also been troubled by the case. And after talking to Stoutsenberger, she became even more suspicious. She began to restudy her collection of tissue slides from the mysterious corpse and to consult with her colleagues and superiors.

On August 25, Stoutsenberger learned that on the previous day a Franklin County, Ohio, court had issued an order prohibiting John Hawkins from spending any of the insurance money from the death of Gene Hanson. It came far too late. Hawkins had cashed the check and vanished with all the money, plus more he had looted from Just Sweats.

Stoutsenberger was dismayed to learn that the Columbus news media had reported this story. With no reason to keep his investigation quiet, he began contacting the county bureaucracy, but met massive disinterest from officials who stated that it wasn't *their* problem.

Finally, he reached Mike Jones, one of six investigators in the Southern California offices of the state department of insurance. At thirty-one, Jones was one of his department's ablest investigators. Working full-time and going to law school at night, after five years he had recently graduated and was preparing to take the tough bar exam.

Jones found Stoutsenberger's fragmentary information tantalizing. With permission from supervisors, he contacted L.A. County deputy DA Albert MacKenzie, an expert on white-collar crime who handled major fraud cases.

On MacKenzie's urgent recommendation, Jones and Stoutsenberger went to see Boggs to confirm the existence of a medical file on Gene Hanson so they could list it in a search warrant.

After Boggs ducked several phone calls, Jones and Stoutsenberger paid an unannounced visit to his office. The doctor was not around. Nevertheless, that same day he called Stoutsenberger's boss to complain of harassment, intimating that he had powerful friends among county officials.

Not intimidated, the two investigators returned to the building where Boggs kept his offices the following day. With them they carried photos of the real Gene Hanson and of the corpse. They showed these photos, among several others, to a pharmacist and to his clerk. Both identified Hanson's photo, but had never seen the man who had died in Boggs's office.

Boggs had finally consented to an appointment though he'd planned to leave before the investigators arrived. Taking him by surprise just as he was about to depart, Jones handed Boggs a subpoena for Hanson's medical records. After some resistance, Boggs allowed the investigators to copy the file.

Next, Jones questioned Boggs. He found that his memory of dates and places was conveniently poor. One thing Boggs said he was sure of, however, was that the man who died in his office was Gene Hanson. He said he didn't recognize photos of what the investigators knew was the real Hanson. Instead, Boggs said that the man depicted in the coroner's photo of a corpse was indeed Hanson.

"You're full of shit," said Jones.

"No comment," said Boggs, looking away.

Boggs refused to admit that the man who died was anyone other than the man he had treated as "Gene Hanson."

The investigators left, sure that he was lying.

A few days later, Jones and Stoutsenberger, armed with search warrants, raided Boggs's office. They were startled at the filth, accumulated debris, and shabbiness, but delighted to find that Boggs apparently threw nothing away—and among the documents seized were many that helped the authorities piece together the bizarre story of how the corpse came to be in his office.

But before proceeding further against Boggs, they felt it was crucial to learn the real identity of the victim. And, if possible, what had killed him.

Like many in law enforcement, Jones was responsible for an enormous caseload, including many cases requiring urgent attention. It was several weeks before he could even contemplate blocking out the hours required to look through hundreds of missing-persons reports in hopes of finding one that might be the man who died in Boggs's office.

While Jones was working to free some time to spend on the project, Stoutsenberger sought to use a nationwide computer network provided by the U.S. Department of Justice. The coroner's office had a terminal linked to the National Crime Information Center (NCIC). But the coroner's staff was so buried by their day-to-day workload that almost no one in the office ever used it—no one even knew *how*.

Eventually, Stoutsenberger sat down at the computer console with the system's manual and laboriously taught himself how to gain access to the NCIC database. After a lot of trial and error, he was rewarded with a multipage printout of missing persons who fit the mystery corpse's general description.

Jones and his partner split up the printout and went through it a case at a time. There were seventy-six men who had disappeared from virtually every part of the country in the months preceding the death in Boggs's office.

But only one from the Los Angeles area: Ellis Greene, a thirty-two-year-old accountant, last seen on the night of April 15 in a North Hollywood gay bar. A comparison of fingerprints from the corpse with those provided by the U.S. Army, where Greene had served in 1972, made it certain: he was the man who died in Boggs's office.

Next, Stoutsenberger and Jones set out to reconstruct the events of his last days. They learned that Greene worked for his uncle in Burbank. At three P.M. on April 15, after the last state and federal returns were mailed, he joined his uncle at the Rawhide, a North Hollywood bar, to celebrate the end of the tax season. Greene didn't stay long; he said he was going to Long Beach for the weekend with a friend. His uncle never saw him again.

About eight P.M., Greene went to the Bullet, another North Hollywood bar, where he met his friend Chip Suntheimer. Chip had finished his tax return and was going to take it to the post office, but when Greene saw that it was handwritten, he offered to go back to his office and type it. After he'd done that, Chip and Greene and another friend, Billy Ray, drove to the Van Nuys post office, the nearest that was still open. Chip and Ray went in, but Greene remained outside to help an older woman—a stranger—who had mistakenly written her California return on a federal form.

After eating, the trio made it back to the Bullet. Chip was tired and left.

Later, in bed, Chip heard his phone ring. An answering

machine picked up the call. The caller, Greene, said only one word, "Chip," then hung up. Suntheimer didn't like the way Greene's voice sounded and he didn't like the abrupt way the call ended. He was worried. He pulled on his clothes and went back to the Bullet. Just before Chip had arrived, the Bullet's bartender had decided that Greene was drunk and refused to serve him again. He called for a taxi to take Greene home. But not just any one. He called Checker Cab and asked for a driver named Russ. Russell Leek arrived just before midnight and drove Greene, a valued customer, away in his cab.

Between two and three hours later, by the coroner's time-of-death estimate, Greene was dead. Leek, under intense questioning from investigators, could not remember where he left Greene. Except for the murderer, he was probably the last person to see him alive.

Late on the Friday night of September 30, 1988, just a day after learning Greene's true identity, police and investigators descended on Boggs's office and apartment.

Jones went to the doctor's home, where among other contraband, he found an incredible assortment of drugs— prescription tranquilizers, marijuana, LSD, and cocaine, plus heroin, morphine, and other opiates—and a handbook for the manufacture of methamphetamines and other illegal pharmaceuticals.

A locked closet yielded chains, whips, ropes, dildos, masks, and an assortment of devices whose only application was in sadomasochistic sex rites.

Meanwhile, another team at Boggs's office was discovering a laboratory filled with the precursor chemicals and vessels used to manufacture methamphetamines.

Boggs was arrested on narcotics charges, then released on bail raised by relatives. There was almost enough cause to arrest him for the murder of Ellis Greene—except for a technicality: the death certificate, signed by Dr. Sy, still "proved" that the man had died of natural causes.

Sy was working hard to remedy this, reading the latest medical literature on heart disease and reviewing her tissue samples and other evidence, all that was left of Ellis Greene's cremated body. In November 1988, she officially reopened the case. Soon she was able to rule out any kind of heart disease, then any kind of disease at all. Since this was not a suicide, that left homicide. On January 4, 1989, Sy amended the death certificate, listing "undetermined" as the cause of death.

The Glendale PD belatedly opened its own homicide investigation after Boggs's arrest on drug charges. The case was assigned to Detective Jon Perkins, a short, dark, intense man, arguably the department's best homicide investigator. With Stoutsenberger's role finished, he returned to his coroner's office duties. Perkins was teamed with Mike Jones.

Hanson's disappearance had been far from seamless. He flitted back and forth between Florida and California for several months after Greene's death. As the "perfect crime" began to unravel with the discovery of Ellis Greene's identity, Hanson was able to follow the case in the newspapers. He grew progressively more wary, changing addresses and identities frequently.

He had good cause to worry. On his trail were California authorities, the FBI, and a team of detectives led by Vince Volpi, the private investigator hired by Farmer's New World Life. Volpi took the courteous and sensible first precaution of notifying every jurisdiction that had any interest in the convoluted case of his own investigation.

Although Volpi ran a local operation around Columbus, through friends, relatives, and acquaintances he could draw on the services of some twenty-five investigators around the country, including his brother, Vaughn, based in Tampa.

Volpi used several ruses to interview Erik De Sando, John Hawkins's sometime roommate and occasional Just Sweats flunky. While he told them little, De Sando's garbage, snatched off the curb by one of Volpi's operatives, yielded several clues. One was a phone bill, which included a number either Hawkins or De Sando had called in Miami.

Private eyes like Volpi cultivate contacts at telephone companies. For ready cash, it's not hard to find someone with access to the right computer. Thus it took Volpi only a few hours to learn that the phone in Miami belonged to someone who called himself "Wolfgang von Snowden."

It was a rather obviously contrived name. Volpi had done his homework and was well aware that Gene Hanson had been born Melvin Eugene Snowden. But by the time his people got to the Tony Brickell Avenue penthouse that Hanson had rented, he was long gone.

Jones, too, had pinpointed south Florida from a review of phone records seized from Boggs's home and office. Another interesting result of this analysis was the emerging pattern of calls. A flurry of Boggs's calls to Hawkins and Hanson in Ohio coincided with times just before and after the unsuccessful attack on Pomeroy—and then, again, with the death of Greene. It was strong circumstantial evidence.

Jones and Perkins picked up Hanson's trail in Key West, where he'd briefly rented a cottage in the name of Ellis Greene. But it was Volpi who laid the critical groundwork for Hanson's arrest. Working with Just Sweats attorneys and a friend in the FBI, he convinced an Ohio magistrate to issue a federal warrant for Hanson on charges of unlawful flight to avoid prosecution. Then he persuaded a friend, a U.S. Customs agent, to enter Hanson's name and known aliases in the Enforcement Communications System, a special Treasury Department computer network. Customs agents routinely consult this system to check out suspicious characters at most U.S. ports of entry.

The names were in the computer when Dave Berry, a customs inspector at Dallas–Ft. Worth airport, spotted a suspicious-looking traveler on the evening of January 29, 1989. The traveler, just off a flight from Acapulco, was a middle-aged man in shorts and tennis shoes. Something in Berry's gut told him that this was not an ordinary tourist. He watched him from a distance, discreetly observing that the man seemed extraordinarily nervous as he waited at a baggage carousel.

When the man had picked up his suitcase, Berry came up and asked if he was returning from Acapulco and if he was a U.S. citizen.

"Yes," said George Soule, who identified himself with a Massachusetts driver's license and a birth certificate.

"Soule" had nothing to declare, according to his customs declaration, but it was Berry's legal right to inspect his luggage. Going on nothing but instinct, Berry asked to look inside a leather knapsack. He found plastic bags with $14,000 in fifty-dollar bills. It's a federal crime to bring more than $10,000 into the country unless this fact is entered on the customs declaration.

Also in the bag were several different identity documents, including a license for "Wolfgang von Snowden," a checkbook from a Key West bank in the name of Ellis Greene—and a Miami Public Library book, eight months overdue, *How to Create a New Identity.*

After arresting "Soule," Berry ran all the ID names through the Treasury computer. Gene Hanson, fugitive from justice, was in the bag.

Questioned by FBI agents, Jones and Perkins, Volpi, *Columbus Dispatch* reporter Robin Yocum, and by an Ohio assistant prosecutor, nearly the only thing Hanson would say for sure was that neither of the attorneys retained by Just Sweats was involved in the fraud.

Allowed to use a phone, Hanson phoned his mother, the first time they had spoken in many years. He began his conversation, "You know, Mother, I'm gay."

But Hanson steadfastly refused to admit his identity. Even when Jones confronted him with evidence proving that Hanson had flown into Los Angeles just hours before Ellis Greene's murder and left for Miami hours afterward, and that Hawkins had told several friends Hanson was alive and the whole affair was an elaborate scam, Hanson refused to cooperate.

Hanson was held by federal agents in Texas. A judge set his bail at $5 million, then asked Hanson if he could afford that much. "If they let me die a few more times, I can," he said.

Hanson went back to Columbus in handcuffs, while Ohio and California authorities worked out the details of who would have first crack at him.

Once Hanson was in custody, Jones and Perkins put twenty-four-hour surveillance on Dr. Boggs. They were ready to pounce at the first sign of flight. Five days later, on February 3, 1989, Boggs was arrested as he left his Glendale offices carrying boxes. But Boggs wasn't trying to run—$20,000 behind in his rent, he had merely been evicted from his office.

In custody, Boggs arrogantly proclaimed his innocence, claiming that he made over $200,000 a year from his practice and had no reason to get involved in insurance fraud, let alone murder. He was arraigned on charges of murdering Ellis Greene.

Catching John Hawkins was to prove far more difficult. Carrying a huge amount of cash, after disappearing from Columbus he flew first to Los Angeles. There he pulled yet another common scam. Hawkins bought ad space in a newspaper, offering "credit repair" for people seeking to improve their credit ratings. When people called his hotel room, Hawkins asked them for their date and place of birth, their Social Security number, driver's license number, and other information.

With this data he wrote away for duplicate documents: birth certificates, Social Security cards, driver's licenses— and passports. Within weeks he had several new identities.

Using at least six different aliases, Hawkins jetted around the country, sometimes with different female friends, staying in various cities under one or another of the identities he had pirated, occasionally telephoning or mailing letters to Just Sweats management.

Upon learning that Hanson and Boggs had been arrested, Hawkins headed for Canada. From there he traveled throughout the Caribbean and to Australia, then to Europe, staying briefly in France, Spain, Holland, England, and Greece. Always the high roller, Hawkins made no attempt at inconspicuousness and did little to alter his appearance. Tips on his current whereabouts steadily trickled into the Glendale PD.

All these tips were relayed to, among others, John Hogan, a Naval Investigative Service agent based in Sardinia. In July 1991, Hogan learned that Hawkins might be headed for Sardinia.

This tip came from a beautiful young woman living in Amsterdam. She had chanced to see a syndicated episode of a very popular American television program, *The Oprah Winfrey Show*. The episode dealt with a phenomenon of

American broadcasting, reality-based crime shows. One of these shows, not seen in Europe, was *America's Most Wanted*, which was introduced with a video clip describing the manhunt for John Hawkins.

The Dutch woman was outraged to learn that the man she had known as Bradley Bryant during an intense, passionate few weeks in Ibiza was a bisexual hustler named John Hawkins. Certain that he was sailing from Ibiza in a red catamaran, she contacted *America's Most Wanted*. Another Dutch citizen, the father of a young man accompanying Hawkins, also called to say Hawkins might be on the Italian isle of Sardinia. Producers passed both tips along to authorities in California.

One of these was Jerry Treadway, Mike Jones's supervisor at the California Department of Insurance. (Jones had moved on to a new career as an attorney.) Believing that Hawkins was traveling by sea, Treadway called the Naval Investigative Service and requested assistance.

Agent Hogan staked out several marinas, and after a few weeks spotted a man closely resembling Hawkins. Italian authorities, responding to Hogan's request, arrested the man without incident. Once in custody, however, Hawkins denied his identity, refusing to give any name. After a detailed medical examination, authorities discovered Hawkins had altered his appearance with a chin implant and injections in his lips. Aside from his fingerprints, however, there was one telltale detail of his anatomy, a peculiarity well known by his legions of lovers, and one that he could not disguise: his genitals lacked skin pigment.

Italy has no capital punishment, so Italian officials extracted a promise from California authorities that Hawkins would not face the death penalty. In return, they agreed to turn him over to U.S. law enforcement. In January 1992, however, Hawkins attempted to escape from Buancammino Prison after removing several bars from a cell window with a smuggled hacksaw blade. Guards caught him before he could leave the prison grounds.

Hawkins, still refusing to give a name, was extradited to California in July 1992. His mother retained famed attorney

Melvin Belli. Hawkins faces charges of murder for financial gain, insurance fraud, and grand theft.

"He was a playboy dancing around the world," said Glendale PD detective Jon Perkins. "He knew how to have fun."

Dr. Richard Boggs, still protesting his innocence and insisting that no murder had occurred, went on trial May 29, 1990, for murder in the first degree and eight counts of fraud. Among the critical evidence presented by prosecutors Al MacKenzie and Mike Jones (the same who had been a state insurance investigator): record of a phone call made at 1:22 on the morning of April 16, 1988, from a pay phone at the Rawhide Bar. The call was charged to Boggs's telephone credit card. Witnesses placed Greene in the bar when the call was made.

Prosecutors also showed that Boggs had been paid $6,500 by Hawkins several weeks after the murder. And the cause of death? Dr. Michael Baden, the New York State Police director of forensic sciences, veteran of over twenty thousand autopsies, concluded that Greene almost certainly died of suffocation.

Boggs was convicted of murder under "special circumstances." The first jury deadlocked, ten to two, for the death penalty. A second jury, which did not hear all the blood-curdling details introduced during the trial, sentenced him to life in prison without the possibility of parole.

When a *60 Minutes* investigation began probing medical licensing procedures in 1992, however, they discovered that despite the murder conviction, Boggs still had a medical license. It was revoked only after *60 Minutes* producers harangued the head of California's medical quality assurance board with this fact.

Gene Hanson and John Hawkins are expected to stand trial for murder in 1996.

Al MacKenzie believes that Boggs, Hanson, and Hawkins came very close to pulling off a perfect crime. The only reason things unraveled can be traced back to the confrontation between Boggs and Glendale patrolmen Tim Spruill and James Lowrey. "If they had believed Boggs, then no one would have taken Greene's fingerprints or pictures," opines MacKenzie. "But they didn't like his attitude, and they didn't believe his story."

Even then, says MacKenzie, building a case against Boggs and the others required beyond-the-call-of-duty efforts from many. "Instead of the usual bureaucratic shuffle," says MacKenzie, "police, pathologists, coroner's investigators, the state insurance department, even industry—insurance companies and private investigators—a lot of different people pulled this together."

# Goodbye, Mr. Chips
(1986)

**T**HE SORT OF PEOPLE WHO PLAN TO COMMIT PERFECT CRIMES *believe very strongly in themselves. They view themselves as bold, intelligent, and resourceful. They understand that what they are undertaking, the calculated commission of a serious crime, is the riskiest of businesses, the ultimate gamble. And they believe firmly in their ability to plan and execute a series of complex activities and cover their tracks afterward.*

*This case revolves around a man with nerves of steel and veins filled with the proverbial ice water, an intrepid adventurer secure in his abilities after a lifetime of meeting the most severe tests, a man serenely sure of his brains and fortitude—and long past fear of law enforcement.*

*He conceived a brilliant, intricate scheme. But filled with self-confidence and blind to his own shortcomings, he failed to consider that almost any unanticipated event might threaten a crucial part of his elaborate web.*

*And as he executed the most critical part of his plan, there was a sudden, unexpected change in the weather.*

A few days before Thanksgiving, just before they flew to Frankfurt, West Germany, Helle Crafts told her good friend Rita Buonanno—like Helle, a Pan American World Airways flight attendant—"If anything happens to me, don't think it was an accident."

Rita and Helle were very close. Rita had consoled and supported her through the years of Helle's painful marriage. So she made a point of remembering her friend's exact words.

Helle Crafts was thirty-nine, tall, fair, blond, fashionably slender, a warm and most attractive woman. Danish by birth, she had married an American.

In the week after Thanksgiving 1986, many people began to wonder where she was. The last time one of her friends could recall seeing her was at seven o'clock on the evening of November 18. After returning from a flight to Frankfurt, coworker Trudy Horvath dropped Helle off at her home in Newtown, Connecticut.

Confounding weather forecasters, a powerful storm blew in later that night. High winds, accompanied by thunder and lightning, blew several inches of snow onto Connecticut, burying roads, downing power lines, and disrupting many normal activities. By midmorning of the nineteenth, as the community began to dig itself out and restore basic services, some of Helle's friends tried to reach her.

But Helle did not return the phone calls left with either her husband, Richard, an Eastern Airlines pilot, or Marie Thomas, the young woman who looked after the couple's three children. A few days later, Helle was absent from a routine training session at Pan Am's airport facility. She did not report for her scheduled flight to Frankfurt.

Most mysteriously, Helle had invited friends and family to her home for a Thanksgiving feast—but when they arrived, she wasn't there. Her husband, Richard, said she was working.

Later, Richard reported that Helle had gone to Denmark to be with her aged mother, who was recovering from major surgery.

But it was not like Helle to just take off. She was a responsible woman who had worked for Pan Am for seventeen years. When her Pan Am friends checked, they learned that Helle had missed her scheduled flight and failed to notify her supervisor about her trip to Copenhagen. That was a serious omission: She stood to lose her job unless her husband had phoned in a request for emergency vacation time. But Richard Crafts had not phoned. .

Her closest friends knew that Helle was planning to divorce Richard, that she had spoken with an attorney and had drawn up papers. They began to wonder if maybe something had happened to her.

On the twenty-fifth of November, a week after the last time she saw Helle, Rita Buonanno, who lived in the countryside near Newtown, called Richard Crafts to ask for Helle's mother's telephone number. Dialing it got her the voice of a strange man who could speak no English. With the help of a Danish-speaking telephone operator, Rita called again. The man who answered assured Rita that she had dialed the right number—but it didn't belong to Helle's mother, whose family name was Nielsen. In fact, the number was in a different town, far from where Mrs. Nielsen lived.

Rita called Richard back to confirm the number. He gave her the same sequence of digits that had proved incorrect. It might be wrong, said Richard, but it was the only number he had for Helle's mother.

The Buonannos raised chickens in their backyard and sold eggs to neighbors. Not long after Rita's unsuccessful attempt to reach Mrs. Nielsen, Marie Thomas, the Craftses' nanny, came by their home for some eggs. A few hours later, she came for more. When she returned a third time on the next day, it occurred to Rita that Marie had bought far more eggs than two adults and three small children could eat. Was there another reason for Marie's visits?

There was. Marie wanted to talk to someone. Somebody sympathetic to Helle, who could help make sense out of the dark thoughts that were so frightening to her that she could hardly sleep.

Richard Crafts, said Marie, had just removed the rug in the bedroom he shared with Helle and another in the room where their two boys slept. A few days earlier, Marie recalled, she'd seen a dark stain several inches wide on the master bedroom rug. Richard had explained then that it came from kerosene—he had spilled some while filling a heater he had lit after the power failed on the night of the big storm.

Marie knew that kerosene has the properties of a solvent and evaporates cleanly. It shouldn't leave a dark stain.

But that wasn't all, said Marie. Richard had recently bought a dump truck, saying he intended to build a house on a piece of property he and Helle owned on nearby Currituck Road. Rita thought it odd that Helle was planning such an investment at the same time as she'd initiated divorce proceedings. And why hadn't she mentioned anything about it?

Then there were the two address books. Marie had one for emergency numbers that she could contact, if necessary, while Richard and Helle were away. Marie couldn't find her book, and thought Richard might have taken it. The other book was Helle's. Marie had seen Richard studying it a few days after Helle vanished, but now it, too, was gone—and Richard denied that he'd seen it. Also missing was a list of family and friend's numbers taped to the back of a kitchen-cabinet door.

As Rita and Marie spoke at length, the young nanny revealed information about herself. In addition to her position with the Craftses, Marie had two part-time jobs. One was at a McDonald's. About two o'clock on the morning of November 19, Marie returned from her restaurant shift, entering the house through the garage, her usual practice, and going to her room above it. Marie remembered hearing Helle, who had complained of catching a cold in Frankfurt, coughing from behind the closed door of the master bedroom. The house was otherwise quiet, and soon Marie fell asleep.

She was awakened at six by Richard. With his hair clinging damply to his head, he looked like he'd just stepped out of the shower. He said that because of the storm, the power was off and the house very cold, and so they would take the children to the nearby home of his sister, Karen Rodgers, where service had already been restored.

The Craftses' oil furnace required electricity to blow heated air throughout the house. Marie wondered why Richard didn't start the gasoline generator he kept in the basement, or why he didn't simply light the kerosene heaters they kept for just this sort of emergency. But she said nothing as she helped dress and feed the three children for the trip.

As they were leaving the house, Marie said, something very peculiar happened.

The family rarely used the front door, preferring to avoid the high, slippery concrete stoop. Instead they left the house via its attached garage, which led to a walkway that was less dangerous. This morning Richard insisted on using the front door. Although it was cold and windy, when his daughter, Kristina, age five, began to wail for mittens she had left behind, he refused to go back to get them. He all but threw the children into the back of his Toyota pickup.

Before they left, Marie glanced around but couldn't see Helle's little Toyota Tercel. Marie had driven it to work the night before and left it in the driveway. Now it was nowhere to be seen. Where, Marie asked Richard, was Helle?

She had already left the house, he said, and would meet them at Karen's place. But when they arrived at the Rodgers house, Helle was not there. Marie asked Richard again: where is Helle?

This time, Richard said he didn't know. And after fixing everyone a pancake breakfast in his sister's kitchen, he left to return to his own house while his sister went to work. The children were left to play with their three young cousins under Marie's watchful eye.

The next day, when the power was back on and the Crafts family back at home, Marie noticed that Helle's uniform and the special Pan Am suitcases and folding travel cart that she always took on overnight flights were missing from their usual closet.

Several days had passed with no word from Helle. Marie knew her to be a good mother, a conscientious woman who kept track of her children with frequent phone calls, even when she was overseas. She could not recall Helle ever being gone this long without calling to see how her children were.

A few days later, Richard left Marie a note: Helle had

called from Denmark. She was with her mother, but would return in a few days.

At the same time, Rita, upset and wondering now if Richard might have done away with Helle, confided her suspicions to two friends. All three decided to talk to Helle's attorney, Diane Andersen. On December 1, the three calls were logged within minutes of each other just before nine in the morning.

Diane Andersen was one of Darien, Connecticut's busiest and most respected divorce attorneys. Helle had retained her services in early September, not quite sure if she wanted to divorce Richard or explore other options, but almost sure that Richard had been seeing another woman. If that was so, she told Andersen and her closest friends, then it was the last straw. All his promises and assurances were so much hot air. As far as Helle was concerned, if her husband was still behaving like the carefree bachelor she'd married eleven years earlier, then he could go back to being a bachelor. She'd get a divorce.

Richard Bunel Crafts was born in 1937 in New York City, the first of three children. His father was a successful CPA and founder of a tony Park Avenue accounting firm. After the family moved to Connecticut, his mother opened a children's clothing store.

Richard grew up as an extraordinarily secretive child with a passion for collecting all sorts of odd things. An indifferent student, slight of build, he dropped out of college after one semester and joined the Marines.

There he found his vocation. Richard wanted to fly. After boot camp, he survived the harsh winnowing process to graduate in 1958 from the naval aviator's program at Pensacola, Florida. He pinned on his aviator's wings and second lieutenant's bars the same day.

In 1960, Richard Crafts, still a Marine, went to work for Air America, an airline secretly owned by the CIA that performed a multitude of hazardous tasks during the undeclared war in Southeast Asia. After a year flying helicopters, primarily in Laos, he returned to uniformed duty with the Marines. In May 1962, Richard accepted an honorable discharge and went back to work flying Air America choppers as a civilian, at substantially higher pay than marine officers rated.

By all accounts, Crafts was a superior pilot, brave but not foolhardy, calm and in control no matter the circumstances. Flying under extremely hazardous conditions, he survived several crashes and was hit in the leg by flak fragments in 1962.

Aside from the hazards of war, Southeast Asia in the sixties was something of a sexual supermarket for Americans. Tens of thousands of young women and girls, a few by choice but most out of dire circumstances, became prostitutes and party girls. For a young pilot with money in his pocket, virtually everything sexually imaginable was available. Crafts, like most of his comrades-in-arms, was a regular patron in Bangkok's notorious red-light district.

He quit Air America in 1966 to fly as a firefighter in Idaho and Utah. But this proved even more dangerous than hauling guns and opium in and out of Laos, and he quit after two months. He found safer employment flying helicopter tours around Manhattan. In January 1968, with over five thousand hours of flight time, he signed on with Eastern Airlines as a flight engineer.

Crafts graduated from turboprop Lockheed Electras to DC-8 jets and then wide-body L-1011s. He quickly earned the reputation for levelheadedness, a pilot who could be relied on to make a safe landing no matter what conditions he flew under. He earned a commendation from Eastern in 1971 for his assured handling of an in-flight emergency. Crafts's friends and fellow aviators saw him as a superb pilot, an extremely patient man, pleasant company on a long trip, reliable, efficient, and possessing stamina remarkable even among pilots. He could go without sleep for days.

Crafts enjoyed his bachelorhood. If he didn't have a girl in every airport city, it was because he hadn't visited them all. He juggled several simultaneous long-term affairs, often with flight attendants, and still found time and energy to prowl for a succession of one-night stands. According to envious friends, Crafts never worked hard at womanizing.

Women just flocked to him. He almost had to fight them off.

In 1969, Richard, then thirty-two, met Helle Lorck Nielsen, who was ten years younger. Within a few months, they shared a New York apartment with four other flight attendants.

Helle was crazy about Richard. She liked the way he moved, the way he talked, the way he made love. At this stage in their relationship, however, he was not ready for commitment. There were too many available women and too little time to bed them all.

Nevertheless, their relationship continued, in an on-again, off-again fashion. Eventually, they took a new apartment, just the two of them. After a few months, he moved out, but their intermittent relationship continued. She put up with his moods, his unexplained absences, his petty cruelties, and occasional physical abuse. At first, Helle accepted his desire to see other women, but by the early seventies she pressed him to get married. Believing that she might be unable to have children, she extracted a promise from Crafts that if she became pregnant, they would marry.

The first time she conceived, he beat her until she agreed to an abortion.

The next time she got pregnant, after angry arguments, Crafts agreed to marry her. They married on November 29, 1975. Several months later, they bought the house in Newtown, just over an hour's drive from JFK Airport or midtown Manhattan.

Many of those close to the couple were mystified at what Helle saw in Richard. From her bruises and black eyes and occasional public humiliation, it was clear that he frequently used her as a punching bag.

While he could be very severe with his children, slapping them hard in the face and demanding a standard of obedience and discipline rarely achievable, Crafts seemed at other times like an excellent father, lavishing gifts and attention on his children.

But he was not generous with Helle. He earned three times her salary but insisted that she pay for their nanny, for their children's clothes, for household expenses, and for her own car. For his own amusement, Crafts bought dozens of firearms and all sorts of expensive "toys"—several vehicles, including a backhoe, a large assortment of power tools and chainsaws, a top-of-the-line Hasselblad camera and lenses, air compressor, welding equipment, cement mixer, etc.

Much of this equipment was intended for home-improvement projects. But Crafts had a habit of starting an excavation or construction, only to abandon it before completion. From the outside, the Crafts home was an eyesore.

Crafts was not home as often as his schedule permitted, in part because he maintained a steady pursuit of "targets of opportunity"—one-night stands, usually flight attendants from other airlines. He also dated a few other women for extended periods.

Then there was his time-consuming "hobby": police work. He served several nights each month as an auxiliary patrolman, first in Newtown (population 20,000) and later in Southbury (population 7,000), six miles away. Outfitted with uniform, badge, and gun, Crafts drove a police cruiser, attended training sessions, and widened his circle of contacts in law enforcement.

It was for this reason that in November 1986, Rita Buonanno decided not to share her fears for Helle's safety with the Newtown police. Richard, she thought, was entirely too cozy with his former squadmates. If something had happened to Helle, Rita didn't want to put him on alert that she had asked for an investigation. Because the more she thought about all the little ways that Richard was not like other men she knew, the more fear she felt for Helle. And for herself.

When Helle retained Diane Andersen, in September, the lawyer suggested that her client obtain proof of her husband's infidelity before proceeding. Helle hired a private investigator, Keith Mayo, thirty-four, to put Richard under surveillance.

In 1984, Richard had surgery for cancer of the colon. Despite the high odds against recovery, after chemotherapy and Helle's nursing, he had resumed a near-normal life by

July 1986. He was scheduled for a semiannual exam on October 2, and Helle had decided to wait until the state of his health was known before deciding about divorce. If the cancer had returned, she reasoned, there was little point in putting both of them through hardship. But after the exam, Richard's doctor told him that he had apparently beaten the odds: there was no sign of cancerous tissue.

On October 7, Mayo delivered to Helle a set of photos to support his surveillance report. On several recent days when he had told Helle he was working, Richard had been with petite, pretty flight attendant Nancy Dodd at her New Jersey apartment. In fact, Nancy and Richard had been seeing each other, on and off, for some twenty years.

The photos of Richard and Nancy hardened Helle's heart. She told Andersen to go ahead with the divorce action. With such good evidence of adultery, Andersen told Helle, getting a favorable settlement would not be difficult. Based on Crafts's salary from Eastern and his other income, Helle could expect about $30,000 a year in child support and alimony, plus a large cash settlement from the eventual sale of their home. Helle told Richard of her decision, and that he could expect to be served with papers by the local sheriff's office.

Richard instead called the sheriff to tell deputies not to bother coming out. He'd stop by the station to accept service within the next few days. But as of December 1, when Diane Andersen heard from Helle's worried friends, Richard had yet to appear at the station. He had not been served.

Thinking over what Helle's friends had told her, Andersen recalled that she, too, had been unable to make contact since just before Thanksgiving. Andersen asked Keith Mayo if he would help find out what had happened to Helle. Rita and several of her friends chipped in a few thousand dollars to pay for his services and Andersen contributed the unused portion of Helle's retainer.

Mayo's first move was to tell the Newtown Police Department that he had information that had led him to conclude that Helle had disappeared and that Richard Crafts might have something to do with it.

The Newtown PD did not want to hear it. Chief Louis Marchese, at seventy-two Connecticut's oldest chief of police, had some years earlier suffered a political double cross that abruptly ended his promising career with the state police. He didn't like outside interference and didn't have much use for private investigators, especially those, like Mayo, who were former police officers. Marchese ran the Newtown department with the subtlety of a locomotive and a charm worthy of Attila the Hun.

Mayo, however, was concerned not only about Helle's whereabouts but about Marie Thomas, the nanny who had become the prime source of information about what was going on in the Crafts' house. But Newtown police were in no hurry to open a case against Richard, and when Mayo tried to press them to investigate, he got the bureaucratic bounce from one disinterested officer to another.

Eventually Mayo used personal contacts, among them an assistant prosecutor and friend, Walter Flanagan, the local state's attorney. He set up a meeting with Marie Thomas. With Flanagan pressing, a Newtown PD officer, Henry Stormer, was dispatched to attend the meeting as an observer.

Marie repeated to Mayo essentially what she had told Rita, adding a few details that she had remembered about the early-morning departure from the Crafts' home. She now recollected seeing a set of footprints in the snow around the house when they left, though she couldn't say for sure if they had looked like the smaller feet of a woman. Marie also recalled that although the windshield of Crafts's Ford sedan was covered with several inches of snow, the Toyota pickup that she and the children piled into had almost none on its windows. She remembered noticing that the lever that was used to put the pickup into four-wheel drive was engaged. From all that, she concluded that Crafts had driven the car earlier that morning. Now, she told Mayo, she wondered why Crafts would get up before dawn and drive the pickup somewhere where he needed four-wheel drive.

A Newtown PD detective spoke to Marie almost immediately after she spoke to Mayo. But he was about to go on vacation and didn't seem too interested in what she had to say. After perfunctory questioning, he turned her over to Stormer, a rookie patrolman who interviewed her for more than two hours and took a statement.

Such casual treatment outraged Mayo, but there was nothing he could do. He had asked Rita and another Pan Am flight attendant, Sue Schneider, to go to police headquarters and give their statements to Stormer. Among the new information now on record from Rita was one curious fact: Helle's car was parked in the Pan Am employee lot at JFK. Just where it would be if Rita had caught a flight to Denmark.

Mayo didn't believe it. He telephoned the state police office in Southbury and walked the resident trooper through the facts of the case, sharing his suspicions that Crafts had killed his wife.

The trooper was not impressed. There just wasn't any evidence of a crime, he told Mayo, ringing off. Mayo was frustrated and furious. With every day that passed, Crafts had more and more opportunity to destroy evidence and further cover his tracks. And the police did nothing at all.

With the help of Rita and Sue Schneider, Mayo learned that if Helle had gone to Denmark, she had not gone on Pan Am or SAS. There were messages in her Pan Am box at JFK. And her car was still parked in the employee lot.

Mayo pushed the Newtown PD to impound the car, which might contain evidence, but they did nothing. So far, they said, Helle was only a suspected missing person—and her husband, Richard, had yet to report even that.

On December 2, Crafts finally spoke to the Newtown PD. A detective asked him to come down to the station, where he admitted that he knew Helle wasn't visiting her mother. He didn't want the embarrassment of telling everyone what he'd known for days: Helle had a boyfriend, some sort of Asian, and she'd gone off with him, abandoning her family. And that, said Crafts, was nobody's business but his own.

Would Crafts be willing to take a polygraph examination? asked the police.

Certainly, said Crafts. He knew that the nearest polygraph was at the state-police barracks in Meriden—and that the machines stayed busy. It usually took several weeks, often longer, to get an appointment.

The next day, however, Newtown PD called Crafts and told him there had been a cancellation. His polygraph appointment was for the following morning, December 4, at eight.

The polygraph measures changes in a subject's respiration, pulse rate, blood pressure, and perspiration. Success in determining the truthfulness of a subject is predicated in large measure on the subject's fear of being caught in a lie.

Crafts was questioned by two experienced polygraph examiners. They asked, in addition to control questions (such as his place of birth and age) designed to establish a basis for comparison, several questions directly bearing on the issue of Helle's whereabouts. And they asked Crafts if he had killed Helle, or if he had caused someone else to kill her.

Crafts's responses indicated no deception. As far as the polygraph examiners were concerned, he was entirely truthful.

There was one small, puzzling thing, however. The examiners couldn't recall seeing another exam where a subject had displayed so little physiological response to *any* question. Crafts was the coolest person they'd ever hooked to their machine. He was calm, controlled, completely assured—just what they expected in an airline pilot. He was either totally innocent—or the most diabolical fiend they'd ever met.

To make sure Crafts hadn't taken some funny drug to disguise his responses, immediately after his test, police had Crafts submit a urine sample, which was sent out for analysis. The results were negative.

Polygraphs are not infallible. There is controversy over their effectiveness, although most police think they are very effective tools. The result of polygraph exams are not admissible as evidence in any state—a fact that Crafts, a reserve officer, must surely have known—but police find them useful in deciding whether to continue an investigation.

When Richard passed the polygraph, most of the Newtown PD higher-ups thought there was no reason to suspect him of having any part in his wife's disappearance.

Keith Mayo, who also believed in polygraphs, was shook up, but undeterred. He *knew* Helle was dead, knew her husband had killed her. Without a shred of proof, he just knew it in his bones.

On December 8, Rita Buonanno, at the request of a Newtown PD detective, opened a safe-deposit box she shared with Helle, an arrangement that Richard had no reason to know about. In the box police found, among Helle's family documents, passports, and other things, her will, leaving most of her worldly goods to "my beloved husband."

Also in the box were Helle's few pieces of good jewelry pearls, gold chains, a turquoise necklace, bracelets, a locket. Richard had told many people that Helle had taken her good jewelry with her.

Rita had supplied police with the numbers of some of Richard's credit cards. Using a "snitch"—someone inside the credit-card company who used his access to the company's computer in exchange for small, regular payments— police had begun to develop a list of Crafts's recent credit-card purchases. One that would later be significant was for $257.96 at Caldor's, a department store in Brookfield, about thirty minutes from Newtown.

Other Newtown officers contacted the Danish consulate in New York, seeking help from Danish authorities in locating Helle. Lieutenant Mike DeJoseph, one of Newtown's most experienced officers, discussed the possibility of getting a search warrant and looking at Helle's car, still parked at JFK. Chief Marchese vetoed the search. It was expensive, and probably would yield nothing of value, opined the chief. And surely, Helle's body wasn't hidden in the car, which had no trunk.

Newtown, in its limited and plodding way, was pursuing Helle's disappearance. But they weren't issuing progress bulletins and they weren't telling Keith Mayo. As far as Mayo knew, they were doing nothing at all.

He decided that he would try to find the stained rug that

Marie Thomas had noticed before Crafts replaced it. If he could find it, and find blood on it that matched Helle's, then maybe he could get the state police to enter the case.

Mayo tracked the garbage collected in Newtown the week of Helle's disappearance to a landfill in Canterbury, clear across the state near the Rhode Island border. Using all his charm and sincerity and the dwindling remnants of the cash put up by Helle's friends, he mobilized a small force—off-duty volunteer firefighters, a police friend, a visiting Englishman, and a day laborer—to pick through layers of nauseatingly odoriferous garbage. An off-duty state trooper who had heard about Mayo's rug hunt joined the search. After a Herculean effort, Mayo's men turned up a blue rug that seemed to match Marie's description of the one Crafts had removed from the master bedroom. On it were dark stains that the state trooper said looked very much like blood.

The rug was turned over to the state-police lab for analysis. Weeks later, the lab would conclude that this was *not* the rug from the Crafts home—but before this conclusion was reached, the seeds that Mayo had sowed trying to alert and involve the state police had begun to sprout.

Mayo was frantic to get an official investigation started. But the Newtown PD wasn't sharing information with anyone, and especially not with Mayo and the state police. When Mayo found the blue rug, the head of the Western District Crime Squad, a state-police unit supporting local law enforcement in the Newtown area, wondered if he ought to enter the case.

Marie Thomas, now fearing for her own safety, moved out of the Crafts house, telling Richard that although she would continue to care for his children, she didn't feel comfortable living in a household without another woman in residence. A few months later, Marie quit the job. Richard's sister, Karen Rodgers, began looking after the three children.

As part of their low-key investigation, the Newtown PD had checked on Crafts's whereabouts on the nights of November 20 and 21, when he was scheduled for duty with the Southbury PD. Records showed that he had a near-perfect work record, and that he had reported for work promptly. He had also turned up for a training session on November 20, but the class had been canceled because so many roads were snowed in.

Nevertheless, Newtown's Lieutenant Mike DeJoseph invited Crafts back for a second interview on December 11. This time Crafts was told that Helle had hired a private investigator, who had photographed him kissing and fondling Nancy Dodd. Crafts now revealed that he had been seeing Dodd for twenty years.

Crafts said he couldn't imagine Helle telling friends that if anything happened to her, it wasn't an accident. And he explained that he had taken up the bedroom rug because he had spilled kerosene on it, and replaced it with new carpeting from a local store. He had taken up the rug himself to save paying for installation. And he said that he cut up successive two-foot strips to make the task of removing the rug easier.

Helle had been missing nearly a month, said DeJoseph. Had she received any mail in that time?

"No," said Crafts and no letters had arrived for her since she left.

DeJoseph saw himself as playing a complicated game with Crafts, a sort of mental chess match. His approach was to keep asking questions while noting Crafts's answers. When he had caught him in enough lies, he would be able to prove, at least by inference, what he was trying to hide.

After this second interview, DeJoseph suspected that Crafts had lied about the rug and about Helle's mail. He also thought that Crafts might have lied about being unable to imagine his wife worrying that he might harm her.

Crafts told DeJoseph that after the snowstorm, power had been restored to his street, Newfield Lane, about 3:00 or 3:30 in the afternoon. DeJoseph didn't check this, because someone he knew who lived nearby also told him the power had come back on in late afternoon.

Nevertheless, DeJoseph now felt that Crafts had moved himself into the "suspect" category. He would have liked to put five or six officers on the case full-time.

But Chief Marchese did not agree. Helle was a missing

person. Nothing more. There was no need to waste taxpayers' money on a costly investigation when the missing flight attendant might turn up, alive and well, at any moment.

Lieutenant James Hiltz, boss of the Western District Major Crime Squad, knew all about Marchese's reluctance to allow outside agencies to get involved in Newtown matters. Nevertheless, alerted by reports filtering upward from state-police investigators, he phoned DeJoseph on December 12 to offer assistance. DeJoseph, placing loyalty to his chief at the top of his agenda, suggested that there wasn't much to the case against Crafts. Somewhat disingenuously, he described it as "bullshit." He suggested that Hiltz contact Chief Marchese.

To Hiltz, it looked like DeJoseph was stonewalling. Rather than call Marchese, whom he knew hated the state police and everyone in it, Hiltz called Flanagan, the state's attorney. To Flanagan it was one more indication that the Newtown PD either couldn't or wouldn't investigate.

By December 18, Flanagan, the district's senior law-enforcement officer, felt he could wait no longer. He called a meeting between Marchese and Hiltz in his own office. From that meeting emerged an agreement that the two agencies would share information. The state police would take overall charge of the investigation and provide forensic services to back up the Newtown PD's limited capabilities.

Despite this agreement, in the months that followed, Newtown and state investigators often pursued parallel tracks, covered the same ground, and failed to share both investigative leads and collected evidence. Hiltz's people eventually began to act as though there was no Newtown PD, while Marchese's officers, who interpreted the agreement between the two agencies very differently from Hiltz and Flanagan, felt as though their efforts were belittled or ignored. These conflicts delayed the investigation.

It is impossible to believe that Richard Crafts, former Newtown patrolman and current Southbury reservist—wouldn't know how little cooperation Chief Marchese could be expected to give the state police and how few investigative resources the Newtown PD possessed.

* * *

On the theory that Crafts had killed his wife and disposed of her body, the investigation assumed that Helle had died the evening of November 18. If Crafts had disposed of her body on the night of November 18–19, during or just after the big storm, then someone might have seen him driving around the Newtown area that night. Major Crimes began looking for witnesses.

At the same time, DeJoseph at the Newtown PD sent Harry Stormer to canvas Newfield Lane, looking for neighbors who might remember seeing anything unusual the night of the storm or the next day. Stormer spoke to eight families. One thing he learned was that power had been restored at eleven in the morning, *not* at 3:30, as Crafts had said. Stormer didn't know if this was important or not, but he wrote it down.

And, Stormer learned, several other neighbors had seen a small silver car, possibly a Volkswagen Rabbit, parked at the end of Newfield Lane, a cul-de-sac, after November 19. Near the silver car was a dump truck.

Against the possibility that Crafts had rented the silver car for some nefarious reason, DeJoseph told Stormer to check on car-rental agencies, but his search yielded no record.

On December 20, when Karen Rodgers came by the Crafts' house to pick up the three children, Marie showed her some stains on the mattress in the master bedroom. They were rust-colored, and looked like dried blood. Similar stains were on a recently washed rag she found in the laundry.

Karen was by now deeply worried about her brother— sure he had done something terrible—but she didn't want to get further involved in building a case against him. So, Karen suggested that Marie talk to Sue Lausten, another of Helle's close friends. After they spoke, Sue asked her husband, Lewis, to look at the stains.

Marie showed him through the house. In Helle's absence, the usually neat and clean interior had become wildly chaotic. For some reason, Crafts had moved his children's beds into the master bedroom, and the whole family, less the missing Helle, now shared a single room. The box frame and headboard of Crafts's bed had disappeared, and he slept on the queen-sized mattress, which rested on the bare floor.

Lewis Lausten took careful note of what he saw and told Stormer about rust-colored stains about the size of a quarter on one side of Crafts's mattress. Also on the mattress were much smaller spots similar in color and a smudge that appeared to have been made when something was wiped on the mattress. The smudge, too, bore the familiar brownish-red stain.

On that same day, Newtown detective Harry Nororian heard back from his "credit-card snitch." According to his charge records, Crafts had rented a large woodchipper on November 18, returned it on November 21, and rented it again on December 3, returning it the next day.

A woodchipper is a large, noisy, gasoline-powered device of channels and swiftly rotating, razor-edged wheels. It is capable of reducing small logs to mounds of wafer-thin chips in a few seconds.

Detective Nororian confirmed by phone that Darien Rents had rented Crafts a woodchipper. That night Nororian told his wife, "It looks like the Crafts guy put his wife through a chipper." The grisly rumor swept through the Newtown PD, though it would be some time before they shared this information with the state police.

By December 23, Walter Flanagan, the state's attorney, had concluded that Newtown would never cooperate with the Major Crime Squad. Flanagan told Hiltz to establish probable cause and to get a search warrant for the Crafts house. Hiltz had his team go through the statements of Marie Thomas and others. On Christmas Eve, Hiltz took his request for a search warrant to Judge Frank McDonald. McDonald signed the warrant, protesting that this was a case where "you're damned if you do, and damned if you don't."

Before serving the warrant two days later, Flanagan had one more thing to do. Invoking an old, rarely-used Connecticut statute, he ordered the Newtown PD to yield jurisdiction in the case. Chief Marchese was instructed to turn over Newtown's investigative files and notes to the state and to stop all further independent investigation.

At four in the afternoon of December 26, state police investigators knocked on Crafts's front door. He wasn't home. Sergeant Martin Ohradan had to remove a pane of glass from the kitchen door to gain access. On a cabinet he saw a note, dated December 23:

*Helle, I'm at mother's with the children. Please come. We love you. R. I have your car with me and keys for the truck and Rabbit are on the stairs. The Ford is out of commission.*

Hiltz, very suspicious, surmised that Crafts had expected his house would be searched and had written the note for the benefit of the searchers.

Later, police would discover that Crafts had left Newtown on December 22 and driven to Florida with his children to visit his mother. The next day, presumably on his way south, he stopped in New Jersey and bought medicine for his son's aching ear. If the note was actually written on the twenty-third, it meant that Crafts had turned around and driven all the way back to Newtown to leave it, then headed down to Florida.

There were other oddities about this note. Crafts's Ford worked just fine when police seized it. And the Volkswagen Rabbit was secretly purchased by Crafts; Helle had learned about it only after going through his papers. She suspected the car was for one of his girlfriends and had discussed it with her attorney. But Helle and Richard never spoke about the car—unless it was on the night of her death.

Police brought in still and video cameras and carefully photographed every room in the house to note the position of every object, a step designed to make it harder for defense attorneys to claim police had planted evidence.

Detectives were surprised to note that the apparent chaos in the house had been carefully contrived. Crafts had swapped the tables in his dining room and kitchen. He had disassembled his children's bunk beds and placed them in the dining room. Boxes and drawers were scattered everywhere. The fireplace could not contain the mound of ashes overflowing from its hearth. On examination, the ashes were from burned paper.

In the master bedroom, investigators noted that the rug had been removed but some of the padding had been ripped out in two-foot strips. Why take out some of the padding and leave the rest? On further investigation, police would learn that Crafts had ordered a new rug, paid a cash deposit, but never took delivery.

Police divided the house into a grid, then carefully searched every square inch, logging each of 113 items taken as evidence to show where it was found on the grid.

In the basement police found an arsenal: over fifty rifles, shotguns, and handguns, along with a live hand grenade. The guns were taken into evidence as a matter of routine. If Helle's body were ever found, and if she had been shot, they would test-fire the guns.

Police found several power tools scattered around the property, including two chain saws. Little attention was paid to tools so common to the community.

Crafts's Ford was found behind his backhoe at the Currituck Road property. The mat lining from the trunk was missing, but there were a few woodchips in the corner recesses, a fact to which no significance was attached until much later.

Thinking about it, Hiltz concluded that Crafts had moved the furniture around to confuse investigators. To defeat this attempt, Sergeant Ohradan asked Sue Lausten, a frequent visitor to the house, to put everything in the master bedroom back the way she remembered it.

After doing so, she concluded that a dust ruffle that had been around the bed was missing. With the mattress returned to its former position and night tables in their usual spots, police noted a pile of women's magazines on the bathroom side of the bed. They concluded that Helle had slept on this side. The dark spot on the rug that Marie had noticed was near the foot of the bed on Helle's side— exactly the area where Crafts had removed both carpet and padding.

The forensics team very carefully went over every inch

of the room, including ceiling and walls. They used a chemical stew called orthotolidine to look for traces of blood. When orthotolidine comes into contact with blood, even in minute quantities, it turns bright blue. The spots on the mattress and newly laundered washcloths and towels turned blue. Police took samples of these for lab analysis.

Based on the position of the blood droplets, Henry Lee, M.D., one of America's most respected forensic pathologists, determined that the blood droplets had hit the bed at an angle, indicating medium velocity. Dr. Lee deduced that if the blood came from Helle, she had been sitting or kneeling on the end of the bed, or on the floor, at the time. The blood could not have come from a gunshot wound or from a stabbing, which would have thrown droplets at *high* velocity. Helle did not cut herself accidentally and later drip on the mattress; that would have caused *low*-velocity characteristics.

So, concluded Dr. Lee, she had most likely been struck with a blunt object that broke the skin and scattered blood.

Taking all that into account, Sergeant Ohradan theorized that Crafts had killed Helle in this bedroom with something large and heavy. Further, before six A.M., he had disposed of the sheets, comforter, box spring, and other bloodstained items.

But it was just a theory. There was no body. No witnesses to the murder. And it had yet to be established that the bloodstains were of the same blood type as Helle's.

A few days later, Ohradan carefully inspected the Currituck Road lot. Covered with brush in places, it included an abandoned mine shaft, its entrance screened by thick brush. Ohradan brought along Lady, a bad-tempered bloodhound. The dog gave no sign of anything unusual in or near the mine shaft.

Later that day, the twenty-ninth of December, Ohradan stopped by the Southbury PD. He was fishing, looking for someone who had seen anything unusual the night Helle disappeared. Someone had.

Southbury constable Richard Wildman had worked the graveyard shift on the night of November 20. He had run into Crafts, who was in uniform, and they chatted briefly.

About four that morning, checking the parking lot of a local school, Wildman saw a U-Haul truck with a large wood-chipper behind. Nearby was a Southbury police car. Wildman saw Crafts, wearing an orange poncho, transfer-ring his police equipment from the cruiser to the U-Haul. Assuming that Crafts, whose shift ended at two, hadn't been able to find a parking space to leave the cruiser in the Southbury PD's lot, he'd stopped to tell Crafts there was now space.

Wildman offered to follow Crafts back to the lot and then bring him back to the U-Haul. On the way over, Wildman asked what he was doing with a woodchipper. Crafts replied that the heavy snow had brought down tree limbs near his house.

Ohradan found this very interesting. What was Crafts doing between two, when his shift ended, and four, when Wildman gave him a lift?

Later, when Crafts was asked about this, he claimed to have hung around the police station for about half an hour after his shift, filling out his report and a pay sheet and checking the bulletin board. He claimed to have gone straight home at 2:30.

But Wildman had seen him at four, and again at 4:30, behind the wheel of the U-Haul, the woodchipper still be-hind, in a parking lot.

Ohradan was beginning to piece it all together. Could Crafts have killed his wife and disposed of her body by putting it through a woodchipper? It was too grizzly to contemplate—until Ohradan found another witness who'd seen a woodchipper that night parked on the bank of Lake Zoar, a wide, sluggish bend in the Housatonic River near the edge of town. Joey Hine, who drove a truck for the county road department, was sure he'd seen the chipper around midnight on the twentieth.

Late that afternoon, just before dark, Harry Stormer, at DeJoseph's order but without Chief Marchese's knowledge, met with Ohradan. Stormer told Ohradan, who had re-quested the meeting, that he had credit-card receipts con-firming that Crafts had rented a woodchipper.

The next day, Ohradan sent two men to interview Joey

Hine, a muscular, tattooed man in his midthirties. Working a second shift because of the heavy snowfall, Hine cleared River Road with his snowplow. Then he'd gone up a secondary route, Purchase Brook Road, until a fallen tree barred his way. He turned the plow around and returned to River Road. There, sometime between 3:30 and 4:00 A.M., he encountered what he described as the strangest thing he had ever seen. On the side of a lonely road in a roaring snowstorm, a man in an orange poncho stepped out from behind a truck. He held up one hand, like a traffic cop, then signaled Hine on with a wave of his other arm. Behind the truck, Hine noted, was a large woodchipper. He didn't hear its loud, unmuffled engine, so he assumed it wasn't in operation.

Two hours later, Hine saw the truck and the woodchipper near a bridge over the Housatonic. As the sky brightened he spotted several small clumps of wood chips along the road between the bridge and the spot of his original siting.

Hines led the investigators to a culvert on the bank of Lake Zoar. An inch-thick carpet of wood chips covered the ground. Walking through these, a detective came across an envelope. Sealed but nicked, its preprinted return address was the American Cancer Society. Through the glassine window, officers read the addressee's name: Mrs. Helle K. Crafts. Also mixed in with the chips, the officers noted, were shreds of bright blue cloth, and other scraps of paper.

While one of the officers stood guard over the wood chips, the other raced back to find Sergeant Ohradan. Minutes later, Ohradan, Hiltz, and both investigators were on the scene. Pawing through the chips, they found return-address stickers with Helle's name and address.

Ohradan was filled with rage and loathing. But he was convinced that Crafts was playing with the police, spreading false clues. "I'll retire if this guy put her through a chipper," he said.

All eight members of the Major Crime Squad were summoned. They inspected the riverbank for a mile in either direction, photographing everything, tagging all objects found among the chips before placing them in envelopes and bags. In addition to the envelope, labels, other scraps of paper and shreds of blue cloth, officers found strands of blond hair and many small fragments. Everything was frozen solid. The items filled some thirty bags.

The evidence was laid out to defrost on large sheets of plywood. Sifting it through a wire screen, police found a small chunk of gray metal that looked like a dental crown. Fragments of bone were noted. To those schooled in such macabre matters, they looked like they came from a human cranium.

Dr. Lee examined the trunk of Crafts's Ford on January 2, 1986. Among the wood chips, he found scraps of human flesh, bone fragments, and blue fibers.

Hiltz now assumed that Crafts had killed his wife and sent her body through the chipper. He further assumed that he had tried to put most of the chips into Lake Zoar and that those on the bank had fallen short of the mark. He asked for a dive team to explore the frigid, nearly opaque waters near the bank.

On the morning of January 6, the first divers, all volunteers, slipped into the lake. The water temperature was two degrees above freezing, so they were severely limited in their underwater time. Nevertheless, they recovered a polished fingernail with a tiny piece of flesh attached. Settled into the bottom mud, they found a Stihl chain saw with its serial number filed off. Three days later, divers brought up the saw's cutting blade.

The bank of Lake Zoar became the site of one of the most intensive hunts for evidence in forensic history. A huge tent, borrowed from the National Guard, housed a large plywood-and-sawhorse table. Under the glare of portable floodlights, police sifted through every bit of the material that could be recovered from the lake bottom and the shoulder. Hundreds of bits and pieces thought to have been human were recovered, including part of a finger and the cap of another tooth.

Meanwhile, other police tracked down the U-Haul truck that Crafts had used to pull the chipper. With a magnifying glass and tweezers, they probed the interior of the cargo space and picked out blue fibers, bone fragments, and chopped bunches of hair.

It was more than enough to convince Ohradan that Richard Crafts had cut up Helle's body with a chain saw and fed the pieces through a woodchipper.

Attorney Flanagan faced a major challenge in convicting Crafts. He had circumstantial evidence that Crafts had put his wife's dismembered body into a woodchipper. But disposing of a dead body is only a misdemeanor. The state would have to prove that Crafts had *murdered* Helle before disposing of her body. And that, Flanagan knew, was not going to be easy.

The unprecedented activity along Lake Zoar had attracted the media, which responded with cameras, helicopters, and reporters. But all the police would say is that they were looking for Helle's body.

Crafts continued to maintain his innocence, but clearly needed a lawyer. He found one in the Yellow Pages. The attorney called Flanagan's office to find out what the state had. Flanagan didn't want to reveal what had been recovered from the lake until he had a chance to question Richard Crafts. He wanted Crafts to tell his story, give him facts that could be verified or contradicted through investigation. Or maybe, thought Flanagan, Crafts might simply confess. He'd seen it happen.

Not this time, though.

Crafts, without his attorney, drove over to meet with Ohradan and one of his investigators. After being read his rights, he said that on the night of November 18–19 he had awakened between two and three in the morning, as he often did due to a stomach disorder, to find the house very cold and the power out.

Police would later determine that the power had actually failed at 3:44 A.M. It would have taken the house about an hour to get "real cold."

Crafts said that his wife left the house about six o'clock that morning. He hadn't seen or heard from her since. He was not unduly worried because she had done this sort of thing before, once or twice a year. He had no idea where she was, unless it was in Denmark with her mother, or someplace with her boyfriend, or perhaps visiting a cousin in California. Crafts said he phoned Dana Dalton, Helle's Pan Am supervisor, and was told Helle had already requested emergency leave. Actually, Dalton later confirmed, she told Crafts that Helle had *not* requested leave.

Asked about his children, Crafts dissolved into tears. Moments later, talking about other matters, he was back to his cool, confident self.

During three hours of interrogation, Crafts displayed emotion only when talking about his children and then but briefly. Ohradan decided he had never met anyone who could control his feelings so thoroughly. Richard Crafts, thought Ohradan, was exactly the sort of man who could land a wide-body on one engine in a hurricane and never break a sweat.

The sort who could feed his wife to a woodchipper.

Richard was arrested for Helle's murder on January 13, 1986. Before he came to trial, police interviewed Crafts's neighbors and friends, and followed his trail of credit-card and cash purchases, to piece together their case.

- On October 29, Crafts bought a well-used silver Volkswagen Rabbit for $2,500. He paid three hundred down, in cash, and the balance with a cashier's check on November 17. The date on that check, however, was November 3. On November 20, Crafts told his neighbors that he would be parking the Rabbit and a dump truck on the street near his house. Crafts would later tell police that he bought the car for Marie to use because she was a bad driver who kept running into things and denting the fenders on Helle's Toyota. It occurred to police that if Crafts was planning to murder Helle and had left her Toyota in the Pan Am lot to make people think she was in Europe, then he would have needed a car so Marie could drive his children around town. Crafts gave Marie the Rabbit's keys on November 22.

- On November 10, a Monday, while Helle was away at work, Crafts bought a new Ford dump truck from a local dealer for $15,000. He told the dealer it was to put gravel on the driveway of his lot on Currituck. Crafts paid an extra $350 to have a pintle hook put on this truck. This is a hitch used to tow a trailer—and would have been required to tow a woodchipper. Installing the pintle hook required driving the truck to a contractor; on the return trip, a fuel line leaked. The dealer said he'd have it fixed and deliver the truck by Crafts's requested date, November 18.

- The same day, November 10, Crafts made phone inquiries in Norwalk, over twenty miles from Newtown, about renting a woodchipper. He was referred to Darien Rents.
- Three days later, Crafts ordered a large freezer chest from a Danbury dealer. He specified the required inside dimensions. The interior was nearly five feet long, large enough to hold a woman Helle's size if her knees were folded.
- The next day, November 14, Crafts called Darien Rents to reserve a large woodchipper for November 18.
- The Westinghouse freezer he ordered was ready to go on November 17. Crafts paid cash, and when the manager insisted on a name for the receipt, Crafts told him to put down "Mr. Cash." Crafts took the freezer away in his Toyota pickup. He stopped by the Volkswagen dealer where he'd purchased the Rabbit and took possession of the car. Since he was driving his pickup, he asked a salesman to drop the car in a nearby shopping center lot. He said he'd come back for it later, with his wife.
- Darien Rents called Crafts at home the next day, leaving a message with Marie to confirm that the "Badger Brush Bandit" chipper he had reserved was ready for pickup. When Crafts came by later that day, the manager observed that he would need a bigger truck to tow the chipper. The dump truck he'd ordered had yet to be delivered, so Crafts told the manager he would pay an extra day's rental ($260) if he'd hold the chipper twenty-four hours, when he would have a proper truck. The manager agreed. Crafts put the charge on his MasterCard.
- About eight o'clock on the morning of November 19, after Richard had taken Marie and his children to his sister's house, fixed breakfast, and left, Bonita Cartoun,

a neighbor on Newfield Lane, rang the doorbell and knocked on the door. She wanted to borrow firewood, but no one was home.

- At 12:31 on the afternoon of November 19, Marie called Crafts at his home. He said that the power was still off. In fact, it had been restored at 10:44.

- About an hour after talking to Marie, Crafts bought comforters and pillows at a Caldor's department store in Brookfield, seven miles from his home, paying for them with his MasterCard. He bypassed the Caldor's in Newtown.

- Twice on the morning of November 20, Crafts phoned the Ford truck dealer to inquire about his dump truck. The manager had promised to lend him a truck, and when he hedged on a time, Crafts got nasty and threatened to cancel the purchase. The manager found him a Ford U-Haul, which he delivered to Crafts about two P.M. Crafts, who had to work his Southbury PD shift that night, put his gear in the U-Haul and drove to Darien, where he hitched the Brush Bandit to the rental truck.

- Crafts was scheduled for a six o'clock training class at the Southbury PD, but because of poor weather and icy roads, it was canceled while he was en route from Darien to Southbury. He was due to go on patrol at ten that evening. Since he was only five minutes from his home, he might have driven the U-Haul back to Newfield Lane to have dinner with his children. Crafts's whereabouts until he reported for duty are a mystery. Clearly, however, he had plenty of time to tow the woodchipper to his lot on Currituck Road, where, Crafts had told the manager at Darien Rentals, he intended to clear brush. He also had plenty of time to drop the U-Haul at home and get his car or pickup, either of which would have been easier to drive on the slick roads that evening. But when Crafts reported for work at ten, he was driving the U-Haul and towing the chipper.

- Around seven in the evening of November 20, a witness, Joe Williams, noticed a truck and a woodchipper on Silver Bridge, which crosses the Housatonic between Southbury and Newtown. Williams heard a loud noise, which he assumed was the woodchipper in operation. As he drove by he saw a man who appeared to be hiding between the truck and the chipper. Since the man wore the poncho and campaign hat worn by many small-town Connecticut police, Williams didn't stop.

- Danny Lewis, a driver for Southbury's road maintenance department, saw a U-Haul truck towing a woodchipper cruising the jam-packed town parking lot about nine P.M. on November 20. It seemed to Lewis that the driver was trying to find a parking space. About two hours later, he saw the U-Haul and the chipper parked at a school about two hundred yards from the parking lot.

- Police noted a Honda gasoline-powered generator in Crafts's basement; it had more than enough power to run the water pump, furnace, and refrigerator. Yet, according to his statements, when Crafts rose at three A.M. on November 19 to find the power off, he didn't attempt to start this generator. Doing so would have made it unnecessary for his children to leave the house.

From these facts, and from evidence already in their possession, Flanagan, Hiltz, and the prosecuting team came up with a scenario that would explain how and why Crafts had murdered his wife and disposed of her body:

He probably took her unaware as she prepared for bed late on the night of November 18. Probably she was wearing her blue cotton nightshirt with unopened mail in a pocket to read before she went to sleep. Since there was no blood on blankets or sheets, Helle might have been making the bed.

Dr. Lee's interpretation of the blood-droplet evidence pointed to a blunt object as the death weapon. Crafts had any number of tools in the house, but had Helle seen him approach with a wrench or a club, she might have screamed or struggled or attempted to flee. There was no evidence she did, so chances are that Crafts used something familiar—something that would not have frightened Helle if she saw it in his hands.

Probably nothing in the house fit this description as well as Crafts's police-style multicell flashlight, which has many qualities of an ideal club. Killing Helle probably required several blows to the head.

That would have broken her skin and accounted for a relatively small amount of blood—just enough to stain pillows, comforters, box spring, and dust ruffle, the items Crafts replaced. The smudge on the side of the mattress might have been made by Helle's head as she fell. Blood could have stained the rug and the pad underneath as it seeped from her wound.

Crafts neglected to replace the mattress. It was, perhaps, a simple oversight, but more likely because he needed a place to sleep and thought he could explain away a few drops of blood on a mattress: people have nosebleeds, cut themselves on paper, reopen unhealed scabs. Women sometimes leave menstrual bloodstains.

Crafts put Helle, unconscious but perhaps still alive, into the Westinghouse freezer chest he'd bought the previous day. He had left the freezer, covered with a tarp, on the Toyota and unpacked it while Marie was away at work on the eighteenth. After Helle returned from work on the evening of the eighteenth, he moved the Toyota to a spot near the kitchen door where it was not visible through a window and plugged the freezer into an extension cord running to the basement. If left at its lowest temperature setting, the freezer would have been at minus-ten degrees Fahrenheit within a few hours.

Crafts froze Helle's body because it made disposing of it far less bloody. The chipper would handle logs only up to twelve inches in diameter, which meant that he would have to dismember Helle's body before feeding parts through it. Had her body not been frozen solid, there would have been pools of blood everywhere. No such stains were found.

Crafts used a chain saw, one that he had owned for some time, to cut Helle's body into small pieces. To make sure it couldn't be linked to him, he filed down the serial numbers stamped into the frame. Sophisticated X-ray technology, however, has made it possible for investigators to read serial numbers by examining metal crystals *under* the filed spot. This is what the state police did on the chain saw recovered from Lake Zoar. The restored serial number led police to its purchaser: Richard Crafts.

When Marie Thomas returned to the house about two o'clock, Helle was probably dead. It's likely that the coughing she heard coming from the master bedroom was Crafts, imitating his wife's shallow cough to make Marie think she was still home. Crafts waited for Marie to go to sleep before leaving the house.

Heavy snowfall was the one contingency for which Crafts had not planned. But he probably killed Helle just about when the first flakes began to fall. From that moment on, there was no going back.

Crafts told police the power had failed between two and three in the morning; it had actually failed about 3:45. Crafts lied because he wasn't in bed when the power failed—he was out moving Helle's Tercel to the shopping center where he had earlier parked the Rabbit. Then he took the Rabbit to his Currituck Road property and parked it.

Crafts jogged back to his house. He backed the Toyota pickup into the garage and used the truck's special ramp-cum-tailgate and a two-wheeled hand truck to off-load the freezer with Helle's body. He hid the freezer in the rear of the garage, covering it against the possibility that someone might peer through a window and see it. Before leaving the garage, Crafts plugged the freezer into a wall socket. This might have been when he discovered that the power was out.

He then hooked up the Honda generator and readied two extension cords. He didn't start the generator because it made a lot of noise and he knew that power could be restored at any time.

To make sure that no one entered the garage, the family's usual route in and out of their house, Crafts jammed the overhead garage door.

Next he had to get the bloody box spring, comforters, pillows, etc., off the property. The snow was heavy and traction difficult. But he was an Air America pilot, bold and clever. He put the Toyota pickup in four-wheel drive, circled around the big spruce tree in the front yard to gain momentum, and easily moved up the steep driveway into the backyard.

Ordinarily, someone might have heard the truck racing around in four-wheel drive. But thick, falling snow muffled all sound, and neither his children, Marie, nor the neighbors heard anything.

When the snowplow operator came by a few hours later, however, he noticed deep tracks in the snow, coiling around the spruce. He remembered this because it was so odd.

With all the bloody items from his bedroom in the pickup, Crafts drove to his Currituck property, where he hid everything until he could dispose of it at his leisure.

Crafts had not anticipated the mess his murder had made at home. But he did know that with so much snow, local authorities would probably close the schools. In that case, his three kids and their nanny would be underfoot just when he was trying to clean up the murder site and dispose of the body. So at six o'clock he woke everyone, told Marie that Helle had left in the Tercel, and took his children and their nanny to his sister's house. As everyone left the house, he made sure they didn't go through the garage. It was in the pickup that Marie noticed the truck's four-wheel-drive lever was engaged, that the windshield was almost clear, and that Crafts's hair was damp, as though he'd showered.

Crafts's hair was damp because he'd been out in the snow, working to dispose of all traces of his wife's murder.

Late that afternoon, while Marie and the children were still away, he again backed the pickup into the garage. The bed contained a lockable "cap," a space to store valuables. There was just room for the freezer. Crafts used the hand truck to load not only the freezer chest but also the generator, and drove both over to Currituck Road. The property was heavily wooded and had areas that could not be viewed from adjacent lots. The generator was used to keep the freezer operating for several hours, until the body was frozen solid.

Most likely, Crafts's plan had been to dispose of Helle's body the same day he killed her, the nineteenth. That would explain why he had reserved the woodchipper for the day before. But when the dump truck he'd ordered didn't arrive, Crafts had to scramble around for a substitute. He could not have been happy about having to accept an orange-and-white U-Haul with Ohio license plates—but that was all he had.

So, like the resourceful pilot he was, he made do. Helle's body was probably dismembered with the tip of his Stihl chain saw, a technique that would have minimized the amount of tissue spewed out. Doubtless he spread plastic sheets on the ground to confine the frozen fragments. And the same storm that had interrupted power had brought down tree limbs all over Newtown, so the bellow of his chain saw was only one of many on the bright, snowy morning the day after the storm.

Crafts probably put the sawed chunks of Helle's body into several plastic bags, which he stored again in the freezer until he had gone to Darien and returned with the woodchipper. After dark, he drove the U-Haul to River Road, towing the chipper. He stopped on Silver Bridge and, with wood he'd cut on Currituck Road and stored in the U-Haul, fed the grisly remains through the woodchipper into the river below. Helle had been wearing her blue nightshirt when she was killed, but Crafts ignored the garment as he froze and then cut his wife's body. The nightshirt and the letters in its pocket went through the chipper along with the body. But a few cotton fibers had stuck to the insides of the chipper, along with bits and pieces of flesh.

Crafts had anticipated having to clean the chipping machine's innards. He brought along a quantity of wood to send through the machine. Most of what remained of Helle would be cleaned out by the passage of wood chips.

Crafts decided to move before cleaning the chipper. He drove to River Road and continued his chipping, shooting the chips into the back of the U-Haul, where he could later dispose of them. But it was dark. Crafts couldn't see that the heavier objects spewed from the chipper, and lighter objects like paper, fell short of the U-Haul. Wind scattered them around.

Crafts then drove back to Southbury to get ready for his

police shift. He claimed to have arrived around eight P.M., but no one remembered seeing him much before nine.

Crafts's shift ended at two in the morning. But he was seen, first by Constable Wildman and then twice by Joey Hine, at 4:00 and again at 4:30.

Before going home to his family, Crafts had to dispose of the wood chips and any remaining fragments of the body. He used a rake and a shovel that he'd purchased a few days earlier to leave the chips in shallow mounds along the road. He must have believed that wind and weather would scatter them in a few days. Then he went back to River Road and got rid of the chain saw and its bar.

Still, not all the chips were gone. Crafts shoveled a few of them out of the U-Haul when he returned to Currituck Road. He got rid of the rest on the way to Darien on the afternoon of November 20, when he returned the woodchipper. Then he went back to Currituck and carefully swept out the back of the U-Haul, placing the remaining chips in the back of his Ford Victoria sedan, and disposed of them along yet another road.

Crafts must have realized that these chips were mixed with bits of Helle's flesh. He removed the mat that lined the Ford's trunk, and discarded it. He never got around to replacing it, however, and when police carefully examined the trunk, they found shreds of blue fiber and wood chips.

Now Crafts faced the problem of creating the illusion that Helle had left to be with her lover, or her mother, or with anyone. He left the U-Haul in a parking lot until he could get the Ford dealer to recover it, and went back to his house. He burned many of Helle's papers and clothes, some in the fireplace and others in barrels lined with charcoal at the Currituck Road property.

Police never ascertained how Crafts had moved Helle's Toyota Tercel to the Pan Am parking lot at JFK Airport. He might have driven it down and caught a bus back to Connecticut. Or he might have towed it behind his pickup, which did have a tow bar. When state investigators went through the car, they found no useful evidence.

But Flanagan and his prosecution team had a theory that fit nearly all the evidence. It was this theory, along with the evidence, that was presented to a New London jury—the case was moved there because of massive pretrial publicity in Newtown—in March 1987.

The state bore the burden of proof, and one of the most challenging issues lay in convincing the jury that a few shreds of human flesh and a few bits of bone and teeth had once been Helle Crafts.

The first trial ended in a hung jury, with a single juror holding out for acquittal. His reason, he explained, was that when Elizabeth Nielsen, Helle's mother, took the stand to testify that, after Helle's disappearance, she had never contacted her in Denmark, the elderly woman had smiled at Richard Crafts. The juror could not be swayed that the smile, if there had actually been one, had been meant for someone else—or that it had been meaningless. The judge declared a mistrial.

A second trial began September 7, 1989. When she testified this time, Mrs. Nielsen did not smile. Richard Crafts was convicted of murdering his wife and sentenced to fifty years in prison.

Richard Crafts had constructed a bold and quirky plan to rid himself of a wife who would no longer tolerate his infidelity and duplicity. A divorce would have greatly complicated his life, cost him considerable money, severely dented his macho pride, forced him to see his children far less often, and robbed him of the convenience of a secure home.

His plan was imaginative and complex, and might have succeeded. The unexpected snowstorm, however, forced him to improvise away from his original plan, which was to kill and dispose of Helle's body in a single day. The snow caused Crafts to leave deep tracks in his front yard, noted by a snowplow operator. And it led two men to drive lonely roads at unexpected times, witnesses who would remember the woodchipper and the U-Haul, so police knew where to search for evidence.

Even so, Crafts might still have succeeded. He failed to commit the perfect crime because he did not treat details with the importance they required. He failed to remove all the padding from his bedroom floor. He kept a bloodstained mattress. He used credit cards for key purchases. He didn't replace the mat in the Ford's trunk. He hid the chain saw near where he'd been seen with the woodchipper—where police would surely hunt—and failed to obliterate its serial number entirely. He neglected to dispose of contaminated wood chips, never imagining that police would invest the labor and time required to recover material he dumped into the river.

Crafts was bold, he was imaginative—and he was fatally lazy.

Behind bars but resolutely maintaining his innocence, Crafts remains something of a celebrity to fellow inmates, a murderer who had conceived a novel approach to corpse disposal. And like most high-profile prisoners, Crafts acquired a prison nickname.

They call him "Mr. Chips."